THE WITNESS OF
THE OLD TESTAMENT TO CHRIST

THE WITNESS OF THE
OLD TESTAMENT TO CHRIST

By

WILHELM VISCHER

Volume I

THE PENTATEUCH

Translated from the 3rd German Edition, 1936

By

A. B. CRABTREE

LUTTERWORTH PRESS
LONDON

PRINTED IN GREAT BRITAIN BY UNWIN BROTHERS LIMITED, WOKING

CONTENTS

5

Note

The original edition in German was published by Evangelischer
Verlag—A. G. Zollikon, Zurich.

INTRODUCTION

Search the scriptures;
for in them ye think ye have eternal life:
and they are they which testify of me.

(John 5: 39.)

(1)

THE Bible testifies beyond doubt, with the attestation of the Holy Spirit, that Jesus of Nazareth is the Christ. This is what makes it the Holy Scripture of the Christian Church. For the Christian Church is the company of all those who, on the basis of the biblical testimony, recognize and believe that Jesus is the Christ, i.e. the Messiah of Israel, the Son of the living God, the Saviour of the world.

The two main words of the Christian confession "Jesus is the Christ"—the personal name "Jesus" and the vocational name "Christ"—correspond to the two parts of the Holy Scriptures: the New and the Old Testament. The Old Testament tells us *what* the Christ is; the New, *who* He is—and indeed in such a manner as to make it clear that he alone knows Jesus who recognizes Him as the Christ, and he alone knows what the Christ is who knows that He is Jesus. So the two Testaments, breathing the same spirit, point to each other, "and there is no word in the New Testament that does not look back to the Old, in which it is foretold",[1] and all the words of the Old Testament look beyond themselves to the One in the New in whom alone they are true.

Strictly speaking only the Old Testament is "The Scripture", while the New Testament brings the good news that now the

---

[1] Luther, sermon on John 1: 1–14 in the Kirchenpostille, 1522 (Weimar Ed., Bd. X, 1 Abt., 1 Hälfte, S.181 f.). "Above all, we must realize that the apostles drew all their doctrine and writings from the Old Testament, wherein is prophesied that which should later come to pass in Christ and be preached concerning Him, as St. Paul says in Rom. 1: God promised the gospel of His Son by His prophets in the Holy Scriptures. For this reason all their preaching is based on the Old Testament, and there is no word in the New Testament which does not look back to the Old wherein it was already declared. Thus in this epistle (Heb. 1: 5–12) we see that the apostle confirms the divinity of Christ by the utterances of the Old Testament; for the New Testament is nothing more than a revelation of the Old—as if one should open a closed letter which he holds in his hand. The Old Testament is thus the testament of Christ—a letter which He caused to be opened after His death and read and proclaimed in the light of the gospel, as is portrayed in Rev. 5 by the Lamb of God who alone could open the book with the seven seals—a book which none other in heaven or on earth or under the earth could open."

7

meaning of these writings, the import of all their words, their Lord and Fulfiller, has appeared incarnate. Every book of the New Testament, each in its own way, makes this pronouncement.

(2)

Let us hear, for example, Luke's account.

He begins by summarizing the Old Testament as a promise of advent. Once again a priest of Israel prays for the arrival of him who should come. Then he is silent. In answer to his prayer an angel tells him that his wife, who is one of the daughters of Aaron, shall bear a son who as the last forerunner shall prepare the way of the Messiah. Six months later, the angel Gabriel is sent to Nazareth, to a girl betrothed to a man of the house of David and tells her that she shall be overshadowed by the power of the Most High and bear a son. This son is the Messiah, described thus by the angel: "He shall be called Son of God, and the Lord God shall give unto Him the throne of His father David, and He shall reign over the house of Jacob for ever, and of His kingdom there shall be no end."

At the circumcision of the last forerunner the tongue of the priest Zechariah is loosed for the proclamation of the new message that the Lord God of Israel will visit His people to fulfil all that He had intimated to the fathers in His sacred covenant and promised by the mouth of His holy prophets. Then comes the night in which Mary brings forth her firstborn son in the manger of Bethlehem, and to the shepherds in the open fields lighted by the glory of the Lord, the angel brings the glad tidings which shall be to all people: "unto you is born *this day* in the city of David a Saviour, which is Christ the Lord."

The birth of the Son of God coincides with the census which Caesar Augustus had ordained for the whole world, and so the child is enrolled in the place of His citizenship, in the messianic dynasty. Eight days later He is received into the covenant of Abraham by circumcision and given the name JESUS, as the angel had named Him before He was conceived in the womb. As faithful subjects of the Law His parents then take Him to Jerusalem to present their firstborn with the prescribed sacrifices in the temple. During this act the old man Simeon takes the child in his arms, and thanks God that, having seen the One looked for through the centuries by the righteous in Israel, he may now depart to his fathers in peace.

8

In true humanity the Son of God grows up in Nazareth, and as He reaches His twelfth year and thus becomes a Bar-Mizva, a responsible son of the Law, His parents take Him again to Jerusalem. There He discusses the meaning of the Holy Scriptures with the learned in such manner that all marvel at His understanding and answers. Alike in the Testament of God and in the House of God He moves with the confident familiarity of a son—"Wist ye not that I must be about my father's business?".

Nevertheless He accompanies His parents to Nazareth and remains subject to them until years later the voice of the desert preacher rings out proclaiming the immediate appearance of Him who brings the final decision. At this, Jesus comes to the Jordan and is baptized by John in token of His complete solidarity with sinful men. In this moment the heaven is opened and the Holy Spirit descends upon him in bodily form and a voice sounds from heaven, "Thou art my beloved Son; in thee I am well pleased".

The glory of His divine sonship, to which this voice from heaven bears witness, is veiled by the lowliness of His incarnation. Luke expresses this by the human genealogy of Jesus which runs back through David and Abraham to Adam—"who was of God". The divine sonship, ruined in Adam and all his children by their obedience to the voice of the tempter and their desire to be equal with God, is restored and offered to them by Jesus through His divesting Himself of His divine form in becoming a son of man. He cannot be seduced by the devil because, in complete contrast to Adam, He is resolved to serve God alone.

After the temptation He preaches throughout Galilea in the power of the Spirit. The staggering thing about His message is His claim, *Through my presence the scripture is fulfilled.* To emphasize this Luke places the appearance of Jesus in the synagogue at Nazareth programmatically at the beginning. It is in Nazareth itself where He grew up that Jesus during the Sabbath service opens the book of Isaiah at the section relating to the Messiah, at whose appearing the acceptable year of the Lord dawns. Having read the passage, He sits down saying, *To-day is this scripture fulfilled in your ears*. At first, knowing Him since He was a child, all who hear are astonished "How can He call Himself the Fulfiller of the Holy Scriptures—is He not Joseph's son?" At last, enraged that He offers no proof but His word, they hurry Him out of the town to cast Him over the hill on which the town stands.

From such a beginning of His public ministry one can foresee the end. The messianic claim of Jesus is bound to cost Him His life. When He asks His disciples the question, "But whom say ye that I am?" and Peter replies, "Thou art the Christ of God", in that same hour He begins to tell them of the approaching change of fortune—"The son of man must be rejected by the elders and chief priests and scribes, and be killed, and the third day rise again."

A few weeks later He stands accused before the High Council of the chosen people. To their question, "Art thou the Christ?", He replies: "If I tell you, ye will not believe. And if I also ask you, ye will not answer me, nor let me go. Hereafter shall the son of man sit at the right hand of the power of God." With one voice they ask. "Art thou then the Son of God?" And He replies, "Ye say that I am" (i.e. "It is as you say; I am").

For this testimony to Himself Jesus of Nazareth is crucified. The inscription upon His cross, written in Greek, Latin and Hebrew, reads: "THIS IS THE KING OF THE JEWS."

The evangelist manifestly believes that this inscription reveals the true nature of Jesus. But is it not in reality the most annihilating judgment upon the messianic claim of Jesus, and, as an inscription over the head of one crucified, a mockery of the whole messianic hope of Israel? Were the Jews not right in demanding of the governor its removal? If Jesus really were the Christ, should He not—at least at the last hour—have come down from the cross? Is not the fact that He failed to do so the clear and final proof that, whatever else He may be, He is at any rate *not* the Messiah of Israel? Or was perhaps the judgment of the high council based on inadequate knowledge of the Scriptures?

No, reply the New Testament witnesses; the Jewish elders and chief priests and scribes *had to* condemn Jesus to death. By this decisive judgment the High Council and Pontius Pilate officially executed the Testament of God.[1] Jesus the Christ was crucified not *contrary* to scripture but *according* to it. In this act are fulfilled the writings of the prophets concerning the Son of Man. Jesus had said the same to His disciples when He spoke to them of His coming death. "They however failed to comprehend it; the word was hidden from them, and they understood not what was said." When they saw their Master cast out from the holy place and hanging on the accursed tree

[1] "To an ignoramus such as I am, after the preacher of the Old Covenant, the wisest writer and profoundest prophet is the executor of the New Testament, Pontius Pilate". Joh. Georg. Hamann in a letter to Lavater (*Hamann's Writings*, ed. Friedr. Roth, V, 274).

they themselves despaired of the faith that He was the Promised One. How disillusioned were the two who left the Holy City and made their way disconsolate towards Emmaus—"We trusted that it had been He which should have redeemed Israel, and beside all this to-day is the third day since these things were done". But a stranger who has joined them on the way reproaches them—"O fools, and slow of heart to believe all that the prophets have spoken. Ought not Christ to have suffered these things, and to enter into his glory?" And beginning at Moses and all the prophets, He expounded unto them in all the Scriptures the things concerning Himself. Who was this stranger? From the way He broke bread at the evening meal they recognized him—Jesus. The women's story of His resurrection was then no fable. The risen Lord Himself by His spirit gave, not to these two alone, but to all the disciples, such understanding of the Old Testament that their hearts burned within them. From the Old Testament He proved to them that as the crucified one He was the Saviour, and in doing so placed in their hands the key to the Scriptures. When He had ascended to heaven and taken His place on the eternal throne at the right hand of the Father, He sent them the promised Holy Spirit, who endued them with knowledge and power to testify that God had made Jesus of Nazareth crucified in Jerusalem to be Lord and Christ.

(3)

Such is the fundamental import of the evangelical message. It is simply the final realization of the Old Testament writings. The coming of Jesus means that all that happened, and was said, to those of the old covenant is realized *to-day* and *now*. "Moses and all the prophets from Samuel onwards, as many as have spoken, have proclaimed *these days*."[1]

In their preaching of Jesus the Messiah the apostles in no way desire to declare anything else than that which is written in the Old Testament. Nor do they wish to give to "the life of Jesus" (*"das Leben Jesu"*) in the Old Testament an arbitrary Christian interpretation, and still less to assert the embodiment of some "Christ-idea" (*Christusidee*). Anyone who construes the declarations of the New Testament as arbitrary or mythological interpretations should realize that he thereby ascribes to the witnesses a standpoint which they would have held to be the direst blasphemy. In regarding their witness as arbitrary interpretation he conceives it to be something quite different

[1] Acts 3: 22 ff.

from what the witnesses intended. That is, he no longer understands the Fact which is witnessed, but sets something different in its place. The gospel of Christ Jesus means neither the apotheosis of a man nor the embodiment of an idea; it means that the miracle has happened:

> Never destined by mankind,
> Him on Mary's lap we find;
> A child so small is born to-day,
> Who rules the universe alway.[1]

That is the fact they declare when they proclaim that Jesus is the Christ of the Old Testament. Their conviction is that whoever does not recognize Jesus as the *Christ* has completely failed to understand Him, and whoever is ignorant of Christ *Jesus* does not know what the Christ is. Christ Jesus is not an idea that results from theological deductions or philological interpretations, but is the Word spoken by God Himself, from which theology flows, and which opens the closed Bible, If we really mean to deal with *this* fact, we must listen to the witnesses and try to understand them in the way they desire to be understood. But if, distrusting them, we attempt to infer from their words a "historical Jesus" instead of Christ Jesus, we palpably reconstruct in place of the fact which they assert something quite different. In place of the *testimony* to Christ which we received, "even as they delivered them unto us, which from the beginning were eyewitnesses and ministers of the word",[2] we project a *picture* of Jesus according to our own predilections. We may have scholarly motives for so doing. Nevertheless, the effort to replace Christ Jesus by the historical Jesus remains, in view of the historical documents on which it must be based, a procedure which from a scientific standpoint is highly dubious. Wellhausen believed that "we cannot return to him (i.e. the historical Jesus) even if we so desired. To make the historical Jesus into a religious dogma is to be ultimately compelled, as were the rationalists of old, to remove from Him all traces of "historical contingency" . . . to replace the historical by the rational, of which there are widely differing conceptions. The historical Jesus, as the foundation of religion, is a doubtful and unsatisfying substitute for that which is lost when the gospel is discarded. Apart from His death Jesus would never have become historical."[3] His death is His claim to

[1] Luther's *Christmas Hymn.*   [2] Luke 1: 2.
[3] Julius Wellhausen, *Einleitung in die drei ersten Evangelien*, 2. Ausgabe, Berlin 1911, S. 104. Dazu S. 153: "Not as a religious teacher, but as the crucified and risen Lord who shall return again, is Jesus the Christian Messiah.

be the Christ. He would not have been killed had not His whole
life confronted His contemporaries with the question whether He
be the Christ, and had He not confessed this before the high
council. His death is His "yes", and His accusers' "no" to His
messianic claims. Whatever may be said, His death—by which
alone He became historical—is undoubtedly as a fact of history
simple the verdict upon the question of messiahship at a
specific point of time. The historian who ignores this in speaking
of Jesus has lost sight of the historical fact on the basis of
which he speaks.

Similarly anyone who, on the basis of the Biblical documents
which testify to Christ, talks about the embodiment of the
"idea of Messiah", is merely indulging in speculation. The
two arbitrary interpretations of the testimony to Christ, the
one leading to the historical Jesus and the other to the "Christ-
idea", are mutually conditioned and arise side by side as soon
as the testified unity of Jesus and Christ is torn asunder. The
Bible knows neither a historical Jesus nor a Christ-idea, but
simply Jesus the Christ to whom it bears a double witness in
the Old and New Testaments. According to this testimony
He is an historical event which happened once for all at a
particular time. This event is the source and goal of all history;
the centre of the circle. That the concept of history is here
transcended is obvious. And yet the Biblical witnesses maintain
that history is not thereby dissolved but fulfilled. That is either
a contradiction or a miracle. The fact is a miracle; if it is not
seen as such it is not seen at all. For it is more than a fact. It is
an event which is only understood when it is seen as the act
of God through which He becomes present in the midst of
history. That does not mean that the historicity of this act
may be impugned. The birth of Jesus Christ is dated as a
historical fact which once happened: *"Factum est autem in
diebus illis, exiit edictum a Caesare Augusto, ut describeretur
universus mundus. It happened in those days . . ."*[1] The event
is circumscribed in space and time by the Roman tax registra-
tion which recorded the wealth and ancestry of all the inhabitants of the earth when Quirinius was legate in Syria. The
christological dogma can never be severed from the "dogma"
(the Greek expression in the text for "decree") which went out

Not the gospel of Jesus which prescribes the Church's ethic, but the apostolic
gospel which preaches faith in Christ, is the essential element. The duplicity
cannot have existed in the beginning, and Harnack's dictum that 'only the
Father, not the Son, belongs to the gospel' is fundamentally erroneous if it
intends to affirm a fact and not merely assert a postulate."

[1] Luke 2: 1.

13

from Caesar Augustus. Jesus the Christ is a real man. His death proves that even more clearly and decisively than His birth. For the seal of historicity is placed upon any character of this world not by his life but by his death. Had Jesus Christ ascended to heaven before His crucifixion from the mount of transfiguration He would not be in the strictest sense historical, but simply a superhistorical phenomenon. But in point of fact after Moses and Elijah, the two representatives of Old Testament witness, had spoken to Him of "his decease which he should accomplish at Jerusalem", He descended the mount of transfiguration to go to His death. "Apart from his death he would never have become historical". That is in entire accord with the fact that the one article in the Apostles' Creed which is historically dated is the death of Jesus: "crucified under Pontius Pilate". That is the knot on the thread of Christian declarations.

(4)

A historical fact can only be established by *historical documents*. If Jesus Christ were a purely superhistorical figure historical documents would be superfluous. In token that He is not superhistorical, but a fact of history to be known only through the medium of historical documents, we have received the Old and New Testaments. They form the selection of "genuine" documents, approved by the Church and attested by the Holy Spirit which, with their "dead" letters, authentically define the historical event, "Christ Jesus", who through His death has become historical.

Christians who think that the Bible can only be "Holy" Scripture if it be, so to speak, fallen from heaven, are mistaken. The contrary is true; the Bible is the Holy Scripture only in so far as it speaks of Christ *Jesus*, the incarnation of the Son of God. It can only do so if its writings consist of the words of men. It is the abiding merit of the historical-critical investigation of the nineteenth century to have revealed the error of the seventeenth-century doctrine of inspiration, and to have shown the historical-human aspect of scripture. The Word became flesh. In their fleshliness, in their temporal contingency and historical fortuitousness, the writings of the Old and New Testament bear witness to this incarnation. "This shall be the sign; ye shall find the babe wrapped in swaddling clothes, lying in a manger." For us the Scriptures are these swaddling clothes, given us as a sign.

I would earnestly beg and warn every devout Christian not to be offended at the homely speech and story which so often meet him in the Old Testament, and not to doubt, however poor it appears, that here are words, works, judgments and deeds of supreme divine majesty and wisdom. For this is the scripture which makes fools of the wise and prudent and lies open only to the humble and simple. Therefore away with your conceit and sentiment, and learn to see in these writings the highest, noblest sanctuary, a mine whose wealth is inexhaustible, so that you may discover the divine wisdom which God here displays so simple and poor in order that he may subdue all pride. Here thou shalt find the swaddling clothes and crib in which the Christ lies, and to which the angel directs the shepherds. Poor and tiny clothes they are; but precious is the treasure, Christ, who nestles in them.[1]

If the words of the Bible were not really words of men they would not be the true swaddling clothes of the Son of Man. The *scandalon* of the human contingency of the Bible, which historical and literary criticism has brought to our attention, corresponds precisely to the *scandalon* of the incarnation of the eternal Word in the historical appearance of Jesus of Nazareth at a certain point of time.

It pertains to the unity of the divine revelation that just as the whole of creation is a work of the greatest humility, so the Holy Spirit, to guide the pen of holy men, stooped and divested himself of majesty, as did the Son in taking the form of a servant. And because the divine handwriting chooses even the simple—the shallow, the ignoble—to put to shame the strength and ingenuity of profane writers, we must have the enlightened, enthusiastic, jealous eyes of a friend, a trusted companion, a lover, if we are to discern in such disguise the rays of divine glory.[2]

Exactly in line with the great paradox of the incarnation of the Word in Christ is to be found the meaning of the sentence: "The Bible is the Word of God." "No recognition of the Bible as the Word of God without concrete knowledge of its historical character."[3] Therefore to deny that the Bible is conditioned by and rooted in history is to fall into the same error as to reject the incarnation of the Word. Rejection of the real incarnation

[1] Luther's *Vorrede auf das Alte Testament*, Abs. 3.
[2] Hamann im 1. *hellenistischen Brief* (Ausg. Roth 2 Bd., S. 207).
[3] Karl Barth. *Prolegomena*, S. 338 u. 344.

15

of Christ is just as much a sign of unbelief as rejection of His divinity. If then we are really concerned to understand the Bible as God's Word, if we wish to read it as a testimony to Christ, we cannot ignore what the historical and philological sciences have to say about the Old Testament. For those seeking exact knowledge, understanding of the historical character of these records becomes "concrete" when the findings of the historical research which pertains to them are taken into account. Of course scientific findings themselves, being historically conditioned, cannot claim absolute validity, and must be regarded critically. Nevertheless even in their relativity we must take them seriously. For decisions of faith have to be made not in heaven but on earth, not in the realm of the absolute but in the sphere of the relative. We have to make them, not as angels but as men whose knowledge is always relative, never absolute. As the contemporaries of Jesus stood over against His historical appearing, so we stand to-day over against the Biblical records. Just as each of them had to use his eyes and ears and employ his intelligence to test what he saw and heard, so we to-day with our relative knowledge are placed in the valley of decision whenever we read the Bible. "And blessed is he who is not offended in me." That is true here; for not directly, but rather through the words of men, God deigns to speak to us. Facts of history point us to the truth of God.

In this we are not seeking to maintain that "contingent truths of history are the proof of necessary truths of reason". What is contended is that a certain section of accidental truths of history, Jesus, is the truth before which the historical facts of all the ages stand or fall. "Contingent truths of history can never prove necessary truths of reason". We should have misunderstood the doctrine of the canonical authority of the Biblical writings if we were to imagine ourselves called upon to attack this dictum of Lessing,[1] or to prevent its application to the Bible. On the contrary, we have every reason to accept it, in order to protect the doctrine of the canon from misunderstanding. The purpose of the Old Testament is not to prove necessary truths of reason, but to bear witness that Jesus is the Christ of God. Jesus Christ is no necessary truth of reason. To regard Him as such is to misunderstand Him completely; to proclaim Him as such is to deny Him. Jesus Christ is neither a truth of reason nor the truth of reason, but a historical fact which took place once for all; He is the Galilean crucified outside

[1] *Uber den Beweis des Geistes und der Kraft*, 1777.

the gate of Jerusalem under Pontius Pilate. That He was "declared to be the son of God with power, according to the spirit of holiness, by the resurrection from the dead",[1] that He is the Logos who was in the beginning with the Father, is anything but a necessary truth of reason. It is the divine foolishness by which God has put to shame the wisdom of this world. This divine foolishness is in every sense the wisdom of God, but in no sense necessary. So utterly free is it in every meaning of the word, that it is only true because it chooses to be so, and only true to him to whom it reveals itself. Never revealed but in grace; never perceived but in faith. For this reason the preaching of Christ Jesus is to the Greeks foolishness and to the Jews a stumbling block. We need to take Lessing's dictum seriously, lest the amazing counsel of God be imperceptibly transformed into a speculative idea, and the Logos into a necessary truth of reason. And it is precisely the recognition of the historical contingency of the Biblical writings which guards us against this confusion, because the offence of the historical contingency of these documents indicates and characterizes the incarnation of the Logos.

The writings of the Old Testament no less than those of the New are for all who seek Him signs and tokens of the Son of God who was born in a manger; crib and swaddling clothes they are, not the Child Himself; testimonies in dead characters, not the living Christ. Unless the Holy Spirit breathe through them they remain dead. The Holy Spirit, as both the Bible and Church doctrine declare, is not to be sundered from the words of scripture as those wild enthusiasts imagine who despise the written word and appeal only to the Spirit. "*Est enim Satanae spiritus qui divellitur a Verbo*, it is the spirit of Satan which breaks loose from the Word with which the Spirit of God is always united."[2] As the Father in heaven acknowledges the Son of Man born of a woman and crucified on the cross, so the Holy Spirit promises by His breathing through the dead letters of scripture so to attest them that whoever hears perceives therein the voice of the living God. There is thus an indissoluble connection, a closed logical circle: through the incarnation of Jesus Christ God speaks the word by which He reveals Himself; the human words of Holy Scripture testify to this Word become flesh when and where and as they are attested by the Holy Spirit.

[1] Rom. 1: 4. [2] Calvin, *Commentary on Isaiah* 59: 21.

(5)

In their unity the Old and New Testaments define the fact of Christ Jesus in such a manner that it cannot be understood as merely a historical event alongside others, but as the presence of the Lord of history: the source and goal of all history has here become an event of history.

> Th' Eternal Father's only Child
> Now lies in manger meek and mild.
> In our poor nature's flesh and blood
> Is veiled the everlasting Good.[1]

The witnesses of the New Testament relate Jesus in the strictest sense, that is messianically, to the Old Testament. And that is quite different from saying, "Jesus is the highest point in the unfolding of Israelite-Jewish religious history, and cannot be understood apart from the Old Testament". Indisputable though such a statement is, it by no means implies that Jesus is the Christ. Even when we heighten it to: "As the highest point of Israelite religion Jesus is the crown of all religious history", we have still not said that He is Christ, the Lord.

According to Biblical testimony, Jesus the Christ is the "corner stone" of the edifice of God's revelation; and the controversy of the exegetes, whether the corner stone should be understood as the keystone of the arch or as the foundation stone, can only be settled by the realization that Jesus Christ is both the foundation stone and the keystone—and therefore the stone of stumbling, the "skandalon" in the eyes of reason.[2] "I am Alpha *and* Omega, the beginning *and* the end, the first and the last."[3] He could not be the true goal unless he were also the origin. The Word which, as one of the apostles expresses it, "we have seen with our eyes and touched with our hands", is, according to the testimony of the same writer, the same Logos which was in the beginning with God, and which was God. He who at a certain time became flesh is He through whom all things were made, and without whom was not anything made that was made.[4] The last prophet, who, because he can point to the One who should come as a contemporary, is more than a prophet, says of Him, "This is he of whom I said, *after* me cometh a man who is preferred *before* me, for he was before

---

[1] Luther's *Christmas Hymn*.
[2] Ps. 118: 22 f. Is. 28: 16. Matt. 21: 42. Mark 12: 10. Luke 20: 17. Acts 4: 11. Rom. 9: 33. Eph. 2: 20. 1 Pet. 2: 7.
[3] Rev. 22: 13.
[4] 1 John 1: 1. John 1: 1-18, 30; 8: 56-58; 12: 38-41.

me". This Son of Man, offspring of Adam's race, is the firstborn before all creatures. This son of Abraham, in whom is fulfilled God's promise to the patriarch, tells the Jews that Abraham had already seen His day, and to their protest, "Thou art not yet fifty years of age, and hast thou seen Abraham?", retorts, "Verily, verily, before Abraham was, I am." His glory was seen by Isaiah, who prophesied that those contemporary with His incarnation would have blind eyes for Him. The son of David who as the legitimate heir ascends the throne of David, is David's Lord, the founder of the messianic dynasty: "I, Jesus, am the root and offspring of David."[1] He is the finisher and author of faith, who sets His seal upon all the faithful from Noah to the last generation. It is not merely that His faith is greater than theirs, but rather that their faith is directed to Him.[2] He is their life. He is the head of the body, namely the Church. The relationship of His life to the lives of those mentioned in the Bible is such that He dies through them and for them in such a manner that they live by Him and through Him. Without Him they are dead. He, "the prince of life" brings life to those who kill Him.[3]

The death of Jesus is the decisive event by which the sin of the world is taken away not repeatedly but once for all. The High Council sacrifices Jesus in order to purify the Church of the Old Testament from the stain of contact with Him, and by this very death Jesus as the High Priest after the order of Melchizedek offers the spotless sacrifice which blots out the offences committed under the first covenant, and ratifies all sacrifices through which in the old covenant forgiveness was accorded to the guilty. His death, through which He founds the new covenant, is also the death of the testator without which there would never have been a commencement of the first testament. Now those who are called can receive the inheritance pledged in the testament.[4] In the moment when the authorized judges condemn Him as a blasphemer He becomes by the ordinance of God the Expiator through the pouring out of whose blood is achieved the justification of all sinners who believe in Him.[5]

(6)

All these insights follow logically from the unity of the two Testaments. Through His death Christ has transformed the two

[1] Matt. 22: 41–46. Rev. 22: 16.   [2] Heb. 11: 1–12.
[3] Col. 1: 14–20. Matt. 20: 28; 26: 26–29; John 3: 14–16. Acts 3: 15.
[4] Heb. chs. 7–10.   [5] Rom. 3: 21–26.

into one. Now there is one Church, one Body and one Spirit; one faith and one hope; one Lord and Mediator; one God and Father of all. The variety of religious discernment and experience characterizing the diverse types of people who at various times have belonged to the Church in no way abates this unity. "There are diversities of gifts, but the same Spirit. And there are differences of administrations, but the same Lord. And there are diversities of operations, but it is the same God which worketh all in all. For as the body is one and hath many members, and all the members of that one body, being many, are one body, so also is Christ. And those members which seem feeblest are the most necessary, and upon those which appear least honourable we bestow abundant honour."[1] This description, by which the apostle reveals a cross section of the Church of his day, is equally true of the history of the Church through the ages. And it has not been proved that differences in religious discernment and experience are greater among Christians living at various times than among those living at the same time. Who has not at some time found it grievously hard to be one in spirit with contemporary Christians? And who on the contrary has not found comfort in the fellowship of Christians of past centuries? Is Abraham, the "Father of faith" really more remote from me than the Christians of to-day? It is remarkable how many Christians and free religious spirits of our day regard it as self-evident that they know more about God than Abraham, "the friend of God", simply because they live a few thousand years later. Have they perhaps never reflected that, however creative they may be in such matters, what they say and write concerning God can be at best but a few drops by the side of the living spring which flows joyously through the chapters about Abraham in Genesis, from which through the ages men have allayed the thirst of their hearts? Was not more insight displayed by that extraordinary man who, whenever he accompanied Abraham in thought to Mount Moriah, sank down exhausted, and with hands clasped exclaimed, "None was so great as Abraham. Who can understand him?"[2]

In any case, if the Testaments truly form a unity—and only if this is so, is Jesus the Christ—the men of faith under the old covenant were, through one and the same Mediator, partakers of the same salvation as the Christians. *"Patrum omnium foedus adeo substantia et re ipsa nihil a nostro differt, ut unum*

[1] Eph. 2: 14; 4: 4–6. I Cor. 12.
[2] Sören Kierkegaard, *Furcht und Zittern*, Stimmung (Schluss).

prorsus atque idem sit: administratio tamen variat." In its nature and essence salvation under the old covenant was in no way different from ours; only in the way in which it was dispensed and offered is a difference discernible. The difference is that the Church was then at a childlike, youthful age, and spiritual promises were appropriately adumbrated by earthly forms: *"Aetas adhuc puerilis erat. Sub hac ergo paedagogia illos continuit Dominus, ut spirituales promissiones non ita nudas et apertas illis daret, sed terrenis quodammodo adumbratas. Hoc tantum dico, beatum et foelicem Ecclesiae statum semper in Christi persona fuisse fundatum. Eadem illis haereditas eadem inter illos Ecclesia."*[1]

Such is the Church of Christ—a Church linking the ages and running through all centuries before and after Christ, sharing one salvation and upheld by one Mediator. In her, Abraham, though a sinner, enjoyed fellowship with God—let us say 1933 years before Christ—because Jesus under Pontius Pilate atoned for his (Abraham's) sin, just as a Christian 1933 years after Christ has fellowship with God only because Jesus bore to the cross nineteen hundred years ago the sins which this Christian commits to-day. The doctrine of the unity of the Bible establishes the genuine historicity of the incarnation, the fact that it happened once for all in space and time, and equally assures the recognition that the events which happened in the life of Christ as temporal history form an eternal *now*: "Jesus Christ, the same yesterday, to-day, and for ever."[2] In every generation every true Christian is contemporaneous with Christ. A man can be contemporary only with the time in which he lives—and with one other: with Christ in His life on earth. His life on earth moves forward with humanity, and in particular accompanies each generation as eternal history. It possesses eternal simultaneity."[3]

---

[1] Calvin, *Institutio*, II. 6. 2; II, 10, 2; II, 11. 2.　　　　[2] Heb. 13: 8.

[3] Kierkegaard, *Training in Christianity*, 4. Christianity as the absolute; contemporaneity with Christ. Compare Christoph Blumhardt jun. in a sermon of March 23, 1898, on the word of Isaiah 63: 4: The year has dawned when I redeem my own.—"Thus from the remotest ages there are men who are called 'my own'. Through men God says, 'Though all should forsake their high destiny, yet there remain men who are mine. In that moment a new year begins. In the year when men began to forsake their destiny, all seemed lost. But now begins a year in which God restores His own to their true destiny. It is the beginning of the year of redemption. The one man to whom God says, 'Thou art mine', opens a new epoch. The years of God are unique. They are not related to each other like human years, so that where one ends the next begins. All years begin with God. The year of redemption has its beginning at man's very creation. Thus Jesus, who belongs in matchless fashion to God, does not say, 'Now begins the year of redemption, for in this year I begin to

(7)

"Now I say that the heir, so long as he is a child, differeth nothing from a servant, though he be lord of all; but is under tutors and governors until the time appointed of the father. Even so we, when we were children, were in bondage under the elements of the world. But when *the fullness of time was come*, God sent forth his Son, made of a woman, made under the law, to redeem them that are under the law, that we might receive the adoption of sons."[1] "Then was *fulfilled* that which was spoken by the prophet . . ."[2] The Anointed, Jesus, has fulfilled the promises of the Old Testament. Such is the unanimous testimony of the New Testament.

But what does "fulfilled" mean here?

Does it mean that we now see what the men of the old covenant were obliged to believe? If that were so the Old Testament would possess but purely antiquarian value. It would be no longer the indispensable source of Christian knowledge from which we learn what otherwise we could not know. It would merely provide us with the means of ascertaining whether the ancient Israelites did or did not yet know that which we know far better. Is that really what the witnesses of the New Testament meant by saying that "the prophets have inquired and searched diligently, who prophesied of the grace that should come unto you".[3] "Christ is the *telos*—goal and end—of the Old Testament."[4] Does that really mean that the Old Testament can now be discarded since we have reached the goal whereas the men of the old covenant were still only on the way? "And He turned Him unto His disciples and said privately, Blessed are the eyes which see the things that ye see; for I tell you that many prophets and kings have desired

---

belong to God', but rather He says, 'Before Abraham was, I am'. The essential nature of Jesus begins with creation, and yet it is a new year. As shafts of light radiate from one sun, so the year of redemption for God's own in Jesus is present at the very creation of the world. In the beginning was the Word, and the Word was with God, and the Word was God. All things were made by him, and without him was not made anything that was made. The same was in the beginning with God. . . And the Word became flesh. Now it is present.

"So it is when we become His own. Abraham became God's, for he was begotten at the very creation of human nature. For this reason Paul is able to affirm that we were chosen before the foundation of the world, when man first appeared in God. If today I belong to God, this fact had its origin in the origin of man himself. And the year which begins for you and me when we become God's own is one which comes into broad daylight only in the course of time, but its beginnings were long ago. When I am convinced that I belong to God, then I know that redemption is come."

[1] Gal. 4: 1-5. [2] In many passages of Matthew.
[3] 1 Pet. 1: 10-12. [4] Rom. 10: 4.

to see those things which ye see, and have not seen them; and
to hear the things which ye hear, and have not heard them."[1]
Does that mean that the disciples and we ourselves see in such
a manner that we no longer need to trust, and hear in such
fashion that we no longer need the word of the Old Testament?
As Jesus stood in the flesh before His disciples, could they
recognize in Him the Christ without believing on the basis of
the Old Testament witnesses—in the strict sense *believing*—
what they did *not* see, namely that this lowly one was the
exalted one? And as He lay slain upon the cross between two
thieves they had nothing left but faith—the faith of hearts
not slow to believe the scriptures.[2] And when the Lord was
risen and ascended to heaven and had sent them the pledge of
the Holy Spirit, did they cease to be on the march as men of
faith? Were they from that moment seated with Him in the
kingdom of His glory, removed from all darkness and fear?
Must they not rather in all seriousness wait in patience and
faith for the end when their Lord should return? The brother
of the Lord after the flesh, who had seen the human nature of
Jesus nearer and more often than others, fortifies his brothers
with the closing words of the book of Daniel, "Blessed is he
who waits", and exhorts them in the time of waiting to take
the prophets who spoke in the name of the Lord as an example
of suffering and patience.[3] And the risen Lord Himself praises
the blessed who have not seen Him and yet believe.[4]

No. "There is no trace in the New Testament of a loosening
and dissolution of the promise through its fulfilment; or of any
kind of salvation meeting men in Christ and entering their
lives through the Church, sermon or sacrament, which is not
in itself essentially a promise, a sign, a pledge of hope; or of
the founding of an island of the blessed in the stream of time;
or of any understanding of the appearing of Christ other than
the 'eschatological'. What we do find is a hundred indications
that the men to whom we owe this authoritative testimony to
Christ realized that they stood in complete solidarity with the
figures of the Old Testament from Abraham to David and on
to the prophets, that is with those who received and proclaimed
the promise which is now alleged to be out of date. Not that
the Kingdom of God has come, but that it is *at hand* is the
meaning of the words 'the time is fulfilled' after the coming of
Christ as well as before (Mark 1: 15); not the presence of a
better world, visible or invisible, but the *expectation* of a new
heaven and a new earth which through the coming of Christ

[1] Luke 10: 24.   [2] Luke 24: 25.   [3] James 5: 7-11.   [4] John 20: 29.

23

has become necessary and vigorous; no other blessedness than blessedness in *hope* (Rom. 8: 24). 'The promise is fulfilled' does not mean that the promise ceases and that which is promised takes its place, but that the promise itself is now complete, perfect, clear, and therefore powerful. If anywhere, it is precisely in the light of the coming of Christ that faith becomes 'advent faith', an expectation of future revelation."[1]

The prophecy is fulfilled in Jesus Christ, in that all the promises of God are yea and amen in Him.[2] Jesus is "the Amen, the faithful and true witness",[3] declares the last book of the New Testament, which shows more clearly than any other that the Church of Jesus suffers and lives in Old Testament expectation. Anyone who, because of this "judaising tendency", wishes to erase the Revelation of John from the Christian Bible, has apparently not realized that the visions of this book are nothing but images of the petitions and the amen of the Lord's Prayer. "He which testifieth these things saith, surely I come quickly. Amen. Even so, come, Lord Jesus."[4]

Faith in Jesus Christ means in every age faith in Him who was and who shall come, and only so is it faith in Him who is. To the witness of the old covenant Jesus is near as the Coming One; to those of the new covenant as the Returning One. Whether praised or afflicted the Church abides in every age a community living in hope; for she is the Church of the *crucified* Christ. If, according to New Testament testimony, Christ had really appeared on earth in messianic *glory*, Old Testament prophecy would have been completely satisfied by His first advent. His appearing, however, was in the form of a servant; His glory veiled by His cross. For the scribes this was as unacceptable as it was unexpected. To all, however, who believed that the crucified was the Messiah it was natural to live in tensest expectation of His imminent appearing. For only His return in glory brings "the return of all things in which all comes to pass which God spoke by the mouth of all his holy prophets since the world began".[5] The end of the path trod by the men of the old covenant is reached only when Jesus appears in glory. Until that day we walk by their side as companions of the same promise; by faith, not yet by sight. All the characters and words of the Old Testament go before and with us as a cloud of witnesses as we hasten towards the coming of Jesus Christ.[6]

[1] Karl Barth, "Verheissung, Zeit—Erfüllung." *Münchner Neueste Nachrichten*, 23. 12. 1930.
[2] 2 Cor. 1: 20.   [3] Rev. 3: 14.   [4] Rev. 22: 20.   [5] Acts 3: 13-26.
[6] Heb. 12: 1.

(8)

Such are the preliminary definitions of the fact "Jesus Christ" resulting from the unity of the Old and New Testaments. If we assume that the two parts of the primitive Biblical documents have really the same purport; that the witnesses of the Old Testament and those of the New stand facing each other like the two sections of an antiphonal choir looking towards a central point, then at this point stands as an historical event Immanuel, God-with-us, the Mediator between God and man, whose life forms that event of world history through which run, as through one point, all lines joining God to any and every man at any time and place. "Neither is there salvation in any other: for there is none other name under heaven given among men, whereby we must be saved"[1] than that which the angel Gabriel named at the annunciation. The birthday of Jesus, which is fixed by Caesar Augustus's register of persons and their possessions throughout the world, is the absolute date from which all other events and figures of history are reckoned and ordered. Jesus Christ crucified under Pontius Pilate is, as Paul declared on the Areopagus at Athens, "the *one man*, attested by God through the resurrection from the dead, through whom God has decreed on the appointed day to judge the whole earth in righteousness". The hour in which He is preached anywhere is the "now" of decision for every man in whatever place.[2]

Is this really true? Does our description accord with fact?

That is ultimately a question of faith. The answer, however, is inextricably bound up with the literary question whether the writings of the Old and New Testament form a unity in the strict sense maintained by the Church. Has the Church made the right selection of "authentic" documents which define the historical fact "Jesus Christ"? It is conceivable that the Church has erred in determining the canon of scripture; that it is exegetically false to combine the Old and New Testament in this way; that Jesus was historically *not* the Christ, but something different.

The recognition of a definite collection of documents as the authoritative canon (i.e. rule and guide) for our knowledge of Jesus Christ, belongs to the confession of the Church.[3] Church and canon mutually condition each other. A different selection of writings would change the very essence of the Church. It is always a serious question whether the Church can continue

---

[1] Acts 4: 12.   [2] Acts 17: 30–31.   [3] Formula of Concord, I. I.

to acknowledge this particular collection. Must we, and can we, do so to-day? Or as a guide to discerning what is Christian must the Old Testament be abandoned completely or in part? Over against the claim of the Old Testament to canonicity we have to set Harnack's contention: "To cast away the Old Testament in the second century was an error which the Church rightly rejected; to retain it in the sixteenth century was a fate which the Reformation had no power to avert; but for Protestantism to conserve it after the nineteenth century as a canonical document is a sign of religious and ecclesiastical paralysis."[1] Those ecclesiastical defences of the Old Testament which allude to, on the one hand, its sub-Christian notes and on the other hand to its abiding religious and ethical worth, in order (through a misuse of one of Luther's sayings) to reach the conclusion that the Christian recognition of the Old Testament restricts itself to that "which deals with Christ" ("*was Christum treibet*") agree fundamentally with Harnack's thesis. Before assenting to such a position we ought carefully to consider where this leads us. One thing is certain: by this step we abandon the Christian confession—the confession that Jesus of Nazareth is the Christ. It may be that one can do this and still remain a devout person whose piety in some way proceeds from Jesus. But why should such devoutness be styled "Christ"-ianity? For Christianity means precisely the confession that Jesus is the Christ in the sense in which the Old Testament defines Israel's Messiah. The New Testament understands it in this way. All its writings, from the Gospel of Matthew to the Revelation of John, testify in manifold ways one thing—that which Philip confessed to Nathanael: "We have found him, of whom Moses in the law, and the prophets, did write, Jesus of Nazareth, the son of Joseph".[2] With complete consistency the early Church took over Israel's entire scripture, since she maintained that "We who believe that Jesus is the Son of God, we who believe His promise that we are His brothers, we—and not the synagogue which has rejected His messianic claims—are the legitimate heirs of the divine Testament." By this appropriation the Church did not design to rob the Jews of the Old Testament. On the contrary the apostles repeatedly emphasized that the Israelites still had the first claim upon them— "To whom pertaineth the adoption, and the glory, and the covenants, and the giving of the law, and the service of God, and the promises; whose are the fathers, and of whom as concerning the flesh Christ came."[3] One thing, however, they must

---

[1] Adolf von Harnack, *Marcion*, pp. 248 f.   [2] John 1: 45.   [3] Rom. 9: 4 f.

recognize—that Jesus whom they rejected is by God made Lord and Christ; one condition only must they observe— *metanoia*, change of heart—and then theirs, pre-eminently theirs, shall be the wealth of the divine testament. "For the promise is unto you and to your children. You are the children of the prophets and of the covenant which God made with your fathers when he said to Abraham, 'By your seed shall all the peoples of the earth be blessed'. For you above all has God raised his servant Jesus and sent him to you to bless you, that every one should turn from his evil ways."[1]

(9)

The Christian Church stands and falls with the recognition of the unity of the two Testaments. A "Church" which disparages the value of the Old Testament in face of the New disbelieves the decisive element in the apostolic teaching, and ceases to be "Christian". For the distinctive doctrine of apostolic preaching is that Jesus is the Christ of the Old Testament. If that is true, if Jesus really is the Messiah, the Old Testament belongs to those who believe in Him, i.e. the Church. That the Old Testament is the sacred scripture of those who truly believe in Christ is not in dispute between Jews and Christians. The difference of opinion arises only in regard to the question whether Jesus is really the Messiah.

This is the question which faces the New Testament and thereby the Church: Is the interpretation which sees in the whole of the Old Testament a testimony to Jesus the Messiah correct, or is it a violent distortion of the Old Testament scriptures? Does it not "perpetrate upon the Old Testament an unbelievable philological farce" (Nietzsche)?[2]

There is no doubt that a Christianity which confesses Christ *Jesus* stands or falls with the unity of the Testaments. But it is equally certain that the one great question which faces every generation of expositors is whether it is true; whether the New Testament is the genuine interpretation of the Old; whether in very truth when the Jews read it even until this day the veil hangs still over the Old Testament, and is only removed when Jesus is recognized as the Messiah.[3] Is it true? The answer, "Faith alone can decide", is an evasion. It is of course true that it is a statement of faith, which as such is not susceptible of

---

[1] Acts 2: 36–39; 3: 12–26.
[2] Cf. Heinrich Scholz, in *Zwischen den Zeiten*, 1931, S. 31 ff.
[3] 2 Cor. 3: 12–18.

27

proof. But here faith makes a statement about a book written in human words. A careful reading of this book must be able to test whether what is maintained is really written there or not. It is true that the eyes of the apostles for the Christian understanding of the Old Testament were not opened until the Risen One revealed it to them. But that in no way prevented their using immediately the proof from scripture even with those who were not yet Christians and who had not received the Holy Spirit, in the manifest belief that the assertion that Jesus is the Messiah is in conformity with the Old Testament scriptures. The proof from scripture is directed in the first place simply to the human intellect. And whilst a mere intellectual assent to the proof from scripture is not true faith in Jesus Christ, yet it remains true that the proof from scripture must be susceptible of verification by intellectual methods. If Jesus is really the hidden meaning of Old Testament scripture an honest philological exegesis cannot fail to stumble across this truth; not in the sense that it directly finds Jesus there, but in the sense that it would be led to affirm that the thoughts expressed and the stories narrated in the Old Testament, as they are transmitted in the Bible, point towards the crucifixion of Jesus; that the Christ Jesus of the New Testament stands precisely at the vanishing point of Old Testament perspective.

The contrary seems, however, to have been proved clearly and finally by the modern study of the Bible, which, especially in the Protestant Church, is imbued with the conviction that the Christological interpretation of Old Testament texts can be substantiated only by an artificial exegesis.[1] But the question

---

[1] The opening words of Paul Volz's preface to his *Commentary on Isaiah II* (1932) are typical: "The exposition of the prophetic word in this commentary is deliberately theological. It rests upon the historical method of viewing religion and literature. This method, whilst absolutely indispensable, leads only to the circumference, not to the centre, of Biblical truth. On the other hand, I hold that the Christological conception and interpretation of Old Testament prophecy which has recently been revived can be sustained only by an artificial manner of exegesis." We would ask what kind of theology Volz has in mind when he pursues an exegesis which is deliberately theological but at the same time deliberately non-Christological. Does Volz realize that such a theology is no longer the theology of the Christian Church? For the hallmark of Christian theology is that it is Christology, a theology that can affirm nothing of God except in and through Jesus Christ, because no man has seen God at any time; the only begotten Son, which is in the bosom of the Father, He hath declared Him—*exegesato* (John 1: 18). Every affirmation concerning God either forms part of this one authentic self-affirmation of God in Jesus Christ or it is untrue. "If the word of Christ be true, that no man has seen the Father but he to whom the Son will reveal Him, then all who desired to know God had to be ready to follow at all times this eternal Wisdom. How could they understand or speak of the mysteries of God unless they were taught by Him to whom alone the mysteries of God are revealed? So the

is whether the methods and results of this kind of research do not arouse legitimate doubts concerning its validity. Is it not influenced by modern philosophy to an extent which is not permissible when we are seeking to understand ancient texts? Does it not introduce points of view alien to the text? Does it not work with ideas and categories which were unknown to ancient authors? Is it, for example, really possible to understand the phenomenon of Israelite history in terms of laws of evolution and tragedy, whereas the ancient chronicles speak of divine commandment and human disobedience, of election and rejection? Is not the historical problem of Israel "the end of Israel", in the same way that without His death Jesus would never have become historical? It is abundantly clear that not only the prophecies but also the narratives of the Old Testament are governed by the conception of divine judgment, which makes of the history of the chosen people a field of dead bones to be made alive again only by the miracle of divine forgiveness. How then can these writings be rightly understood if we refuse to take this seriously, and instead read into them another meaning more consonant with modern views (Weltanschauung).

The new orientation which Karl Barth has brought into Protestant theology constrains and helps us to-day to interpret the Bible once again as the Bible in its own characteristic sense, however strange this may seem to our modern ways of thought. In addition, there are in the realm of Old Testament study itself—to mention the most important for our purpose— Albrecht Alt's territorial-historical investigations and Johannes Pedersen's researches in Hebrew psychology and sociology, which lead us to-day, as it seems to me, to understand the Israelite traditions afresh in a manner which is historically sounder and more consonant with their true nature.

There is, moreover, one outstanding fact which robs of its validity the scientific protest against the Church's insistence upon the unity of the Bible—the fact that it is characteristic of this "scientific study" of the Bible to interpret the Old

saints only knew God in so far as they saw Him in the Son as in a mirror. By that I mean that God never revealed Himself to men except through the Son, i.e. His own Wisdom, Truth and Light. Whatever of divine teaching Adam, Noah, Abraham, Isaac, Jacob and the others possessed, they derived from this source. It was from the same fountain that the prophets received the divine prophecies which they uttered. But naturally this one Wisdom did not always manifest itself in precisely the same fashion." (Calvin, *Inst.* IV. 8. 5.)

From this it is clear that all the knowledge of God which resides in the Old Testament scriptures is mediated through Jesus Christ. Consequently, the theological exposition of these writings within the Church can be nothing other than Christology.

Testament texts, not by reading what is there, but by reconstructing an "original" context and meaning. It interprets the testimony backwards, in order to discover records of something which has happened, instead of being ready to look forward to that which should come as the records indicate. Since it is characteristic of the Old Testament to look forwards and not backwards, that can be done only by a violent dissolution and reconstruction of the text. This is not the place to discuss whether and to what extent such construction is scientifically permissible or necessary. One thing only need be said—that the Church has never maintained that documents of the religious history of Israel-Judah so reconstructed testify that Jesus is the Christ. It is not surprising if such a procedure leads to other conclusions. The Church's doctrine of the unity of the testaments is not so directly menaced as "the modern scientific study" imagines. Naturally, if the Old Testament were a Redaction which grossly distorts the original meaning of the documents, and if the New Testament were a presentation of the person of Jesus cut to fit the pattern of the Old, every scholar would have to consider carefully how far the Bible is credible. The first question, however, with which we are concerned is whether the Old Testament as it has been handed down to us corresponds both as a whole and in its particular books to the New.

To answer our question we must read the Old Testament as it stands, in the best sense of the word naïvely; not as those who know before they read what they will find there. For it is not the case that we know what the designation "Christ" means. When the New Testament declares that Jesus is the Christ it immediately refers us to the Old: Learn there what "Christ" means. With this in mind the primitive Church retained the Old Testament as sacred scripture. We must follow the train of thought through the various books, following each turn of the way without obstinate rigidity but rather with the utmost flexibility, in order that at the end we may see whither our glance is directed.

In this we shall not proceed by any pneumatological method or pneumatic exegesis. If it is to remain scientific (Wissenschaft) theology must never become theosophy, as we are reminded by Kant's limiting condition, which theology, to its cost, has too little regarded.[1] Nor must Biblical philology—the psychic-rational process of reading and understanding—become pneumatology. We must keep this boundary in mind although we

[1] Kant's *Critique of the Aesthetic Faculties*, p. 89.

know, or rather *because* we know that the Holy Spirit alone can open the Bible and reveal its true meaning. The Author has hidden Himself in such a manner in His work that no exegetical art can bring Him forth. He must of His own free choice be His own interpreter if the reader is to find Him. The Holy Spirit can never be a means by which men take possession of God, but is the freedom of God to make Himself present or absent according to His will. The Holy Spirit is the mediator, but not a means; the *dynamis*, the power of God, but not a spiritual dynamic; the way, *he hodos*, but not a method. It pertains to the holiness of the sacred Scriptures that God Himself must so interpret them that the reader finds there not simply other men and their thoughts about God, but God's thoughts about him, the reader; so that in reading the lives of others he hears the words, "Thou art the man", and his Creator and Judge meets him *to-day* in the erring paths of life with the words, "I am the Lord thy God. I have called thee by thy name; thou art mine." Where that happens the reader hears in faith that which he could never say to himself; that which is possible only as a miracle when God says it to him here and now. Then he hears the Word of God not as the word of the witnesses, but as the voice of the Lord to whom they bear witness who now claims him completely; as the Word which casts upon him the responsibility of giving an answer to God. The man who, accepting this responsibility listens to God and answers Him does so in the confidence and obedience of faith in Christ Jesus, who is God's Word to men, and man's answer to God.

The words of Holy Scripture are like countless messengers who go forth on all the roads in the world to meet each of us—just there where we walk or stand or lie half dead—to halt us and summon us to meet the living God. Not that God speaks to men only through the words of scripture. He speaks when and where and as He will, by every word that proceedeth from His mouth—through the works of His creation, through His guidance in history and in our own lives. The Bible itself says that. It begs us remember how He stands on every side of us, so that there is nowhere to flee from His presence. It is the voice of the *Hidden One* who says, "*Seek My face*". How could we seek Him if He did not call? We should never know *that* He is, to say nothing of who He is. Therefore our whole salvation lies in the words with which He calls out to us from His concealment: "Seek My face". And we can never listen eagerly enough to this voice if we would not grope aimlessly in darkness. But we cannot fail to see that precisely then when man sets out to seek God he falls into dreadful confusion. Does not the history of religion reveal this with frightful clarity? If we would not go completely astray in our quest for God we must keep to the *signs* which God has given us in the Bible to show who He is and how we should seek Him.[1] These signs must be our guide which we follow attentively, honestly and without deviation, following the movement displayed in the writings frankly and faithfully in order to discover their meaning. That we can and should do. The discovery is the gift of God. But we have His promise that to those who *ask* the Holy Spirit will be given.

There is always a great danger that we should read our own ideas into Biblical writings. We shall therefore be ready to be instructed by anyone who reads more correctly. Above all, to keep on the highroad of exposition, we shall follow the footprints of Luther and Calvin. That our understanding of the Old Testament is not so perverse as certain modern experts imagine is remarkably confirmed by its unpremeditated coincidence in many points with those of a Jewish expositor. Anyone who knows Martin Buber's *Königtum Gottes* and *Kampf um Israel* will find much in this book with which he is already acquainted. It must here be remarked, not as claiming priority (which would be presumptuous) but simply to rebutt the facile assumption that our correspondence with Buber is due to direct dependence, that we had laid down the main lines of our treatment of the Biblical documents without guidance from Buber. Consideration of his work enabled us later to make a line here and there stronger and better, for which we are gratefully indebted to him. But possibly the reader will find the differences more important than the agreements. To mention immediately the main one: Buber remains a convinced Jew. Despite the considerable concord between his outline of the Old Testament and ours, in the end when we are constrained to say that they point to the Messiah Jesus of the New Testament, Buber allows them to dissipate in a cloud of mysticism.[1]

[1] This is strikingly evident for example in Buber's address on "Biblical Leadership" (*Kampf um Israel*, S. 84–106). There in one passage he says, "In fashioning the conception of the Messianic leader, the Bible . . . intends to signify nothing less than that at last the answer is present, viz. that from mankind itself comes the word akin to the word that was spoken, a word which is the answer to the word of God. It is the earthly fulfillment which is sought after, a fulfillment upon this earth, a fulfillment in and with mankind. And this is precisely the fulfillment towards which the Hand of God moves forward through all creation, through nature and history. This is the meaning of the Messianic faith, faith in the authentic leader, in the happy ensue of the dialogue, in the ending of God's disappointments. And when an apocryptic fragment of the gospels pictures God saying to Jesus, 'In all the prophets I

A Jew who is resolved to remain a Jew whilst taking seriously the messianic factor in the Old Testament—and here we stand again before the decisive fact—must, however great his respect for the figure of Jesus, reject Jesus' messianic claims. He cannot harmlessly and neatly classify Jesus as modern Protestant theory attempts. For him it is simply a case of either-or. If he were to accept the messianic claims of Jesus he would become a confessing Christian. Actually the most cogent proof from scripture cannot constrain him to this, as the New Testament clearly shows. This confession requires, for Jew and Gentile alike *metanoia*, change of heart, faith.

Is it then impossible to prove from scripture that Jesus is the Christ? Yes; for this proof is given only by the Holy Spirit. The question of the truth of Christianity can be decided only by faith and the election of grace. It is, however, to this decision that the proof from scripture leads. From the hearer or reader nothing more is demanded than that he emulate those in the Jewish school at Berea, who were nobler than those in Thessalonica, and gladly received the word of the apostle and searched daily in the Scriptures whether it was there confirmed.

(12)

In conclusion we summarize the thoughts of this introduction in the words of J. G. Hamann:[1] "How can we cast death into the vessels to render the vegetables more palatable for the children of the prophets? How can the angry spirit of scripture be placated? Do you think I should eat the flesh of oxen or drink the blood of bullocks?" Neither the dogmatic thoroughness of the Pharisaic orthodox nor the poetic exuberance of Saducaic free-thinkers can renew the outpouring of the Spirit which drove holy men (εὐκαίρως ἀκαίρως) to speak and write . . .

The disciple who lay upon the bosom of the Only-Begotten,
have expected Thee, that Thou shouldst come that I might rest in Thee, for Thou art My rest', it displays but a late development of a genuinely Jewish conception."

How clearly the messianic idea is here delineated. But at the close of the address it is lost in a mysterious twilight: " . . . And when the Biblical writer raises his eyes to behold the final Messianic triumph over history, he sees how outward history subsides, or rather how outward history and inward history become blended together, and how the mystery of leadership emerges clearly from the darkness and shines forth over the plains of history, so that the meaning of Biblical history is fulfilled in the whole reality."

See also in particular Buber's preface to the complete edition of the books of the Chassidim (Hegner, Hellerau 1928), in which he states his reasons for rejecting the messianic claims of Jesus.

[1] J. G. Hamann, *Aesthetica in nuce*, Ausg. Roth, 2. Bd., S. 295-298. I have added the translation of the citation from Augustine.

who is in the bosom of the Father, has told us that the spirit of prophecy lives in witnessing to the *one Name* by which alone we can be saved and so inherit the promise of this life and that which is to come; the Name which no man knows but he who receives it, the Name which is above every name, that at the name of Jesus every knee should bow, of things in heaven, and things in earth, and things under the earth; and that every tongue should confess that Jesus Christ is Lord, to the glory of God—the Creator who is blessed to all eternity. Amen.

The testimony of Jesus is therefore the spirit of prophecy, and the first sign whereby He reveals the majesty of His servant's form, transforms the holy books of the covenant into old good wine which deceives the judgment of the master of the feast, and strengthens the weak stomachs of the connoiseurs. *"Lege libros propheticos non intellecto CHRISTO,"* says the punic Church father, *"quid tam insipidum et fatuum invenies? Intelligi ibi CHRISTUM, non solum sapit, quod legis, sed etiam inebriat"*— "Read the prophetic books without reference to Christ—what couldst thou find more tasteless and insipid? Find therein Christ, and what thou readest will not only prove agreeable, but will intoxicate thee."

PREFACE TO VOLUME ONE

Had ye believed Moses,
ye would have believed Me;
for he wrote of Me;
But if ye believe not his writings,
how shall ye believe My words? (John 5: 46–47)

THE Law, in Hebrew Torah, consists of the so-called five books of Moses, which in the Latin Bible bear the following names descriptive of their contents: 1. *Genesis*, i.e. The Book of Beginnings, 2. *Exodus*, i.e. The Book of Emigration; 3. *Leviticus*, i.e. The Book of the Service of the Sanctuary; 4. *Numeri*, i.e. The Book of the Numbering of the Host; 5. *Deuteronomium*, i.e. The Repetition of the Law. They contain the primitive documents of the monumental revelations, commands and promises on which rests God's covenant with the chosen people. From a literary point of view this collection is a composite structure of ancient traditions, the nucleus of which goes back to Moses. It was first preserved and developed by the priesthood at Silo until the destruction of this sanctuary in the days of Samuel, after which the tradition became divided into two parts—a southern, which in the early days of the kings took the form of the so-called Jahwist, and a northern, which in the form which it assumed during the middle ages of the kingdom is known to modern scholarship as the "Elohim" source. The archeologist, Albright[1], conjectures that Deuteronomy, which assumed its standard form in the seventh century B.C., is based on a primitive core of far older narratives and laws which were probably preserved in the ark of the covenant at Gilgal near Sichem; and that particular documents of the priestly codes, representing the standpoint of the Jerusalem priesthood after the Deuteronomic reform, go back to literary traditions which were written in the eleventh century B.C. Other literary critics hold different views which we need not discuss here. In any case more than a thousand years have yielded the contents of the Torah.

We may regard Ezra the scribe as the redactor of the Pentateuch, who gave to it canonical form and rank. For this "Book of the Torah of Moses" which he brought from Babylon, and upon which he re-founded the sacred community after the exile,

---

[1] W. F. Albright, "A Millenium of Biblical History in the Light of Recent Excavations" (Proceedings of the American Philosophical Society. Vol. LXIX, Nr. 7, 1930).

making it thereby in the narrower sense the people of the Holy Scripture, this book of the law which the Samaritans also have received, is (apart from a few ordinances which were later added) identical with those books of the Bible which we call the Pentateuch. From his wooden pulpit he read it to the people in the market place before the water-gate day by day from morning to evening. Pierced to the heart, they broke down; but he forbade their weeping—"The joy of the Lord is your strength" (Nehem. 8). The memory of those days lives on in the synagogue as "the time of our joy" which reaches its climax on the day of the "Torah joy" when a sevenfold procession with all the rolls of the Torah which have been taken from the ark makes its way through the house of prayer with rapturous joy. The people embrace and kiss the adorned and coronate rolls and dance with them.[1]

[1] Martin Buber, *Die chassidischen Bücher*, S. 685.

I

THE BEGINNINGS

GENESIS I–II

GENESIS contains the records of the creation of heaven and earth, of the earliest history of mankind, and of the blessing of the patriarchs of the chosen people. In keeping with the condescension of the divine Word, these records are given to us in the form in which peoples preserve the memory of their origins, in the language of legend and saga. "The Spirit of God alone could narrate the miracle of the six days in so profound and comprehensible a manner. What a proof of divine omnipotence— and humility—it is, that He should desire and be able to breathe the depths of His mysteries, the treasures of His wisdom into the tongues of human concepts so halting, so confused, so burdened with the form of a servant.

"He made us in His own image, and because we lost it, He assumed our image—flesh and blood as sinners have. He learnt to weep, to lisp, to speak, to read, to think like a true son of man. He imitated us that we might be inspired to imitate Him. The pagan and the philosopher discover the omnipotence, the majesty, the holiness, the goodness of God, but of the humility of His love for men they know nothing."[1]

Thus what we read at the beginning of the Bible are legends and sagas—one could call them myths if the word were not so misused. "Around the origins of the human race plays the myth", writes Jacob Grimm. Similarly J. J. Bachofen writes, "The beginning of all development lies in the myth. All thorough-going research into antiquity inevitably leads back to it· The myth bears the beginnings within itself, and alone can disclose them. Origins condition the later development and determine the direction which it shall follow. Without cognizance of origins historical knowledge can arrive at no satisfactory conclusions. The sundering of myth and history, which is justified as it refers to the difference in the manner of describing events, loses its significance and its justification when applied to the continuity of human development. The mythical tradition makes its appearance as the faithful expression of the law of life of those ages which form the foundation of the historical development of the ancient world. It is as the mani-

[1] J. G. Hamann, Ausg. Roth, Bd. 1, S. 449 f.

37

festation of primitive modes of thought, a direct historical revelation, and consequently a true source of history marked by high reliability."[1] The interpretation of myths accordingly occupies the same place in historical research as geology in natural science; out of the petrified and incomparably mightier strata upon which rests the shallow humus of the historical it recalls the memory of the determinative experiences of mankind. In this connection we recall the words of Berdyaev,[2] himself a disciple of Schelling and his doctrine of mythology as the primitive history of the human race: "The profundities of the ages are the deepest hidden strata within man himself, strata which are merely concealed . . . The historical myths possess a profound significance for the process of recollection; in the historical myth is found information which is handed on in the national memory, and which helps us to rediscover in the depths of the human spirit a particular layer which is associated with the profundities of time." For according to Berdyaev the myth overcomes the limits of the outwardly and objectively factual which separate those who live to-day from the event of the past, so profusely recorded, and discloses "a subjective-objective fact," so that "a kind of transfiguration of the mighty past takes place in which occurs an inward comprehension of the historical object, an inner process which renders kindred subject and object." Without taking up any particular position regarding Berdyaev's philosophy in general, we may recognize that these citations help us to understand the meaning of the legends and sagas of Genesis. In its own organic (*ganzheitlich*) way, a thinking in terms of roots and their derived branches, the Biblical account of origins contrives to record events of the past which indeed happened at a particular time, but which, far from being distant and strange to those who read of them to-day, form part of their own experience. To confess "I believe that God created *me* along with all creatures" is to understand the story of creation aright. And to believe the story of Adam's fall is to realize that I as a son of Adam am involved, and responsibly involved, in his fall.

Similarly what Bachofen says of myths is true of the Biblical legends, that the historical event provides the content and religion the form. "The treasury of myths in which the ancient world deposited its earliest recollections of history, the whole sum of its physical knowledge, the memory of earlier periods of

---

[1] J. J. Bachofen, in the preface to his principal work, *Das Mutterrecht*, Basel, 1861.

[2] N. Berdyaev, *Der Sinn der Geschichte*, Darmstadt 1925, S. 45–49.

creation and mighty transformations of the earth, becomes the medium for the delineation of religious truth, the illustration of the great laws of nature, the expression of ethical and moral truths, and the fountain of comfort."[1] It is of course precisely this blending of the report and its meaning, whereby the event becomes almost a parable, which awakens the suspicion that there is in the myth possibly truth, but not historical reality. In regard to many myths this suspicion is in fact well founded. But one must remember that whenever and wherever an event becomes history there is interpretation and composition. For to narrate an event is to express it in words which both recount the fact and articulate its meaning. The simplest narration is an interpretation of that which has happened, though not to the same extent and force as in the case of a myth. To speak figuratively, if we regard the normal historical narrative as the wine pressed out from the grapes of events, the myth is the alcohol distilled from the wine. The product of hundreds or even thousands of years may find its impress in a legend or saga, which may be brief and contain only two or three figures and yet lay hold of the whole reality and profoundest significance of the experience. Such legends are, so to speak, written in hieroglyphics rather than in normal characters. Their words are weightier than those of ordinary narratives, and have a higher value just as gold coins have a higher value than copper ones of the same size and design. That must be recognized by anyone who would understand legends.

We conclude these reflections on the literary form of the primitive records of Genesis by pointing out that among the myths of the nations there are some which are not the expression of real history, but are merely disguised speculations. The word myth as employed to-day has usually a significance quite different from that given to it by Bachofen, and is commonly used to describe something which may equally well happen everywhere all the time as nowhere at no time. The category of the myth in this sense does of course utterly negate history as such, and therefore the particular historicity of the Biblical records.[2] In view of this, it is better not to use the word myth, the meaning of which is coloured both by Greek philosophy and more recent idealistic philosophy, but to use instead the word "story" (*Mär*) in the sense intended by the singer of the Nibelungenlied:

Wondrous things innumerable are told in ancient story.

[1] In the selection in three volumes, edited by C. A. Bernoulli in the *Reclamverlag*, Bd. i, S. 282.
[2] C.f. Karl Barth, *Dogmatik*, I, i, S. 347.

This is also the meaning given to the word by Leopold von Ranke,[1] who makes it the goal of his historical researches: "to seek out the story of world history, that surge of human facts and development which is its true content, its centre, its essence."

GOD'S CREATION

I, 1–2, 4a

1. *In the beginning God created the heaven and the earth.*

In its opening sentence the Bible mentions God and the world in one breath. Not as though they were one, which we might call *either* God or the world; but as two, God *and* the world, which are so distinct that one did not arise out of the other. The world is not a part of God, nor God a part of the world (or something which the world brings forth). Between the two is an infinite qualitative difference. None the less, they belong together. Not in |their nature—once again this must be emphasized—or by a metaphysical affinity, but solely in virtue of the power of God's free will. He does not choose to be alone. He desires a world, and creates it for Himself; it belongs to Him. The relationship between Him and it must not be reversed: He is the Creator and it is the creature. He is the Lord who has created it for His service. He whose Being, hid from our eyes, abides from eternity to eternity, without beginning and without end, gave the world both beginning and end. He it is who initiates the first beginning. From His infinite eternity He decrees time and space and fills them with significance. We can never cease to ask what went before, for eternity is set in our hearts (Prov. 3: 11). And yet how can there be a "before" before time, and a "without" outside space? To our understanding there can be nothing, though "nothing" is the most difficult of all things to imagine. By this we realize that we ourselves are merely creatures, and our understanding is not creative power but simply the perception of that which is given. God gives and we receive. And beyond what He gives us nothing is given; God Himself is not given. The Bible does not say, in the beginning or before the beginning there is God (God is given).[2] No, God is not something given, but He is the source of the revelation that He *gives*. In creative generosity He creates what He gives, and gives it in such a manner that through the gift He makes Himself known as the Giver. He ordains that we know that the Giver is not the gift, and also that it is not His will to reveal Himself to us in

---

[1] *Foreword to the Epochs of Modern History.*
[2] German expresses "there is. . ." by "es gibt . . ." (it gives).

His naked majesty, but clothed with His gift; not as He is in Himself, but as He is in His love to us.

God *created*. "Bara which means create can express only a *creatio ex nihilo* (creation out of nothing). God therefore can be the subject of this verb, but not man, and for this reason, in distinction from other verbs of making and constructing, when bara is used no material is ever mentioned from which the thing created is produced."[1] From nothing comes nothing, unless a miracle happens; and that is precisely what the first sentence of the Bible means, that the coming into being of the world can be understood only as a miracle.

> *And the earth was without form, and void;*
> *and darkness was upon the face of the deep.*
> *And the spirit of God moved upon the face of the waters*
> (Gen. 1: 2).

The import of these words is not that some chaotic substance lay before the Creator waiting to receive its form. It is true that this verse is in Hebrew a so-called "nominal clause," and describes the conditions which preceeded the act referred to in the verbal clause, "And God spake". In Hebrew thought the day begins with the evening; thus in this chapter at the conclusion of each day's work we read, "And the evening and the morning were . . ." Accordingly we might conceive of the primitive darkness as the night belonging to the first day; or —and this is more in keeping with the meaning of the text, that the first day of creation really begins when the light is divided from the darkness, whilst the creation of the light is the all-embracing forward-looking act of God's creation, which is given more precise form in the work of the six days. In this sense also the confusion and darkness are created by God as the foil and presupposition to His revelation in light, as is indicated by the prophet (so closely related in spirit and language to the author of this account), who says in Isa. 45 that God has manifestly not made the earth to be a *Tohu*, but a dwelling-place; yet he remains the Creator of light and of darkness.

The moving of the Spirit over the waters belongs also to God's creative act. Luther[2] expounds it beautifully in the following words: "In Hebrew there is one name for wind and spirit, and here you may take whichever you prefer. If it signifies wind, it means that the air moves hither and thither upon the deep as is its wont. Should you choose to call it spirit, you may; for I know

---

[1] Arnold B. Ehrlich, *Randglossen zur hebraischen Bibel*, on this passage.
[2] *Declamationes in Genesis*, 1527, W. A. Bd. 24, 16 ff.

not how to fathom it. But how beautiful if it means spirit! For then one could image God taking the creature which He has created under Himself as a hen broods over the egg to hatch the chicken." Actually the word used for "move" seems to have as its root the physical picture of brooding. In this passage however, as in Deuteronomy 32: 11, the thought is rather of the mysterious movement of great wings over the young brood.

> *And God said,*
> *"Let there be light",*
> *And there was light* (Gen. 1: 3).

In Hebrew more strongly than in English, after the phrases describing conditions, this first phrase of action, "Let there be", suddenly springs forth with dazzling brilliance. When one reads aloud from the beginning—*bereshith bara . . .*—to this *"yehi or"* it is as though one watched in the darkness the glimmering fuse until the moment of explosion. Yet this comparison is bad, for it gives the impression of violence, whereas here every word breathes the infinitely sublime peace of the Lord, whose is the glory and the power. "He spake, and it was done; He commanded and it stood fast"(Ps. 33: 9). By His word He creates the world. In speaking He ends His infinite solitude. It matters little what He says; the simple fact that He speaks is the marvel of all miracles, by which out of nothing the universe comes into being before God. Fundamentally it would suffice could we but really hear this first "And God spake", for thereby we should comprehend the meaning of the entire Bible. The story is told of Rabbi Sussya of Hanipol that when his master, the great Maggid, in reading the passage of scripture which he desired to expound, began with the words of scripture "And God spake" or "And God said", Rabbi Sussya was filled with ecstasy, crying and moving so wildly that he disturbed the company at table, and had to be led out. Then he would stand in the corridor or in the wood room, beating the walls and crying, "And God spake". He regained his composure only when the Maggid ended his exposition. So it happened that he failed to hear the speeches of his master, and yet was perhaps more strongly moved by the message than the learned scholars.[1] In the creation chapter one "And God spake" after another occurs, and all flow from the first, which introduces no monologue of God, but creates the possibility of the mighty dialogue between the One supreme in glory and another being. That God speaks is the strongest expression of the fact that God deigns not to be alone. For

[1] Martin Buber, *Die chassidischen Bücher*, S. 432.

whoever speaks addresses himself to a hearer. Through His word God creates His hearer. In speaking, the "I"—that is the revealed name of the Eternal (Exod. 3: 13 ff.)—confronts Himself with a "Thou". He reveals Himself as "I am" in saying, "Be thou". So arises the world.

In speaking, God expresses Himself. What is the thought, hidden in the eternity of His divinity, which now comes forth?

Let there be light (Gen. 1:3).

In the abstract, says Goethe,[1] we think of darkness without object as a negation. Light, however, can never be thought of in *abstracto*, for we perceive it as the effect of a definite object *in* space which thus makes other objects visible. Through the word, "Let there be light" there is created a reality which (in contrast to darkness which can only be conceived in the abstract as a negation without object), can only be perceived in the affirmation of its effects here and now, concretely in space and time. The world is thus seen as the object of God's activity, an object which the I places over against itself as Thou, because He chooses not to remain in solitude, but to have a beloved who shall love Him in return. And in the one word light all meanings are comprehended. For light is beauty, goodness, wisdom, colour and form, sound and fragrance; light is joy, laughter and singing, is movement and power, order and harmony; light is feeling and knowledge, clarity and truth, warmth and delight; light is life itself. But it is all this before God, as the sight of His love and in the contemplation of His glory. It is of Him, and through Him, and to Him:

Lord, with thee is the fountain of life,
And in thy light we shall see light (Ps. 36: 10).

Here we must sedulously guard against the danger of slipping into natural pholosophy or mysticism. It is even a little dangerous to use the word "love" in connection with our text, for though the Bible as a whole and in particular the Johannine writings give us the right to equate life, light and love, and set them forth as the final meaning of creation, we have to remember that the word "love" is not used in the first chapter of the Bible, and that it all too easily to-day conjures up the false notion of physical love (*naturhafte Erotik*). The categories and ideas of our chapter belong to the stern system of priestly theology. Excluding fantasy and extravagance, the construction of the world is described as a temple which the Eternal provides

[1] *Beiträge zur Optik*, 1. Stück, Einleitung, Nr. 22 and 23.

for the epiphany of His glory to the elect holy congregation. Instead of saying |"to enter the temple" the Israelite says "to appear before the face of the LORD" or" to see the face of the LORD". And according to the main lines of this account, which begins with, "Let there be light," and ends with the world-sabbath, this is the meaning of creation: in priestly garments arrayed all creatures appear before the face of the Lord, serving Him in adoration and rejoicing in Him—for to the Israelite to rejoice before God and in God is an essential element in the service of God. "Let there be light" thus does not mean, "see the light, and be happy a little while in it", but, "See Me". The light which the Creator here sends forth is, far above the brightness of the heavenly bodies called forth on the fourth day for particular purposes, the epitomy of the miracle whereby God allows His invisible Being to be seen. This light is—the expression can no longer be avoided if we are to expound our text fathfully and guard it against every kind of speculative misinterpretation—"the glory of God in the face of Jesus Christ" (2 Cor. 4: 6). Heaven and earth are the scene of this radiant "brightness of His glory" (Heb. 1: 3), and "wherever the eye looks, there is no part of the world where the radiance of at least some sparks of His glory are not discernible."[1] Yet always in such a way that the light by which He reveals Himself is at the same time a garment in which He hides Himself, and His strong tower into which none may enter (1 Tim. 6: 16). Only "by faith", and that means in New Testament language "by faith in Jesus Christ", can we know that the world is completed by the Word of God (Heb. 11: 3), and only by faith in Jesus Christ can "his invisible nature, his everlasting power and divine being, be perceptible in what he has made" (Rom. 1: 20, Moffat).

And God saw the light, that it was good.

The maintenance of the world rests upon the joy of God (Gen. 1:4) who views His work with satisfaction because, as the expression and object of His goodness, it is good. (Ps. 104: 31 ff.). The proclamation that God sees the world and how He sees it is the "Weltanschauung" (world view) taught by the Bible.

And God divided
the light from the darkness.
And God called the light Day
And the darkness he called Night.
And the evening and the morning were the first day.

(Gen. 1: 4, 5)

[1] Calvin, *Inst.* I. 5. 1.

God divided. God's thought of the world, expressed in the word, "Let there be light", is, according to the opening verses of the Bible, if we may express it in Kant's mode of speech,[1] conceived by intuitive intelligence, the power of an entirely spontaneous contemplation. The intuitive intelligence moves from the synthetic-general to the particular, i.e. from the whole to the parts. God thinks as the Creator, we as creatures. God conceives the world, we meditate upon it. He conceives it as archetype (as *intellectus archetypus*), we see it as an object presented to us (*abbidlich*) (with the capacity of the *intellectus ectypus*). But whether by the one or the other, knowledge proceeds by differentiating and defining. Socrates teaches that human perception consists simply in defining what is before one's eyes, and in the Biblical creation chapter the Creator makes His thoughts concerning what He sees clear, visible and conceivable to us by defining, dividing, calling and decreeing.

He who is the light in which there is no darkness (1 John 1: 5), He who is the Father of lights with whom is no variableness neither shadow of turning (James 1: 17), divides the light from the darkness and determines the movement of the created world by constant change. He casts it in the midst of time, so that its character is that of Becoming, not of Being; its condition is restless transition, not repose but movement. Being and Time mutually exclude each other; Being and Eternity belong together. Being is eternal presence. "God alone *is* in such real and actual Being that a single Now embraces Always."[2] The characteristic of the world however is time, the transition from "not yet" to "no longer", from "becoming" to "been", unending change; not the undivided once-for-all of true uniqueness, but the divided, the sub-divided, the numbered and measured. God divided. And the evening and the morning were the first day.

God makes his thoughts clear to us by presenting them in events of space and time. Space and time are the forms both of outward and inward perception by which our mind apprehends the world. Space, however, is not merely that which can be measured by the rod, nor time merely that which is measured by the clock. The account of the six days, which expresses the differentiation of God's thoughts in space and time, can least of all be measured by the clock. These six world-days have an altogether different measure from the earth-days which are determined by the relation of the earth to the sun. They can be

[1] *Critique of the Aesthetic Faculties*, 22.
[2] Michel de Montaigne, at the end of the *Apologie de Raimond Sebond*.

compared only with the last days, when world time will be ended by God, when sun and moon will lose their brightness and the stars fall from heaven and the powers of heaven be agitated. The first day corresponds to the last day.

Speaking figuratively, it is as though the Creator in His work of the days held before the one light He had called into being a prism (that instrument so highly regarded in the orient that the Chinese ruler reserved to himself the exclusive right of possession, as Goethe reminds us)[1], so that the one white radiance is distributed into seven bands of colour. Repeatedly we read "And God divided". There is separation and alignment, dominance and subordination. And before our eyes there arise the firm clear lines, architectural and symmetrical as if drawn with ruler and set-square, of a temple, a palace of light as Herder[2] puts it, making it evident in the following scheme:

I
Light

II	IV	III
Firmament of heaven		Earth

IV
Lights

V		VI
Creatures of heaven		Creatures of earth

VII
Sabbath

Everything moves towards the great Sabbath festival. For this is raised the lofty sanctuary with the heavenly clock of the starry constellations which proclaim the rhythm of the ceremonial seasons, and the sacred "Host" (2: 1, a significant priestly-levitical expression!) of heaven and earth in ordered array of rank and place, each kind ordained to its office in the liturgy, the sacred service. For this reason we have the frequent repetition "each after its kind", and are acquainted with the peculiar vocation of each by the words "and God called it". The whole chapter in its content and the expression it employs is the fundamental document of priestly learning, which divides the totality of creatures into classes in preparation for the cult. "Natura", in Calvin's[3] definition which reflects the meaning of this chapter, "est ordo a Deo praescriptus". Nature is the order decreed by God, in which each part is called to worship. When concerning the sixth day we read, "God saw

---

[1] Beiträge zur Optik, Nr. 33.
[2] Aelteste Urkunde des Menschengeschlects, vi.   [3] Inst. I, 5. 5.

every thing which he had made, and behold, it was very good", we are not to understand "very good" in the sense of the perfection pertaining to a Greek statue, but in the Hebrew sense of "good", i.e. fashioned to perform its appointed rôle in the drama, capable of experiencing and doing that to which it is destined. All creatures are very good in so far as they are suited to enjoy the Creator's goodness and to praise Him for it. Very good are they in that in them He can reveal His glory and they in adoration can glorify His name, so that He may rejoice in them and they in Him.

At the head of the hierarchy, as the creature who should lead all others in sacred roundelay, God places man. It is true that His creation has no day completely to itself, but follows the creation of land animals; yet the fact that this is God's last work gives to man a special eminence. That it is truly the crowning work is shown in the devotion with which the Creator lays His hand thereon:

Let us create man in our own image, after our own likeness
(Gen. 1: 26).

In mankind God created His true "Thou" (*Gegenüber*), to whom He can reveal Himself.

And God created man in his own image,
In the image of God created he him.
(wayyibra Elohim eth ha-adam b-zalmo,
b-zelem Elohim bara otho) (Gen. 1: 27).

This verse, with its perfectly rounded poetic parallelism, hangs like a clear, beautifully-finished gem on the austerely fashioned golden chain of the creation story. The word "created" which forms the title and is otherwise not employed throughout the chapter, is here twice used to express the direct relationship between God and man. So by its position, its form and its meaning, this verse proclaims that of the whole creation to which God discloses His glory, man is the *eye*. "The light of the body is the eye: if therefore thine eye be single, thy whole body shall be full of light. But if thine eye be evil, thy whole body shall be full of darkness." (Matt. 6: 22 f.) In the words "Let there be light", the whole meaning of creation is expressed: "See me". But light is nothing without an eye, and the eye nothing without light. If the possibility of being misunderstood in the sense of mysticism were not so close at hand, we would recall with Goethe[1] the teaching of the ancient Ionic philosophers

[1] In the introduction to the *Entwurf einer Farbenlehre*.

that an equal can only be recognized by an equal, and follow Goethe further and summarize the relationship of light and eye and man's being in the image of God (*Gottenbildlichkeit des Menschen*), in the Neoplatonic saying:

> Were not the eye made like the sun,
> How could we see the light?
> Possessed we not God's strength within,
> Could the divine be our delight?

Perhaps the lovely verse may stand, if we are quite clear that according to the Bible, in contrast to the mystical words above, this power to see is in truth God's own power, His possession, and never becomes an attribute which is ours except by grace. We must not conceive the image of God as something which rests in the creature and is guaranteed as its own, but as something which in the strictest sense he first receives, that is, which comes to him in the fact of revelation; never as fulfilment but as promise. "Grace is our created being, grace also our 'created being in God' (*Izu Gott hin Gerchaffensein*). Grace is always and in every respect the work and act of God, going forth in this or that moment of time in which God chooses to be gracious and acts graciously and reveals his grace."[1]

In every moment creation stands solely by the grace of its Creator. That is true of every creature, but pre-eminently of the last, which the Eternal made in His own image, placing it at the head of the world as His "Thou" over against Himself. Man lives entirely and solely by grace and in faith. So deeply is God concerned that man should be His image, His Thou, that man can only really live as he faces God, lives from God and to God, only as Thou, and in no sense as I.

The second chapter of Genesis emphasizes this same truth once again, and if we fail to understand it we shall not rightly understand a single word of what follows. The message that the whole creation has its goal in this relationship between God and man, and that this irreversible "I-Thou" relationship between the Creator and the creature, this movement of grace and faith, of divine favour and human trust, of command and obedience, of promise and hope, of gift and gratitude, is the real and only motive of the whole commotion of the world, holding together its inmost soul and reaching out to its remotest distances—this message is so astounding that it is nothing less than a miracle when we believe it. It is a message so

[1] Karl Barth, *Zur Lehre vom heiligen Geist*, S. 45.

wonderful that we can at best but confess with the psalmist
(Ps. 8):

> When I consider thy heavens, the work of thy fingers,
> the moon and the stars which thou hast ordained;
> What is man, that thou art mindful of him?
> And the son of man, that thou visitest him?
> For thou hast made him a little lower than God,
> and hast crowned him with glory and honour.
> Thou madest him to have dominion over the works of thy
>   hands
> Thou hast put all things under his feet;
> all sheep and oxen,
> yea, and the beasts of the field;
> the fowl of the air and the fish of the sea,
> and whatsoever passeth through the paths of the seas.
> O Lord, our Lord,
> how excellent is thy name in all the earth!

The whole world is nothing but the proclamation of One
"Name" by innumerable marvels. And the supremely astounding thing is that of all the mighty witnesses in heaven and on
earth man is summoned to be the crowning witness to the
Creator—and at first not man clothed in wisdom and power,
but man as a helpless child:

> Out of the mouth of babes and sucklings
> hast thou ordained strength
> because of thine enemies,
> that thou mightest still
> the enemy and the avenger (Ps. 8: 2).

The prattle and smile which proceed from the mouth of the
little helpless one are the mightiest defence against the hardened
speech of those who deny the divine authorship of the world;
the strongest proof that the omnipotent and infinitely gracious
will of the *Father* called all things into life, and that the meaning
of creation is found in being sons of God.

That is the message proclaimed by the first chapter of the
Bible. "The Spirit of God alone could describe the miracle of
the six days so profoundly and intelligibly. To me it is astonish-
ing that it should occur to the Architect of the world to give
account of His mighty work of creation, for a clever man does
not readily trouble himself to enlighten children and fools
concerning the mechanism of his actions. Nothing but love to

us who are the infants of creation could move Him to this weakness."[1]

The more modern natural science opens our eyes to the immeasurable expanses of time and space in which we are lost as *"infusoria* of a speck of world-dust", the larger grows our astonishment at the Biblical message that the creative motive of the universe is God's fatherly heart directed to us. This astonishment, however, is accompanied by an increasing reluctance to regard what may be called the world-picture of this chapter as a mere form which one can calmly surrender without injuring its content—a sort of ancient bowl which must be broken to enable modern man to accept the Biblical faith in God. For in these swaddling clothes, and in no others, lies the Christ. Of course the chapter reveals the limitations of man, to whose power of apprehension God has adjusted Himself in revealing His thoughts, and most certainly there is no reason to curtail the investigation of nature in any direction. But we should remember that natural science can never penetrate to the first cause of the world; and further that all observation of nature, whether naïve or scientific, is inseparably connected with a certain point of view (*Weltanschauung*) in accordance with which the observations are systematized and ordered in a certain manner, so that the meaning is conditioned by the kind of person who is looking at it. A review of the transformations of the picture of the world through the centuries shows that "the cosmos is a picture of man, and man a picture of his cosmic picture".[2] The conception of the order of the universe and the orders of society and the order of one's personal life form a unity. Every culture has its appropriate picture of nature. It was no accident that the Copernican reversal of the relations between earth and sun was accompanied by a reversal of the relations between man and man, superior and inferior, prince and people, the individual and the community, man and woman. There is a profound truth in the word of the Polish Rabbi of Purim who said, "Since one began to say that the sun stands still and the earth turns, my head has been turned".[3] There is a direct connection between the liberty of modern man and the dissolution of the world of stars into an infinite universe with an infinite number of worlds. Similarly the convulsive attempts of modern Europeans to rediscover a binding order for our common life go hand in hand with the attempt of modern

[1] Hamann in a letter to Kant, R.A. Bd. 2, S. 448 f.
[2] Otfried Eberz, in the magazine *Hochland*, 27 Jahrg. 1929-30, S. 292-295.
[3] J. L. Perez, *Jüdische Geschichten*, S. 30.

philosophy and astronomy to replace the formless chaos of infinity with some kind of limited ordered cosmos.

The picture of the world varies with the changing phases in the history of human thought. This process of change should not be controlled by ecclesiastical doctrine, and to assume that Biblical faith is tied to the Ptolemaic view of the universe would be to jump to a premature conclusion. On the other hand, we must remember that amid the flux of scientific and un-scientific "orders of nature" anyone who would listen to the Biblical message must take the first chapter of Genesis seriously as the groundwork of the divinely decreed order, as the revela-tion of the architectonic mind which cannot be contained in material nature of its intelligible substratum, and which forms a kind of primal causality for the universe which our minds ("*intra humanae pollutionis fines*"[1] i.e. within the limits imposed by a sinful degradation) can in no way discover. The message of these ancient documents concerning the origin of the world in the will of a transcendent God who desires a Thou, and the order of divine service to which the whole sacred host in heaven and earth is ordained with its hierarchy of created beings culminating in man, made in the image of God and as His true Thou—this message dare not be tampered with unless we would shake the whole message of the Bible to its very foundations.

For everything in this chapter proclaims the Christ. "Here in the Pentateuch we have the mine of gold from which comes all that is written in the New Testament concerning the divinity of Christ. The ore, it is true, lies half buried, but anyone who takes time to place alongside this text of Moses the words of the Holy Spirit in the New Testament will find great light, pleasure and joy."[2] Anyone who believes in a Jesus who either has nothing to do with this chapter or only in so far as He is a member— perhaps even the noblest member—of the created world, does not really believe at all in Jesus the *Christ*. For the Christ is more than the ripest fruit of creation; He is its root, its meaning, its truth. He is the Word that was in the beginning, which was with God and partook of the nature of God. "The same was in the beginning with God. All things were made by Him; and without Him was not anything made that was made. In Him was life, and the life was the light of men. And the light shineth in darkness" (John 1: 1–5). "In eternity God in His majesty and divine Being has a word, a discourse, a conversation or a thought with Himself in His divine heart. This Word which

[1] Calvin, *Inst*. I. I. 2.
[2] Luther, *Kirchenpostille*, Weimar Ed., I. I, S. 181.

God the Father has and speaks with Himself is so completely one with Him that there is nothing in God that is not brought forth in the Word, so that when we behold the Word we see the perfect nature of the Father. This Word dwelt from eternity in His fatherly heart, and by it God resolved to create heaven and earth."[1] The Word is the Son. In saying "Son", God is "Father". The eternal dialogue between Father and Son is the ground and meaning of creation. "By His Son God has made the ages; He is the brightness of His glory, and the express image of His person, and upholds all things by His powerful word" (Heb. 1: 1–2). "Christ is the express image of the invisible God, the firstborn of all creation. For by Him were all things created that are in earth, visible and invisible, whether they be thrones or dominions or principalities or powers: all things were created by Him and for Him; and He is before all things, and by Him all things consist" (Col. 1: 15–17; 2 Cor. 4: 4–6).

The apostolic message runs: Jesus our contemporary is this Christ. In the fullness of time He came to us as Lord and brother. "The Word, which was in the beginning with God and by which all was made, became flesh and dwelt among us, and we beheld His glory, the glory as of the only begotten of the Father" (John 1: 14). Jesus is God's "exegete" through whom alone the Eternal utters Himself (John 1: 18), "and no man knoweth the Father but the Son, and he to whom the Son will reveal him" (Matt. 11: 27). In Him alone is mediated to us knowledge of, and faith in God the Father, the Almighty Creator of heaven and earth. In Him and alone in Him, is the truth of what is written in the first chapter of the Bible.

MAN IN GOD'S GARDEN

(GEN. 2: 4b–15)

This passage is a second account of the creation of man from a different and in some sense narrower point of view. In the first chapter we read, "God created heaven and earth"; in the second: "In the day that the LORD God ('Jahweh God')[2] made the earth and the heavens . . ."; here the earth stands first. And another landscape lies before our eyes in this tradition. While the first account, according to which the waters must

---

[1] Luther, in a sermon on John 1: 1–13, cited according to Eberle, *Luther's Evangelienauslegung*, S. 62.

[2] Like Luther in his translation of the Bible, we use the word "Lord" for the name by which God revealed Himself in the Old Testament, JHWH, the pronunciation of which we do not know with certainty, and for which both Jews and Greeks read "Lord".

first be gathered together in one place before the earth becomes visible, reminds us of the conditions of a river valley where the floods must recede before the fields can bring forth; the second account transports us to dry steppe land where nothing can grow until the Lord sends showers upon the earth. The *garden* which the LORD God planted in Eden, and which we are accustomed to call Paradise from the Persian word employed by the Greek translators, is the prototype of an oasis with a *"ras el ayin"*, a source of water, from which the four principal rivers of the earth arise. God creates man before this garden is planted, and the eye of the reader is immediately directed to this event. There was neither bush nor grass of the field, says our narrator, until man was there to cultivate the land. Everything revolves here around the formation and rank of man. We are, so to speak, in the inmost of the concentric circles of the first chapter.

> *The LORD God formed man of the dust of the ground,*
> *and breathed into his nostrils the breath of life;*
> *and man became a living soul* (living creature) (Gen. 2: 7).

Wayyizer ("and he formed") describes the work of the potter, and expresses here two thoughts. First, that man is an earthen creature, nothing but a handful of clay, a frame of dust, a form fashioned by the pure free will of his maker. "Shall the clay say to him that fashioneth it, 'What makest thou?'" (Isa. 45: 9; Rom. 9: 20). Secondly, that man is at the same time the most intimate and marvellous of God's works, fashioned by His own hand. This complete dependence upon God, which means the closest union with Him, is further expressed in the saying that God has personally breathed into the nostrils of this lump of earth *the breath of life*, and thereby transformed it into a living creature. To the Hebrew, the word "soul" which is used here did not mean a part—let us say the spiritual as contrasted with the corporal—but the whole living creature just as it is. Man does not receive a "soul"; he becomes a soul. He lives by breathing, "as a cow, a horse, a stag, and such creatures as have breath. And thus is indicated that our breath is not in our own power and that we cannot of ourselves breathe or draw breath. Yet by this breath we live, and when it ceases we are dead."[1] The distinctive thing, which is not said of any of the beasts, is that God Himself breathes into him the breath of life. Man's life at every moment depends upon the breathing of God's spirit upon him and upon his receiving God's breath.

[1] Luther, in his sermons on Genesis, 1527.

53

As soon as he becomes wrapped up in himself he dies; for he has no life in himself, but has it only from God. From moment to moment he must receive it anew; he possesses it not once for all, but only in a constant receiving and giving. He can never take it away from God and appropriate it to himself; for failure to breathe out leads to suffocation just as surely as failure to breathe in. These are the "two graces in breathing"[1] which form the abounding life of those under grace.

MAN IN THE STATE OF FREEDOM
(GEN. 2: 16–25)

The word "freedom" is not used in this section, yet there is scarcely a passage in the whole of scripture from which man, who has now lost his freedom, can so well learn what human freedom is. Freedom here is pre-eminently the power to obey God because of one's trust in Him.

> *The LORD God commanded the man, saying*
> *"Of every tree of the garden thou mayest freely eat.*
> *But of the tree of the knowledge of good and evil,*
> *thou shalt not eat of it:*
> *for in the day that thou eatest thereof thou shalt surely die."*
>
> (Gen. 2: 16).

Man is thus confronted with choice. Choice and will are one. The Creator in His freedom has chosen him; the eternal I desires him to be "Thou", that is that he is ready to be used in the service of God, and desires God with all his heart and soul and mind and strength. In the Old Testament, the word choose means love. God loves man, and desires to be loved in return. But love is impossible without freedom, for love is the freedom to choose someone. The man who has lost his freedom persuades himself that to be free means to live to oneself. But in reality when man lives to himself he is in the fullest sense bound, for all the powers of his life are fettered. He becomes free and alive when with all his being he lives for Another, when his life is open and not closed to the Other. He is free who can say "yes" to the Other and give himself to him. Man's life consists in this freedom, in this incomparable possibility which the Creator has conferred upon him in making him in His own image and confronting him with the command of life and love: Desire Me, as I desire you. Desire *Me*—not something from Me or alongside Me. Desire My goodness—not something good. Let your

[1] Goethe, *West-östlicher Divan*, Buch des Sängers, Talismane.

will be governed by My will, for it is My will to be good to you. You must be wholly Mine. Listen to Me and obey Me in complete confidence. The man to whom the knowledge that God knows him means everything, who fully acknowledges God's goodness, knows nothing of the ruptured knowledge of good and evil. So completely does the life of man consist in his being chosen by his Creator, so utterly in the love of God which confronts him with the decision to say Yes or No to God, that the faintest No is death to him.

> The LORD God said,
> It is not good
> that the man should be alone;
> I will make for him an help
> as his confronter (Gen. 2: 18).

The reader who is unfamiliar with Hebrew need not imagine that this translation is a more or less violent interpretation in order that I might interpose the word "confronter" (Gegenüber) in the text. "As his confronter" is the literal translation of the Hebrew Kenegdo. The Eternal Invisible offers Himself to man face to face (Gegenüber) gives to man a visible "confronter" in a being who is his equal. Man, whose "nearest relation" is God,[1] may and should become neighbour to a fellow-creature without his intimate relationship to God being thereby disturbed; on the contrary, from the love of God should flow love to one's fellow-men, and one man become to another as a clear mirror in which is reflected a heart kindled by the love of God (Prov. 27: 19). One could express it thus: the moon revolves round the earth and the earth round the sun by one movement and power in the rays and reflection of one sun. The miracle of the duplication of the One Love stands without comparison. Man can only love his equal as himself.

> Out of the ground the LORD God formed
> every beast of the field,
> and every fowl of the air,
> and brought them to the man
> to see what he would call them;
> and whatsoever the man called every living creature,
> that was the name therof.
> And the man gave names
> to all cattle and to the fowl of the air
> and to every beast of the field (Gen. 2: 19, 20).

[1] Heinrich Pestalozzi, Abendstunde eines Einsiedlers.

That is the origin of language. "How could anyone possibly regard language, *'cet art leger, volage, démoniacle"* (to use Montaigne's words taken from Plato), as an independent discovery of human art and wisdom? Remember that Adam belonged to God; and God introduced the first-born and most ancient of our race as the trustee and heir of the world, finished by the word of His mouth. Angels, greatly desiring to see His heavenly countenance, were the ministers and courtiers of the first monarch. With the choir of the morning stars all the children of God sang for joy. All tasted and saw, at first hand and in the light of present act, the graciousness of the Master-worker, who played upon His earth and had pleasure in the children of men. Not yet was any creature against its will subject to that vanity and slavery of a transitory system under which it now gapes, groans and is speechless. Every phenomenon of nature was a word—the sign, symbol and pledge of a new, secret, inexpressible, and therefore more inward unity, intimation and fellowship of divine energies and ideas. Everything that man in the beginning heard, saw with his eyes, beheld, and handled, was a living word; for God was the Word. With this Word in his mouth and in his heart the origin of language was as natural, as near and easy as child's play."[1] The play of children is the origin of language, the play of the glorious freedom of the children of God. The Creator, so to speak, takes man upon His knee and shows him clear living words, as a father shows his little son the picture-book which he has made for him. What the Creator speaks, man repeats after Him; what the Creator has invented he thinks about and comprehends it with the intellect given him as the image of the Creator, and makes it his own with the freedom of a child to whom everything belongs which the father has made.

Here we would recall again the Socratic dictum that all human knowledge consists of defining that which comes before our eyes. "We think in names", says Hegel. "Apart from speech we should have no Reason."[2] And language "unites us by an unbroken chain of words with the fathers of our race, and derives its life from the first expression of thought by the human spirit. Nothing new has ever been added to the substance of language; all its changes have been merely formal; in a certain sense no root, no primitive word, has been invented by later generations, just as no new element has been added to the

[1] Hamann, *Des Ritters von Rosenkreuz letzte Willensmeynung über den göttlichen und menschlichen Ursprung der Sprache*, A.R. Bd. 4, S. 30 ff.
[2] Hamann, *Zwey Scherflein zur neuesten deutschen Literatur*, A.R. Bd. 6, S. 25.

material world in which we live, so that in a certain sense—
and indeed with perfect justice—we can say that we have the
same words to hand that went forth out of the mouth of the
Son of God as man gave names to all cattle and birds of the air
and animals of the field."[1]

Thus as the first man appropriated with reasonable words the
reality in which he was placed, it became apparent that a
peculiar eminence over his fellow-creatures, the animals, was
assigned to him, for though he could give them names and call
them, there was found among them none so resembling him as
to be his "confronter" (*Gegenüber*).

> *But for the man he found no helper as his "confronter"*
> *And the LORD God caused a deep sleep*
> *to fall upon the man, so that he slept.*
> *And he removed one of his ribs*
> *and covered the place with flesh.*
> *And of the rib which he took from the man*
> *the LORD God made a woman,*
> *and brought her to the man.*
> *And the man said,*
> *"This is it, at last—*
> *bone of my bone,*
> *flesh of my flesh.*
> *She shall be called* Isha, *woman,*
> *because she was taken from* Ish, *from man"* (Gen. 2: 20–23).

The Hebraic play of words, designed to show that the two
are equal and are made for each other, cannot be expressed in
German. Jerome imitates it in Latin by the use of *virago* and
vir.

> *Therefore shall a man*
> *leave his father and his mother,*
> *and shall cleave unto his wife,*
> *and they shall become one flesh* (Gen. 2: 24).

Despite his corruption, man still dimly feels something of
this awakening of Adam, this dawning awareness and recognition of another person who belongs entirely to him, when he
makes the great encounter of his life. Then begins the discourse
of lovers: "My beloved is mine, and I am his" (Solomon's Song
2: 16).

[1] Max Müller, *Vorlesungen über die Wissenschaft der Sprache*, Deutsch von
Böttinger, 2. Aufl. 1866, Bd. 1, S. 25.

And they were both naked, the man and his wife,
and were not ashamed (Gen. 2: 25).

So completely are they, each as he is, fashioned for each
other, so perfectly are they one, each being there for the other,
that they have no shame in each other's presence. For "only
because (though rightly because) man and woman in their
manliness and womanliness desire to belong to themselves, and
not to each other, does the manliness of the man and the
womanliness of the woman become an object of shame (and
shame itself most paradoxically a virtue.")[1] So long as the first
man and his wife lived in the condition in which their Creator
had made them, they were not ashamed either before Him or
before each other. They were utterly free in the presence of
each other because they lived in no sense as single but as
married people. And it is just this belonging to each other
utterly in love, so that it is no longer possible to live singly,
that forms the true condition of freedom; as is indicated by the
old German word "frija" which means "love, beloved", and the
old Saxon word "frî" which means "wife, beloved".

SIN (GEN. 3: 1–7)

Our attempt to understand the first two chapters can at
best, if we are honest, lead to the confession that we are unable
to understand it because neither we nor the world in which we
live and die is as it should be according to this narrative; and
yet that this is the only true life, which if we lose we lose our
being. The word of scripture alone can open our eyes to our
lost condition, which does not simply mean that we have lost
this or that, but that we have lost our being, and are utterly
lost. Until the Word of God removes all veils from our eyes and
reveals to us the abyss of our perdition, we deceive ourselves all
too easily with any kind of interpretation of the self or of being.
The third chapter tells us that man and the world are lost, and
how they become lost and yet were not destroyed but placed
under promise.

Now the serpent was more subtil
than any beast of the field
which the LORD God had made.
And he said unto the woman,
"Yea, hath God said:
Ye shall not eat of every tree of the garden?"

[1] According to Barth's *Vorlesung über die Ethik.*

And the woman said unto the serpent,
"We may eat of the fruit of the trees of the garden;
but of the fruit of the tree which is in the midst
of the garden, God hath said;
Ye shall not eat of it, neither shall ye touch it,
lest ye die."
And the serpent said unto the woman,
"Ye shall not surely die:
For God knows
that in the day ye eat thereof
then your eyes shall be opened,
and ye shall be as God
knowing good and evil" (Gen. 3: 1–5).

Cunningly the serpent endeavours to awaken in the woman *doubts* concerning God's goodness. Every word it speaks is artful. "Neither in German nor in Latin can I adequately interpret the Hebrew. The word *Aph ki* conveys the impression of turning up the nose to laugh at someone in mockery" (Luther).[1] With pitying ridicule it begins to undermine her simple good faith by distorting the Word of God to give the impression that the Creator finds amusement in placing men in the beautiful garden and tormenting them by making them afraid to enjoy the alluring fruits. As we have seen, God's commandment that Adam should not eat of the fruit of one particular tree, was for Adam "the gospel and the law" (Luther); the sign that the Creator had given man freedom of choice, placing him in that relationship of love which rests on loyalty and faith, on trust and obedience. This love, being most delicate, is utterly destroyed by the slightest mistrust. Let but the thought arise in the human heart that God's purposes are perhaps not entirely good towards him, that man can find some good outside or against the will of God, and all is shattered. Bravely, though somewhat garrulously, the woman sets the commandment in its true light. But as soon as she allows herself to be drawn into a discussion of the Word of God all is lost. Perhaps after all the serpent is right in suggesting that there is another way of knowledge than the way of love and the simple knowledge that God is good to him. May it not be that in reality this "higher" knowledge will bring freedom from the strict and entire dependence of the creature on the Creator, of the child on the Father, and give him a position in which he is not

[1] In all cases where the context of a citation from Luther on Genesis is not given, it will be found in Luther's exposition of the passage in his sermons on Genesis, 1527, or in his lectures on Genesis, 1544.

simply coming from God and looking towards God, but standing beside God, independent, a master of affairs like God Himself, knowing good and evil? Would not the attainment of this knowledge signify the achievement of full humanity, his freedom from God, his release and the liberation of his divine being? As soon as man begins to think thus his eye is no longer single, but having become evil glances furtively elsewhere than at God. Therewith in his heart he has committed that which severs him from God and cuts the nerve of the world. "Doubt it is which turns good to evil" (Goethe).

The fact, verse 6, that the woman, having plucked the forbidden fruit, partakes of it and gives it to her husband who also eats, seems so insignificant that it only deserves mention because it reveals the act of disobedience and disloyalty in the hidden recesses of the heart.

> *And the eyes of both of them were opened,*
> *and they knew that they were naked;*
> *and they sewed fig leaves together,*
> *and made themselves aprons* (Gen. 3: 7).

They had imagined they would achieve a knowledge resembling God's, and now they know—that they are naked! They are ashamed in each other's presence, and, as the next verse will show, in the presence of their Creator. They who before had nothing to hide, and who could be quite frank with each other and with God, now seek to cover and to hide themselves. In place of the simple knowledge that because God is good to them, all things are good, they have the divided consciousness which perceives the contrast of good and evil, the conscience which frankly can only be a bad conscience, the knowledge that I am evil. Could God then—that is the question repeatedly posed by children and philosophers when this account is read—not avert this catastrophy? If He could, is not He alone responsible for the "Fall"? From the first two chapters comes the clear answer: God had indeed complete power and freedom to create and guide everything so that nothing could happen contrary to His will. He could have created man not quite in His own image, and withheld from him complete freedom. It was His will however that man should be His "confronter" and love Him with all his heart. And love without freedom is not perfect and pure love. Certainly the Creator could have made man so that he could not deviate by the slightest variation from the will of God. But would that have been love? Could man really in that case have answered

God's love by love? "Dost thou desire me as I desire thee?" That is love's question; and it can only be real when the one who is asked has freedom to respond with "yes" or "no". It is the infinite hazard, and whoever risks it hazards himself and everything. The creation of the world is the fathomless and eternally incomprehensible hazard of God's love. The Creator in giving man freedom puts everything at stake. And man answers: No! By this all is destroyed. Anyone who blames God for this does not know what he is saying, for he is blaming God for placing man in the relationship of love.

The whole infinite guilt of this "no" lies solely on man. How was it possible, we ask, that this "no" could arise in his heart? How could he who breathed nothing but trust in God have a distrustful thought? That is the mystery of evil, the frightful riddle of evil. Anyone who in reading this narrative is offended because an animal speaks, and considers this a sufficient reason for rejecting the whole story as a fable, has clearly not begun to feel the "demonic miracle" of the serpent's speech (Delitzsch)[1] The text is also falsely understood if we imagine that the final guilt is here placed upon the serpent or upon Satan who speaks through him. For precisely in attributing the guilt to man this chapter (and the whole Bible) distinguishes itself from every form of "gnosis". Man cannot fix the blame upon another without denying the freedom which is his as a child of God. In so far as he shifts the guilt which is his before God on to the shoulders of another, whether it be Satan or some potency of fate, he surrenders the incomparable nobility to which the Creator has called him in placing him as a son over all angels and devils, powers and dominions. But in truth there is not one who has retained a shred of this nobility. We can learn of this only through the One who called Himself with modest pride "the man" and "who inherited a far more excellent name than the angels" (Heb. 1: 4), and over whom the tempter possessed no power precisely because he refused to rob God of the slightest honour and desired to be nothing more than His obedient servant (Matt. 4: 1–11; Col. 2: 15).

THE MERCIFUL CURSE (GEN. 3: 8–19)

And they heard the voice of the LORD God
walking in the garden in the cool of the day:
and the man and his wife hid themselves
from the presence of the LORD God.

[1] Franz Delitsch, *New Commentary on Genesis*, 1887.

And the LORD God called unto the man,
and said unto him,
"Where art thou?" (Gen. 3: 8–9).

A dreadful reversal of circumstances now becomes evident, for after listening to the voice of the serpent and becoming disobedient the man and his wife no longer find in the voice of God their joy and delight, but are possessed by mortal terror. The Word of God, that converse with Him which had been their true element, has now become their destruction. The voice of the LORD is now the voice of a judge, no longer that of a father. They hide from him in the inmost thicket of the garden, and the voice of God utters but a single word: *"Ayyecka!"*, the terrible sharp word, sharper than any two-edged sword, piercing even to the dividing asunder of soul and spirit, and of the joints and marrow, and is a discerner of the thoughts and intents of the heart (Heb. 4: 12). This voice startles the creature out of every hiding-place and exposes him in his nakedness: "Where art thou?" This "thou" from the lips of the eternal "I", in which had reposed the whole blessedness and majesty of man, becomes, now that He has exalted Himself to "I", the most dreadful indictment. The presence of God becomes the "question of God" in a far more disquieting sense than in our usual discussions of the question of God in which we mean man's quest for God. *God* asks, "Where art thou?" How can man escape this question?

If I ascend up into heaven, thou art there:
if I make my bed in hell,
behold thou art there.
If I take the wings of the morning,
and dwell in the uttermost parts of the sea,
even there shall thy hand lead me,
and thy right hand shall hold me.
If I say, "Surely the darkness shall cover me",
even the night shall be light about me.
Yea, the darkness hideth not from thee,
but the night shineth as the day" (Ps. 139).

From his peaceful security in God man is roused by the voice of the LORD, driven into fearful anxiety. In vain Adam tries to elude the judge by shifting the blame on to his wife. In vain the woman makes the serpent responsible. They merely prove thereby that they have acted inexcusably, that they have failed in the moment of decision, that they have spurned the claims of God's goodness, and responded with No to the

Yes of His love. Can anything other be expected than that
God will requite this deed with complete destruction?

> *And the LORD God said unto the serpent,*
> *"Because thou hast done this, cursed art thou*
> *above all cattle, and above every beast of the field;*
> *upon thy belly thou shalt go,*
> *and dust shalt thou eat all the days of thy life.*
> *And I will put enmity*
> *between thee and the woman,*
> *and between thy seed and her seed;*
> *it shall bruise thy head, and thou shalt bruise*
> *his heel."*
> *Unto the woman he said,*
> *"I will greatly multiply thy sorrow*
> *and thy conception;*
> *in sorrow shalt thou bring forth children;*
> *and thy desire shall be to thy husband,*
> *and he shall rule over thee."*
> *And unto the man he said,*
> *Because thou hast hearkened unto the voice of thy wife,*
> *and hast eaten of the tree,*
> *of which I commanded thee saying:*
> *Thou shalt not eat of it,*
> *cursed is the ground for thy sake;*
> *in sorrow shalt thou eat of it*
> *all the days of thy life;*
> *thorns and thistles shall it bring forth to thee;*
> *and thou shalt eat the herb of the field;*
> *in the sweat of thy face shalt thou eat bread,*
> *till thou return unto the ground;*
> *for out of it thou wast taken:*
> *for dust thou art,*
> *and unto dust shalt thou return"* (Gen. 3: 14-19).

What is this thing which has happened? One can scarcely
grasp it: the miracle of grace has occurred. God has judged
man, yet not destroyed him. He has punished him severely,
yet answered man's "no" with "nevertheless". Thrice He has
pronounced the curse, yet thrice filled it to the brim with
blessing. The serpent, the tempter, is cursed, and mortal
enmity decreed between its brood and the seed of the woman.
Therewith man ceases to enjoy the goodness of God in simplicity
and peace and is thrust into deadly discord and dissension, into
the battle of good and evil. Human life has forthwith become a

mighty conflict from which none can escape. Terrible though this is, is it not at the same time a sign of the wondrous grace and favour shown to man, that in condemning him to this struggle the Eternal Judge also summons him to it, and by His Son, born of a woman, promises victory over evil?

Upon the woman the Creator imposes an unbearable, painful burden in pregnancy and childbirth: at the risk of sacrificing her own life, she who is herself mortal carries within herself the new young life which she brings forth to nurse and care for; under the judgment of wrath and yet in noblest hope; following the instinctive urge yet taking part most intimately in the miracle of creation; groaning with affliction, bent with labour-pains, brought low, overburdened, languid, weeping; and yet graced with delights and joys and abundantly fruitful sufferings. "As soon as she is delivered of the child, she remembereth no more the anguish, for joy that a man is born into the world" (John 16: 21).

And finally the curse upon the man falls like lightning upon the earth beside him. "Because thou . . . cursed be the ground!" The man had tried to tear himself away from his Maker; now he is obliged to spend every hour in the hard struggle for existence. Instead of enjoying the fruits of paradise as the gardener with the care-free spirit of a child, he must work laboriously to win food from the earth. The way of the farmer, the way of hardship! Scourged with hunger, afflicted with care, bent with labour, he toils in the field till he can do no more.

> Is not man's life on earth bitter drudgery?
> Are not all his days like those of a day-labourer,
> who longs for the shade of evening? (Job).

> He digs and shovels as long as he lives,
> and digs—till at length his grave he has made (Schiller).

Seek as he will to prevent it, his warm day of life is extinguished in the cold night of death. "For dust thou art, and to dust shalt thou return." Such is man's life under the wrath of God. And yet, does not even the curse carry with it grace and favour? Does it not summon man to the activity of life, to the utilizing of all his powers? Is there not an inexhaustible promise in the fact that human life is still possible, even though completely sicklied o'er with death? And is it not precious just when it becomes toil and labour? For just because at any moment all may be lost, at any moment all may be won. The more we have to fight for our life, the more we love it. Danger increases our vivacity, suffering deepens it.

And the man called the name of his
wife chavvah, "Life",
for she is the mother of all living (Gen. 3: 20).

Between the curse and the expulsion from paradise, "though sunk in death he gave to his wife so proud a name. And I doubt not that he breathed again as he heard the voice of God speak of the propagation of life" (Calvin).[1] The man destined for death, whose path, turn as he will, must inevitably end in death, trusts nevertheless because of the merciful curse in the possibility of life in his wife, in the possibility that life is not extinguished by his death, but that even in a world of death he who is destined to death may hand on the gift of life. So long as the miracle of the birth of human life from the womb of mortal woman takes place, the possibility is given that all creatures living under the curse of death may be redeemed. Therefore the first man as "Moriturus" greets his wife as the mother of all living, and the name Eva becomes "the cue to the promised grace" (Melanchthon).

Unto Adam also and to his wife did the LORD God make
coats of skins, and clothed them (Gen. 3: 21).

The man has disgraced himself and lost his innocence. He has become "flesh". As a sign of this he is obliged to cover his nakedness. No cult of nudism, however justified its criticism of modern modes of clothing, can restore the innocence of paradise. The Creator Himself clothes the naked with coats of skins, and thereby establishes—again in merciful punishment—the relationship of religion in place of the original and natural fellowship of man with God. For what is religion but man's sense of shame before God, and his attempt to clothe himself in His presence? "Religion, thou receivest the blush of shame in the body of my death" (Pestalozzi).[2] It is a sign of God's grace that He does not completely cast man out of His presence, but clothes him with His own hand. And in taking the life of animals to make clothes for man from their skins He shows that for the religious covering which He in mercy is ready to acknowledge sacrifice is essential.

And the LORD God said,
"Behold, the man is become
as one of us
to know good and evil:

[1] Calvin, *Commentarius in Genesin*, on this passage.
[2] Heinrich Pestalozzi, *My researches concerning the course of nature in the development of the human race*, section on religion in the principal part.

and now, lest he put forth his hand,
and take also of the tree of life,
and eat, and live for ever".
Therefore the LORD God sent him
forth from the garden of Eden,
to till the ground
from whence he was taken.
So he drove out the man; (Gen. 3: 22–24)
and he placed at the east of the garden of Eden Cherubims,
and a flaming sword which turned every way,
to keep the way of the tree of life.

In these words of God, "The man is become as one of us", Luther finds biting sarcasm and scorn. For not only has he destroyed the image of God within him, but "in desiring to be like God he has become like Satan". He has usurped something of God's glory, and acquired a positively satanic knowledge. The dreadful thing about his judgment is that he now has to live with this knowledge, at the heart of which is the knowledge of death. "We have perhaps peered too far into profunditie. and in consequence reached a moment in human history ˷ ˷ ˷ we know too much about everything, even the most hidden and intractable matters, and especially about ourselves and our end—death. We cannot divest ourselves of this knowledge, and are obliged to live with it" (Overbeck).

Man's simple converse with his Maker, his nearness to God, and the way of the tree of life are all barred by the rotating disk of flame. *Caveant mystici.* All attempts to attain the divine bliss of paradise by religious-mystical means lead either to the dreadful experience of being struck with the lightning of the sword of fire wielded by cherubim or to an illusory blessedness. Man is no longer at home with God. "And if he is not at home with God he is utterly without home. In that case he is what he is only in virtue of completely failing to be what he is. Were his humanity, even in the smallest particular and but for a moment, being without admixture of non-being, he would be at home with God. But there are no such particulars and no such moments. Desiring an abiding home, he is condemned to be for ever on the march—with no abiding city either among the angels or among the animals, either in the soul or the body, either in spirit or in nature, either in the infinite or in the finite."[1] He is in opposition to God, and therefore contradiction and discord pervade all his existence, his life and thought. He dies in living.

[1] Karl Barth, *Prolegomena zur Christlichen Dogmatik*, S. 68 and 69.

He wills that which he does not will, His truth is that he is a liar. The *contradiction* of our nature which destroys our peace and which we are powerless to resolve, the incurable *division of* our whole being, the radical yet unbearable *doubt* of ourselves and all we comprehend, is the root and dynamic not only of religion but also of morals; it is the principle of all knowledge, of philosophy and psychology, just as the disharmony which can be resolved partially but never completely is the dynamic of all art. Without the Fall there would be no such thing as the reality we know as internal and external human history, as world history. For this reason Schiller[1] extolled the Fall as the happiest and greatest event of human history because by this fall there emerged from a happy instrument an unhappy artist, from a slave of instinct a creature acting in freedom, from an automaton a moral being, and thus by one giant stride man placed his foot on the ladder which in the course of many centuries will lead him to self-mastery. Anyone who has read and understood the Biblical account of the Fall will speak more soberly, and realize how unwarranted Schiller is in transforming the voice of God in Eden which prohibited to man the tree of the knowledge of good and evil into the voice of man's instinct, and then proceeding to ascribe man's freedom to his disobedience of this divine command. The Bible knows a different freedom, which was conferred upon Adam but which he lost by the Fall, and for the manifestation of which in the children of God the whole creation waits with anxious expectancy. For not only man is subject to vanity, but with him all creatures—*in hope* says the apostle Paul (Rom. 8: 20). This "in hope" expresses the miracle that God has filled with blessing the curse with which He answered man's "No". It is solely by the grace of God that the disobedience of man is not his end, that his revolt does not destroy him and his doubt end in despair, but that where sin abounded grace did much more abound, and that a story begins with the promise that the last shall be more glorious than the first.

That is the act of God in *Jesus Christ*. Through him, God judges the sinner without destroying him. Through Him, God embraces the fallen world which merits only His wrath in love, giving ground for hope. In sending His own Son in the form of sinful flesh and because of sin, God pronounced judgment of death upon sin, and revealed the marvellous righteousness by which He justified a sinful world and reconciled it to Himself

[1] Friedr. Schiller, *Concerning the earliest human community according to the indications in the Mosaic documents.*

67

(Rom. 8: 3 f.). As the crucifixion of Jesus Christ ruthlessly exposes the world's enmity towards its LORD and God's terrible wrath, so His incarnation and resurrection from the dead expresses the Nevertheless of the Creator to the world severed from Him. Christ's birth, life, death and resurrection are the one event, the one act, by which God keeps this world of death alive until the final victory. Jesus is the conquering hero in combat with the old wicked enemy. At every moment from the fall of Adam to the complete extermination of the old serpent, who is called the slanderer and satan (Rev. 12 and 20–22), He is in the midst of the fight suffering victoriously. He alone, who bore the sins of the world and tasted the bitterness of death, can promise His own that they shall be with Him in paradise and eat of the tree of life which is in the paradise of God (Luke 23: 43; Rev. 2: 7; 22: 14).

Christian expositors have good reason to call the words of God in the cursing of the serpent the original gospel (*urevangelium*), and to declare that in these words Christ stoops from heaven to help. For all who believe, Jesus Christ is in these words present in a world of reality which stands in complete contradiction to God. As Adam heard these words "he returned from hell". By faith in these words the first men "lived and died, and the fathers who succeeded them all expected and believed and preached that a descendent would come to tread down the head of the serpent. These few words embrace all that is comprised in our evangel and faith. Behold how bravely the Old Testament speaks of things: there it is written that Adam was a Christian long before the birth of Christ. For he had the same faith in Christ as we. For time makes no difference to faith. The faith is one from the beginning of the world to the end. Therefore he has received by faith the same that I have received; he saw not Christ with his eyes, nor do we. He possessed Him however in the Word, as we possess Him in the Word. The sole difference is that then it had still to happen, now it has happened. Faith remains the same. So all the fathers were justified by the word and faith, and died therein" (Luther).

REPROBATION (GEN. 4)

Cain and Abel

The Bible here records the first birth and the first death among men.

> *And Adam knew Eve his wife;*
> *and she conceived and bare Cain* (Gen. 4: 1).

In the birth of Cain there occurs for the first time the incomparably wonderful and hopeful event that from two mortal men a new life is engendered and born. Adam "knew" his wife —*Adam realiter expertus est suam Hevam, quod esset foemina* (Luther)—and she became pregnant and bare a child. To the new bearer of life the mother gives the name *Cain*:

> *And she said, "Qanithi a man from the LORD"* (Gen. 4: 1).

Qanithi means "I have gained, I have won", and also (as in the related passage Deut. 32: 6), "I have created, I have produced". And indeed a "man". This striking expression can be explained only from a consideration of the rights of the mother: "The woman *is*; the man *develops*; the woman is present originally as mother, the man as son. The man originates from the woman by a marvellous metamorphosis of nature which is repeated in the birth of every boy. When a man is born of woman the mother herself stands in wonder at the appearance of this new thing. For she recognizes in the formation of her son that power to which she owes her motherhood. With enchantment her eyes rest upon the creature" (Bachofen, *Mutterrecht*). This astonished joy of the mother is expressed in the name Cain, and the addition of *eth-Jahweh*, "with Jahweh", is best understood as emphasizing the divine miracle. Can there be a birth which is not illumined with this joy at the reception of new life, a ray of hope that the sin of death which lies upon mankind will at length be overcome?

> *And she again bare his brother Abel* (Gen. 4: 2).

As the name Cain expresses the hope of life, the name of his brother, born probably as his twin brother, is the expression of deepest despair. For Abel is the Bible's word for the disconsolate emptiness and frailty of human life: *"ak kol habel kol 'adam* —every Adam is through and through an Abel"; or as Luther translates Psalm 39:

> Men live so securely, yet in reality are as nothing!
> They move about like shadows,
> and disquiet themselves in vain;
> they heap up riches,
> and know not who will profit by them.
> O LORD, how shall I comfort myself? (Ps. 39: 5–7).

That is the interpretation of the name Abel. It expresses the bitter realization that outside paradise there is no life without death. *"Nascentes morimur"* (Manilius). "To awaken life is to work for death" (Bachofen). Is there a birth on which this shadow does not lie?

My Brother's Murderer

Even the recognition of this fatal frailty does not bring us to the deepest abyss of human nature. That dread precipice yawns before us when man meets his *brother* and sins against him; man stands in the way of his fellow-man and becomes the mortal enemy of his neighbour; the "I" cannot tolerate the "thou" beside it; Cain *hates* "his brother" Abel, whose only fault is that he is there, and there before God. The fever of hate grips the firstborn man, because in his veins courses the serpent's poison which he inherits from his mother and father. As the son of one who was seduced to break down the barriers between God and himself, he cannot tolerate the barriers imposed by the presence of his brother. Thus even in religion, when it is a case of to be or not to be, I or thou, one's neighbour becomes of all men the most insufferable, and hatred of one's brother most fatally poisonous. *"Talis furia in politica ira non est. Furor pharisaicus est furor plane diabolicus"* (Luther: "There is no such rage in the civic anger of citizens. Pharisaic fury is a perfectly diabolical fury").

> *Abel was a keeper of sheep,*
> *but Cain was a tiller of the ground.*
> *And in process of time it came to pass,*
> *that Cain brought of the fruit of the ground*
> *an offering unto the LORD.*
> *And Abel, he also brought*
> *of the firstlings of his flock*
> *and of the fat thereof.*
> *And the LORD had respect unto Abel and to his offering;*
> *But unto Cain and to his offering he had not respect.*
> *And Cain was very wroth,*
> *and his countenance fell* (Gen. 4: 2–5).

It is envy for the grace of God which drives Cain to fury and at last to the murder of his brother. When the brothers bring to their gracious Creator (who even beyond paradise causes the strange and marvellous birth and growth of plants and animals) their tokens of homage, the LORD looks with favour upon Abel, but not upon Cain. Why? For no other reason than that He is gracious to whom He is gracious; that in the homage which men offer Him *everything* depends upon His favour. The offering is *sola gratia* acceptable, i.e. only when it is offered *sola fide,* that is in the recognition that the value of the gift—if it has any value at all—lies neither in the gift nor the giver, but solely in the God who receives it. For this reason the Epistle to the Hebrews says *"pistei,* by faith Abel offered unto God a more excellent sacrifice than Cain". "Cain thought, indeed was confident, that his offering could not fail to please God far better than that of his brother. For thus he reasoned: I am the elder son, to me pertains the priestly service to God, and authority; moreover I bring the best offering. Therefore God will look upon my gift and be more pleased with it than with my brother Abel's. Abel on the other hand thought: I am the least, he is the best, he has the advantage over me and has brought the better sacrifice; therefore God must look upon my offering in pure grace." In this interpretation of *pistei* Luther paraphrases verse 5 with greater faithfulness to the text than many a midrash of ancient rabbinical or modern protestant exegesis which presumes that righteousness depends on works. Cain made his gift not in faith but in the assurance of his own worthiness and with an eye to winning God for himself. "When he failed in this the contents of his heart are unleashed and he becomes embittered against God and his brother. For where no true faith is, the heart beholds God with jealous eyes and says, "I would that God were not God" (Luther).

In the exegesis of the words which follow (which cannot be fully elucidated philologically), in which God warns and exhorts Cain, we shall be wise to follow again the guidance of the Reformers rather than the Greek translaters who, with their distortion of the text "have departed far from Moses' meaning" (Calvin).

> *And the LORD said unto Cain,*
> *"Why art thou wroth?*
> *And why is thy countenance fallen?*
> *Is it not like this?—*
> *If thou doest well, thou mayest look me frankly in the face;*
> *if thou doest not well,*
> *sin lieth at the door,*
> *desiring to possess thee;*
> *govern it* (Gen. 4: 6, 7).

The fatherly admonitions of the LORD show clearly that God's grace in no way annuls man's responsibility, and that justification by faith alone opens no door to sin but on the contrary leads to the recognition of the sin which lies like a lion at the door and summons us to conquer its lusts (cf. Rom. 6

and 7). This is the meaning of God's exhortations, words and commands to men, that they place man in the position of full responsibility, and open the way for the struggle of the spirit against the flesh (Gal. 5: 17). In Cain's case, however, the terrible result is that sin "gains impetus" (Rom. 7: 11) from the good commandment, and the warning provokes him to the uttermost:

> *And Cain talked with Abel his brother:*
> *and it came to pass, when they were in the field,*
> *that Cain rose up against Abel his brother,*
> *and slew him* (Gen. 4: 8).

To emphasize that of all murders the worst is the murder of one's brother, the story constantly repeats the word brother. Yet dreadful though this deed is, it does not reveal the profoundest abyss of the human heart. More dreadful than the murder is Cain's attempt to excuse it.

> *And the LORD said unto Cain,*
> *"Where is Abel thy brother?"*
> *And he said, "I know not.*
> *Am I my brother's keeper?"* (Gen. 4: 9).

Where art thou? was the question of God in paradise which drove Adam to his last refuge. Where is thy brother? is now the same question of God. Cain's reply decides the possibility or impossibility of his existence before God. Responsibility before God is responsibility for one's brother. In vain Cain seeks to evade God's question with the counter-question, "I know not. Am I my brother's keeper?" Could he have accused himself more effectively than with these words of utter irresponsibility? No further trial is needed:

> *And he said,*
> *"The voice of thy brother's blood*
> *crieth unto me from the ground.*
> *And now*
> *thou art cursed from the earth,*
> *which hath opened her mouth*
> *to receive thy brother's blood from thy hand.*
> *And when thou tillest the ground*
> *it shall not henceforth yield unto thee her strength;*
> *a fugitive and a vagabond shalt thou be in the earth"*
> (Gen. 4: 10–12).

Who can endure to live burdened with such a curse? How can

72

man live when he can no longer evade God's question? "Where is thy brother?" and is tortured by the knowledge that he is guilty of the death of his brother? *"Haec tandem est ruina illa de coelo ad infernum*—this is finally the hideous fall from heaven to hell" (Luther).

The Sign

In his profound despair, in his "hellish agony", Cain cries out for God's mercy:

> *My guilt is greater than I can bear* (Gen. 4: 13).

This may also be translated "my error" or "my punishment", and the Hebrew word for bear can also mean "remit, forgive". Whichever translation is preferred, these are the words of a despairing man who can no longer endure his guilty existence, a man who has lost the possibility of life.

> *Behold, thou hast driven me out this day*
> *from the face of the earth;*
> *and from thy face shall I be hid;*
> *and I shall be a fugitive and a vagabond in the earth;*
> *and it shall come to pass*
> *that every one that findeth me shall slay me* (Gen. 4: 14).

"These are sheer words of desperation" (Luther). How does God answer them?

> *And the LORD said unto him,*
> *"No. Whoever slayeth Cain,*
> *vengeance shall be on him sevenfold"* (Gen. 4: 15).

God answers the despairing cry with graciousness. That is the miracle of His revelation, that He kills and makes alive, that having led men into hell He leads them out again. Over the condemned He holds His hand. And to seal His promise

> *the LORD set a mark upon Cain,*
> *lest anyone finding him should kill him* (Gen. 4: 15).

Branded with the sign of Jahweh Cain is able "to live a life which moves on a knife-edge between the possibility of living (*Lebendürfen*) and the necessity of dying (*Sterbenmüssen*)" (Barth). One would think the text so clear as to require no learned investigation such as Stade's[1] to establish the truth that the sign of Cain is a sign of protection which as Jahweh's

[1] Bernhard Stade, *Das Kainszeichen, Zeitschr. für die Alttestamentliche Wissenschaft XIV*, 1094, S. 250 ff.

sign shows its bearer to be inviolable under the protection of Jahweh. It resembles the custom of religious stigmatization which has been shown to exist among many peoples, and which consists in the marking of a sign or "symbol" of the god on some part of the body. "Anyone thus bearing the mark of his God is proof against the dangers of life, both against human enemies and demonic spirits."[1] "This custom belongs to the same category as the marking of cattle, slaves or prisoners of war by branding" (W. R. Smith). The Greeks stigmatized slaves who had committed theft or escaped. Thus by this sign Cain is stamped as Jahweh's own possession, and one would like with Meyer[2] to see his name as a shortened form of the Arabic *qain-el*, i.e. *slave of God.*

The sign of Cain is thus, like all Old Testament signs, a *covenant sign*, and is indeed the first covenant sign in the Bible. By it God not only binds men to Himself, but also—no, not "also", but rather in the first place in the sense of decidedly taking the initiative, binds *Himself* to men. By this sign Cain is not only marked out as a slave of God, who, though he flee to the end of the earth can never and nowhere escape the hand of his "Lord"; he is also, and in the first place characterized as one whose avenger, whose *go'el* is Jahweh. According to Gen. 4: 15 the sign symbolizes and sacramentalizes Jahweh's promise to be Cain's *go'el*, his *avenger of blood* (2 Sam. 14: 11; Job 19: 25). He, Jahweh, God Himself assumes the responsibility of the next of kin (Ruth 4: 4–6; Prov. 23: 10 f.) to him who is despised and exiled, just as later by the covenant at Sinai He becomes Israel's *Go'el* (Isa. 43: 1).

A passage in the book of Ezekiel confirms this conception of the sign of Jahweh as a sign of protection and leads to a conjecture concerning the form of the sign. In the vision described in the ninth chapter of his book the prophet hears the command given by Jahweh to an angel before the destruction of all inhabitants of Jerusalem who had gone over to foreign cults— "Go through the midst of the city, and set a mark (*hithwitha taw*) upon the foreheads of the men that sigh and cry for all the abominations that be done in the midst thereof". The true worshippers of Jahweh thus receive the mark *taw* on the brow in order that they may not be slain by the destroying angel. In the days of Ezekiel[3] *taw* was written X or +. We may thus

[1] Wilhelm Bousset on Gal. 6: 17 in *Die Schriften des NT.*, *neu übersetzt und für die Gegenwart erklärt*, 3 Aufl. 1917. Göttingen.
[2] Eduard Meyer, *die Israeliten und ihre Nachbarstämme*, S. 397.
[3] Cf. the contrary sign, the token which the worshippers of the beast bear upon the right hand and upon the forehead. Rev. 13: 16 f.; 14: 9; 16: 2; 19: 20; 20: 4.

74

with a fair degree of probability assume that the cross with which Cain was branded and which in Christianity received a new significance is the ancient sign of Jahweh. The fact that in Revelation 7 (cf. 9: 4), in almost literal dependence on Ezekiel 9 the 144,000 slaves of our God are marked on the brow with this seal ($\sigma\phi\rho\alpha\gamma\iota\varsigma$ = stamp, seal) before destruction is let loose over land and sea, confirms the view that the Christian seal of the living God is the same symbol as the sign found in the vision of Ezekiel and upon Cain.

The Christian amulet in the form of a cross thus probably had its origin not in the cross of Christ but in the sign which Jahweh set upon Cain, though it remains true that it was filled with new meaning by the crucifixion of Christ, or rather renewed in its inmost meaning. In both cases the sign symbolizes the same most holy paradox—that he who as a murderer falls under the judgment of God is nevertheless upheld by the grace of God. The sign of Cain is at once a stigma and a sign of protection: anyone bearing it is publicly branded by God as a murderer of his brother; at the same time he is by the same sign protected as God's inviolable possession. And in the same way, though in a higher degree, he who bears the sign of the cross of Christ is branded as the murderer of his "Brother" by God, the Innocent and Holy One who was not ashamed to call the one thus branded as the murderer of God and of his neighbour his brother; yet the same sign sets the seal of God's grace upon him, the murderer, and distinguishes and protects him as God's own possession. The Christian sign of the cross, like the sign of Cain, imprints on its bearer the character *indelebilis* of a servant of God. "Servant of Christ Jesus" or "servant of God" the apostle calls himself, and grounds his inviolability which becomes him as a servant of Christ upon the fact that he bears in his body the marks of Christ (Gal. 6: 17).

Even if the conjecture that the sign of Cain was in the form of a cross and identical with the Christian cross-amulet (which does not mean that the Christians who wore it were conscious of this identity) should prove too audacious and untenable, the affirmation that the sign of the cross of Christ renews and confirms the deepest symbolism of the sign of Cain would remain unshaken. For the sign of Cain carries the promise of reconciliation to the man guilty of Cain's sin, the man who must confess before God that he is his brother's murderer. When the Bible speaks of sin it means nothing less than that the sin of Cain is begotten of Adam's sin as inevitably as Cain was born of Adam. Christ Himself places those who seek His

75

life on the same level as Abel's murderer (Matt. 23: 35). Upon him who is guilty of the death of Christ comes the blood of righteous Abel (Heb. 12: 24). And whoever is not guilty of the death of Christ has no part in the reconciliation through His blood, which speaks better things than that of Abel. For Christ dies for His murderers, and His grace is grace to criminals. When the incarnate Son of God dies on the cross for His murderers the curse is removed which exiled Adam from paradise, as is also the curse which made Cain a fugitive and a vagabond in the earth; then the word which shatters the bars of death and hell becomes true of the criminal—and only of him—who confesses that he is really in perdition: "Verily I say unto thee, to-day shalt thou be with me in *paradise*".

That is the fulfilment of the *promise* which God sealed with the sign of Cain, the stigma of a murderer and protecting sign of God's grace.

Driven out accursed from the holy land

And Cain went out from the presence of the LORD,
and dwelt in the land of Nod, "flight",
on the east of Eden (Gen. 4: 16).

In the story of Cain and Abel "the conception of *adama* (ground), the Holy Land, is inevitably introduced".[1] The geographical area of this chapter is Palestine. And we see how the meaning of the story revolves round the thought that Cain, whose original home was the Holy Land, has fled from it and become a fugitive and vagabond like a bird scared from its nest. Cain is *qen meshullach, ka'oph noded* (Isa. 16: 2). Similarly it becomes clear that Cain is the *Heros eponymus* of the tribe of Kenites known to us from the history of Israel. As in the speeches of Balaam (closely related to our text, cf. also the mention of Cain in Num. 24: 21) it is said that Amelek was the first of the nations (Num. 24: 20), so another ancient saga names the tribe of Cain as the oldest race of men. And the 4th Chapter of Genesis relates the legend that Cain was the first-born man and as such the chosen inheritor of the holy land of Jahweh in such a manner that it tells also of his being driven out of the Holy Land. As the first-born of Adam he inherited the service of the *adama* as a husbandman. Therefore he offered to Jahweh, the divine LORD of the holy arable land, the fruits of the land as an offering. But he was filled with jealousy against his

---

[1] Julius Wellhausen, *Die Composition des Hexateuchs*, Skizzen und Vorarbeiten, Heft 2, S. 9.

brother Abel who under Jahweh's favour fed his flocks on the
pastures of the holy land and whose sacrifice God graciously
regarded. In hatred he slew his brother whom he could no
longer bear to have beside him as co-heir of Jahweh's blessing
in the land of Jahweh. Then occurred the dreadful *reversal of
his destiny*: the blood of Abel cried out to Jahweh from the
adama which had opened its mouth to receive his brother's
blood from his hands. The holy land is no longer permitted to
yield its riches to him who through murder has profaned it
and outraged the heritage of Jahweh (Jer. 2: 7). Hence Cain is
excluded not only from the farming of Jahweh's land, but also
from the cult of Jahweh. Hence his lament: "Behold, thou hast
driven me out this day from the face of the *adama*; and from
thy face shall I be hid". For only in the holy land can he
behold God's face; only over the land of Jahweh "shines"
God's countenance. In a strange and "polluted" land (Amos 7:
17; Ezek. 4: 13) he cannot "seek" Jahweh's face with sacrifice
(Hos. 9: 1–7)[1] but must "hide" himself before the face of
Jahweh. It is this which gives the exile its deadly poisoned
sting. Once outside the holy land Cain loses the right of asylum
granted by Jahweh. Moreover the exile becomes an outlaw,
"so that his fate is to be slain by anyone who finds him".

But the enigmatical mystery about Cain is that despite his
being cursed from the ground Jahweh is his avenger, that over
him who may not look upon the face of God the eye of God
keeps watch. That is the mystery of the sign of Cain, which
places its bearer, though he be fallen under the judgment of
God, under the protection of God, and thus renders him
invulnerable.[2]

Do we go too far in saying that this mystery of Cain is the
same mystery which was presented by the Kenites to the
Israelites in historic times? From Judges 4: 11 we may conclude
that individual Kenites, probably smiths, stood in an economic
relationship with Israelitic tribes as *guest craftsmen*. Max
Weber[3] has shown that craftsmen in particular were characterized by their peculiar relationship as clients, in town and in
village as well as in the desert. "It was precisely the smiths,
those craftsmen of greatest importance to the beduin, who

[1] In order that he may worship Jahweh in Damascus, Naaman takes with
him two mules' burden of holy soil, so that in an unclean land he may form
an enclave sacred to Jahweh, (2 Kings. 5.)
[2] *Qain* in Aramaic and Arabic means "smith", and this is evidently the
meaning in Gen 4: 22, where Tubal, the tribal father of the metal workers,
receives the surname qain.
[3] *Die Wirtschaftsethic der Weltreligionen. Das antike Judentum*, S. 34.

were regarded by the beduin as in the position of ritually unclean guest craftsmen, or (more commonly) as craftsmen excluded at least from the connubium and usually also from the commensalia. They formed a pariah caste enjoying only traditional, or at most religious, protection. It was the same with the bards and musicians who were equally indispensable to the beduin. It is completely in keeping with this that in Genesis (4: 21 f.) Cain is the father of the smiths and the musicians and is the first to found a city" (4: 17). Bernhard Duhm points to the analogy between the relationship of wandering Kenites to the Jews and the position of Jews in medieval Germany, where upon payment of a tax Jews could become "chamber-slaves of the Roman Empire" and so avail themselves of a certain legal protection.[1] It was not only the Kenites who as guest craftsmen stood in this strange contradictory position of being outcasts from the Israelitic Jahweh-community and yet belonging to it. The same enigma is presented by the settlers in Palestine, above all by the shepherds of the Negeb of Judah (who Wellhausen sees represented in the figure of Abel), those exotic Kenite figures who, exiled beyond the borders of the land of culture, and pursued by hunger and fear in the "great and terrible wilderness" (Deut. 1: 19), could never find peace.[2]

> By want and hunger "shrivelled",
> they gnaw the withered reeds. . . .
> Nettles they pluck from the bushes,
> and their food is juniper roots.
> They are driven from society,
> and a cry raised after them as after a thief.
> In shuddering valleys they are obliged to live,
> in caves of the earth and in the rocks.
> They bray among the bushes,
> and meet under the thistles,
> A foolish and nameless generation,
> exiles from the land (Job 30: 3–8).

Such are the Kenites, who cannot live and cannot die outside the Holy Land. Such is their life in the "nests of the rocks" (Num. 24: 21), and in the Negeb-hakkeni (1 Sam. 27: 8–10), which with the Negeb-Judah and the Negeb of the Jerachmelites forms a unity against the hostile land of the Gesurites, Girsites and Amalekites. Such is their situation—they are

[1] Erwin Merz, *Die Blutrache bei den Israeliten*, Leipzig 1916, S. 88–93.
[2] According to the translation of A. Menes in *Die sozialpolitische Analyse der Urgesehichte*, Zeitschr. f.d. at Wissenssh. 1925, Heft 1 u. 2.

outside, beyond the borders of the Holy Land, yet not in the same way as the Amalekites, the "enemies of Jahweh", whom to plunder is a "blessing" (1 Sam. 30: 26). If David had broken robbing and murdering into the Negeb of the Kenites instead of into the land of the Amalekites he would "have made himself stink before his people Israel".

This peculiar position of the Kenites, who are outside and yet inviolate, is grounded in the saga of Cain and Abel. It is even possible that the Kenites still bore the sign of Cain in historical times. Stade attempts to demonstrate the possibility of this in his researches concerning the sign of Cain. In favour of this theory is the fact that in Israel in the time of the Kingdom and until after the exile such a sign was known, and was worn in particular by the members of the fanatical prophetic guilds of the Jahweh cult. There is for instance, the Jahweh-fanatic who covered his forehead with a band in order to hide from Ahab his prophetic "character". As soon as he removed the band from his forehead "the King of Israel discerned him, that he was one of the prophets" (1 Kings 20: 35–41). And according to Zech. 13: 4–6 those who attempted to deny that they were prophets by protesting that they are not prophets but farmers who from their youth had served not God but men, are unmasked by the question, "Then what are these scars between your eyes and on your hands?"[1] On being asked, they try to help themselves by attributing their scars to a profane cause: "I was wounded in the house of my friends". Thus even in late times the scar on the forehead was an unmistakable sign of a prophet. Stade renders it also probable that the "totaphot", the phylacteries of Israel, i.e. cult symbols which serve to bring to remembrance one's attachment to the cult of Jahweh, and which were later replaced by "hand-tephilla" and "head-tephilla" which were buckled on for prayer, are identical with, or at least closely related to, the sign of Cain.

The First Rejection

The indications mentioned above—quite apart from the fact that they are in part mere conjectures—must not be allowed to mislead us into interpreting the story of Cain and Abel as it is in Genesis as relating not to primeval Cain but to the Kenites of the days of David or some other historical time. This chapter narrates an event of primeval times—the original event which prepares the way for the special history of God's revelation within fallen humanity and for the election of one race of

[1] According to B. Stade's emendation of the text.

79

mankind to be the bearer of the special revelation of God. *"Hic incipit ecclesia dividi*—here the Church begins to divide", says Luther with profound insight concerning Gen. 4: 4. If we will retain the metaphor used already, according to which the legends of Genesis, as it were, illuminate the geology of the soil from which all later history takes its rise, we may see in the story of Cain and Abel, as the geological presupposition for the rise of the people of revelation, the "Church", a terrible *rejection of certain strata* which fills the beholder with horror. The first-born is rejected with a hard curse in favour of another. For the chapter ends with the setting of Seth ("set") in the place of Cain. Three times successively there occurs this dreadful catastrophe of groups. The first time with Cain and Seth; the second time with Ishmael and Isaac; and then with Esau and Jacob. In each case the election of the later born takes place in such a manner that he inherits the land whilst the firstborn is driven out into "the great and terrible wilderness". In each case, however, we do well to observe that the one rejected is nevertheless upheld by God and is protected even while in exile. That is so not only in the case of Cain but also in the case of Ishmael and Esau. Although outside the borders of the Holy Land they do not pass beyond God's horizon, and at any moment they can be brought within the fold if it so please God. To those who are within, they stand as warning witnesses of the severity and freedom of God. "Because of unbelief they were broken off, and thou standest by faith. Be not highminded, but fear; for if God spared not the natural branches, take heed lest he also spare not thee. Behold therefore the goodness and severity of God: on them which fell, severity; but toward thee, goodness, if thou continue in his goodness: otherwise thou also shalt be cut off. And they also, if they abide not in unbelief, shall be grafted in, for God is able to graft them in again" (Rom. 11).

The elect dare not forget for a moment that they stand or fall with the free grace of God. The Church lives and moves in faith and trust in God's boundless mercy. The election of grace (*Gnadenwahl*) is the foundation which God laid in Christ after Adam's fall as the basis of His rule over those who were fallen. All man's attempts, whether with or without religion, to establish in his own right a foundation on which he can stand are wrecked on the election of grace. The election and rejection upon which God builds His Church in Christ is the stone of stumbling and the rock of offence, the stone which the builders rejected, and which God has made into the cornerstone. Whoever falls upon it will be broken; whoever believes will not be put to shame (Matt. 21: 42–44; Rom. 9: 33). In the story of Cain this stone is laid bare for the first time through the Biblical revelation.

The Development of Cainitic Culture (Gen. 4: 14–24)

These verses relate how away from his homeland the exile Cain propagates human life and how his descendants become the bearers of culture. No longer allowed to pursue agriculture, they become not simply nomadic herdsmen living in tents, but begin to build cities. Jubal is the first musician; Tubal-Cain "discovers the oldest and most important art—that of the blacksmith, whereby arise the sword and bloody vengeance". The Creator's curse has not annulled the blessed command which man received as the image of God: "Subdue the earth". Man has not lost the gifts which render him capable of this either by his expulsion from paradise or by the sharpening of the struggle for existence through his being exiled from the Holy Land to the land of "flight". Now more than ever he busies himself with art and technical skill. Upon Adam's obligatory step from gardening to agriculture there follow the next steps, evoked by sheer necessity yet proceeding with amazing ingenuity, and always under the curse. "As mankind moves forward in culture it moves backwards in reverence. The first stage of civilization is the need to clothe oneself." It is the first fruit of the "knowledge" which man had appropriated to himself. Upon it follow the inventions of Cain and his sons. "The story of the city and tower of Babel points in the same direction. Here we have the founding of great empires and cities of the world which unite the powers of men and aspire to reach to heaven. In all this the emancipation is extended, but the mounting civilization is accompanied by a deepening alienation from the highest good; and—that is clearly the unuttered meaning—the restless advance never reaches its goal. It is like the work of Sisyphus, and the eternally incomplete tower of Babylon is its fitting symbol."[1]

A striking illustration of the fact that this extension of culture has not rendered men more humane is provided by the song of vengeance by the Cainite Lamech.

> Ada and Zillah, Hear my voice;
> ye wives of Lamech, hearken unto my speech:
> for I have slain a man for my wound,
> and a young man to my hurt.

[1] J. Wellhausen, Prolegomena zur Geschichte Israels, 6 Ausgabe, S. 301.

Yes,
Cain is avenged sevenfold,
but Lamech will be avenged seventy and sevenfold
(Gen. 4: 23, 24).

The speech is a testimony to "the gloomy, wild age of blood vengeance, in which every murder brought forth a new one, where blood which is shed is washed in the blood of others, where 'fowls of the farmyard' lacerate each other in endless waves of murders, where the demon of the race descends in peace to the earth only when the last offspring has made atonement with his death for his ancestor's crime" (Bachofen). Lamech's words have the metallic ring of the bronze age as Hesiod describes it. In Hesiod it is succeeded by "the heroes of divine race who in ancient time were also called demigods. But they were effaced by the miserable war". Then comes the iron age, which is harder than the bronze and to which the present time belongs. The Greek singer closes his description of it with the words, ". . . and nowhere help from disaster".

The New Shoot (Gen. 4: 25–26)

And Adam knew his wife again,
and she bare a son, and called his name
Seth—"set":
For God, said she, hath appointed me another seed
instead of Abel, whom Cain slew (Gen. 4: 25).

From the race of Adam there springs a new scion besides slain Abel and Cain in his wild career. Upon this new scion of the race the mother sets all her hope for the salvation of mankind. Therefore she names him Seth, which means "set"— "as if one should lay or set firm a foundation which should stand fast. By this Eve designs to indicate that this son shall be as it were the foundation upon which the promise will stand and rest. And so Eve, the mother of us all, is rightly praised as a holy woman full of faith and love because she so gloriously honours and praises the true Church in Seth and asks nothing concerning the Cainites. She does not indulge her motherly nature and heart. She does not excuse or minimise her son's guilt. But rather, since God has rejected Cain, she rejects him also, and exiles him and all his race among the heathen who live without the assurance of grace, having only that which falls to them, as beggars and not as heirs" (Luther).

82

And to Seth, to him also was born a son;
and he called his name
Enos ("Weakling").
Then began men to call upon the name of Jahweh
(Gen. 4: 26).

The Sethites are in no way relieved of the misery of sinful human existence. They bear the gracious promise amid many trials. The name Enos indicates this. Enos means simply "man", and characterizes him as a quintessence of weakness in contrast to Elohim, God, who is the quintessence of strength and power, whilst Adam, the other word for man, expresses his belonging to the earth, his connection with the Adama, the "red" earth (*Homo ex humo*).

What is Enos, that thou art mindful of him,
and the son of man, that thou visitest him? (Ps. 8: 4).

And so as bearer of the promise Seth's son bears also the mark of distressed and impoverished human nature. "Blessed are the poor, for theirs is the Kingdom of God". Contradictory though it seems, it lies in the very nature of things that in the days of needy Seth, men began to call upon the name of Jahweh. For "all who call upon the name of God must be in their outward nature under the cross. He had to bear this and lay the foundation" (Luther). Jahweh (or whatever be the pronunciation, which we no longer exactly know) is the name by which the almighty Lord of heaven and earth revealed Himself under the old covenant to His people. "I am that I am" is the interpretation of the name which Moses received from the burning bush. I am present in the reality of your world; I am with you despite sin and death, making real my rule and salvation to you and through you, I in the reality of My own self (*Ichheit*), in order that you may both know and confess Me. "Jahweh, Jahweh, I, I, GOD, merciful and gracious, longsuffering, and of great mercy and faithfulness." So He proclaims His own name, so that His own may call upon Him and declare Him (Exod. 34: 5 ff.). Were it not too artificial it would best express the sense if we were to read and write the name whenever it occurs in the Old Testament as I in English. The Jews, fearing lest they should use the holy name in vain, read it as "Lord", so that it was a simple matter for the Christians, to whom the presence of God in Jesus Christ, the Lord, was revealed, to find throughout the writings of the Old Testament traces of the revelation of their Lord.

THE CHAIN OF GENERATIONS (GEN. 5)

This is the book of the generations of Adam.
In the day that God created Adam
he made him so that he resembled God.
Male and female created he them;
blessed them and called their name
Adam ("man") in the day when they were created.
When Adam had lived 130 years
he begat (a son) who resembled him
as his own image,
and called his name Seth.
The days of Adam after he had begotten Seth
were 800,
and he begat sons and daughters.
And all the days that Adam lived
were 930 years,
and he died (Gen. 5: 1-5).

"He lived . . . and begat . . . he lived . . . and died!" These are the words which in mighty rhythm and with the monotony of hammer blows in a forge ring out through this chapter, and forge, ring upon ring, the generations of mankind.

The Numbers of the years strengthen and deepen the rhythm. "The second wisest after name is number" (Pythagoras). The inner order, magnitude and movement, relation and context of forms and events lies in the number and is revealed by it. The length of life attributed to the generations in this genealogy is significant. The Priestly Writing, to which this chapter belongs, "reckons the lifetime of the fathers from Adam to Noah 700–1,000 years; from Noah to Abraham 200–600 years; for the patriarchs 100–200 years; and for the present time 70–80 years. What prodigious strength—so runs the thought which underlies such reckonings—must the patriarchs have possessed to beget the whole human race! The older the world becomes, the weaker and shorter lived do men become; the more sin increases, the more do the days decrease" (Prov. 10: 27).[1] Beyond this general significance, the particular numbers possess special importance, even though we cannot recognize its significance in every case. The total of Methuselah's years show that he died in the year of the great flood, either just before the judgment began or as one of those judged. The 777 years of Lamech's life are connected with the number 77, of

[1] Hermann Gunkel, *Handkommentar zur Genesis*, 3 Aufl., S. 133.

his speech of vengeance. The special position of Enoch is repeatedly emphasized. In one case he is the seventh in the list, and we recall that seven is the sacred number. Then he does not die, upon which we shall comment shortly. Lastly, not only has he in relation to the others a particularly short life, but the number of his years, 365, corresponds to the days in a year; he thus lives exactly a solar year. A special mystery enfolds his life—his very name means that he is an "initiate" to the mysteries of God, which is quite in keeping with the statement that he walked with God and then was removed (cf. Jude v. 14 and Ecclus. 44: 16).

We will content ourselves with this, and refrain from further interpretative detail. The whole period from the creation of Adam to the flood occupies 1,656 years. By adding to these the figures which are given later we reach the conclusion that the departure of Israel from Egypt took place 2,666 years after the creation. 2,666 is two thirds of 4,000 years, and it is manifest that all these figures belong to a chronological system "which has an apocalyptic goal" (Gunkel), for the existence of the world is estimated at 4,000 years.

Time is thus strictly limited. It opens up no endless possibilities of development. Since through the Fall man forfeited time, and no longer has a right to exist, all time has become for him in the strictest sense a "respite of grace" (*Gnadenfrist*). "My times are in thy hand" (Ps. 31: 16). Man has "time" only when God gives it. Its possibility rests solely upon the *covenant* which the Eternal makes. For this reason the times of the Bible are governed by covenants. Each covenant anchors time and fills it with a certain commandment and a certain promise. The place where man stands before God is not in the eternity which lies beyond time, but in the time bounded by eternity. This time, this "now", is at every moment a time of decision. Neither the godless nor the God-fearing can escape from time into eternity. The decision whether God is God; whether human life has meaning, can neither be postponed nor removed from time to eternity. Here and now it must be taken. Therefore all the figures in Biblical history stand in the piercing searchlight of judgment and grace, election and rejection.

Two linguistic observations may serve to clarify the peculiar concept of time in the Bible. The Hebrew verb has no special forms to denote the tenses (past, present, future). To an English-speaking person that is one of the most remarkable things about the Hebrew tongue, which describes an action only as complete and finished or as incomplete, continuing, "becoming". Instead of the tense, the kind of action is expressed; in other words what is stated is whether time still remains open or is already closed. The second linguistic observation is this, that Hebrew uses the same word, Olam, for eternity and for world, and thus does not distinguish as we do in our thinking between eternity and world or between eternity and time. Time is as it were anchored eternity. The Hebrew root *Alam* denotes that which is hidden. *Olam*, time, is veiled eternity which awaits its apocalypse. Biblical history ends therefore inevitably in apocalyptic. Consequently the chronological system of the Bible has an apocalyptic goal. Time becomes "fulfilled" like a vessel that is prepared for a specific content. At the end its hidden divine import will be revealed. That is the apocalypse. Therefore all the days of the world are *numbered* in the strict sense, i.e. not merely from their beginning from which they proceed contingently, but towards their destined end. The last day reveals the meaning of all which preceded it. They all move towards the goal, culminating in the last day which reveals them in fulfilling them.

In this reckoning of time each historical event has its peculiar significance for the whole according to the year in which it takes place. The most important crossroads of Old Testament chronology (the reason for which is given in 1 and 2 Kings), is the building of the temple by Solomon in the 480th year (i.e. twelve generations each of forty years) after the exodus from Egypt. From Abraham's departure for the promised land to the erection of the temple is likewise a period of 480 years, and similarly a period of 480 years is reckoned from the construction of Solomon's temple to the new temple after the Babylonian captivity. It is at once apparent that a certain rhythm is being imparted to history by these figures. The modern historian would, however, be wrong if he were for this reason to cast aside the figures of the Bible as worthless speculation. So far as historical times are concerned the actual conditions are carefully taken into account by Biblical chronology. If errors have crept in they are a sign of human frailty and the historical contingency of these documents. The case is quite different with the prehistoric and primitive epochs. They are distinctly intended to be more symbolic. Therefore when differences occur between the Biblical figures and those arrived at by modern scholarship for those ages for which the chroniclers of the Old Testament possessed no "historical" dates, this need become no occasion for apologetics. Rather should we remember that these

Biblical numbers are symbolic figures which retain their significance despite all differences with the chronology of modern scholarship.

It is in any case most remarkable that the *coming of Jesus Christ*, declared by the New Testament to be the "now", the goal towards which all events of the Old Testament move (and therefore the goal and fulfilment of all divine covenants, the fullness of time and the revelation of the hidden divine import of all ages) should fall practically in the 4,000th year after the creation of the world according to Old Testament reckoning, and thus *fulfil* the time indicated by Biblical chronology.

So much for the numbers in this chapter. Turning to

The Names, we make the important observation that the names of the Cainites in the fourth chapter are found in a slightly different form in the genealogy of the Sethites. It is very easy to resolve this contradiction by saying that we have here two distinct sources, each of which must be taken by itself. Or on the other hand it may be resolved by placing great weight on the differences in the names and assuming that names which are exactly alike designate nevertheless different people, so that we have two completely distinct lists—here the Cainites and there the Sethites. If however we keep to the text, we cull from it the important recognition that God indeed divides men by election and rejection, but it is an invisible division which does not coincide with the racial, ethnological, sociological, psychological distinctions which we make, nor even with the moral and religious. God's demarcation runs hidden through mankind, and we cannot say these are the elect, those the reprobate. To us it pertains simply to hear with fear and trembling the Biblical witness to the divine dividing word and thus face the choice ourselves.

Enoch

> *Enoch walked with God,*
> *and—was no more,*
> *for God took him* (Gen. 5: 24).

From the one Adam the generations are forged, link by link into one chain. They inherit the same life and the same death. "As by one man sin entered into the world, and death by sin, so death passed upon all men, for that all have sinned" (Rom. 5). Under the kingship of death they live their appointed years. There is no suitor, and each child they beget is born a slave of death. Why? To what purpose? Is there hope of deliverance? Will One at length come who can redeem them and make them kings of life? Yes, this promise is written over the chapter. In Enoch a sign is established. In him occurs the amazing miracle that he does not die. He is removed. God, with whom he walked all his life, does not permit death to separate him from Himself. He takes him to Himself. The miracle is astounding, and yet—Enoch does not thereby become a redeemer. He cannot liberate others. But that which has happened to him is a signal of hope. All who see its light lift up their heads to Him who gave power to death and who can again remove its power. The exception provided by one whose life did not end in death does more than confirm the general rule of death; it shows that death, to which everything is subject, is contrary to the order of creation, and that the Lord who made everything subject to death is not Himself in the power of death. Enoch is not the "bringer-in of life" who can deliver the whole chain from the punishment of death by taking away in dying the sting of death ("the sting of death is sin!") and by his innocent death swallow up death in victory. He does not fight with death for the redemption of all; he is removed. Thereby he becomes not the redeemer, but a witness to the promised victory of the power of God.

Twice God raised up a Sign which was unmoved when the cortege of death composed of those forged into the chain passed by. The first was Enoch for the period from Adam to Moses in which men were subject to death before they received the law at Sinai. The second (the law meanwhile having been interposed) was the ascension of Elijah. At last came the resurrection of Jesus Christ from the dead. Jesus had been forged into the chain. "This is the genealogy of Jesus Christ"—so begins the New Testament, and thereby connects itself with the fifth chapter of Genesis. In Luke's gospel the genealogy of Jesus goes back over David and Abraham to the fathers before the flood until it reaches Adam "who was God's". The One who had been forged into the chain draws the whole chain out of death into life. "For since in and through the fall of the one death obtained the mastery, so far more certainly will those who receive the fullness of grace and the gift of righteousness become kings in life through the One, *Jesus Christ*" (Rom. 5).

Noah

When Lamech had lived 182 years
he begat a son,

and called his name Noah,
saying,
"This same shall comfort us
concerning our work
and toil of our hands
upon the ground which the Lord hath cursed"
(Gen. 5: 28, 29).

"These are words of what Paul calls (Rom. 8: 22) the groaning and travailling creature who imagines that the resurrection of the dead, the redemption from sin and the restoration of all lost gifts are at hand. Because God displayed such honour and so glorious a miracle in receiving Enoch, a man such as we are, to eternal life, the holy fathers in great comfort and joy imagined that the happy day was at hand which should fulfil the promise. Just as Adam and Eve, having received the promise of God, came to have such hope that they supposed that Cain would be the same promised seed (Quain = "gained"), so also I hold that Lamech in pious error (*pio errore*) gave his son Noah this name saying, He will comfort us and deliver us from the misery of this life—from the curse which, with all its distress and affliction, oppresses the earth for the fault of Adam, and which because of sin has descended upon the whole human race. Lamech thinks therefore that Noah is the promised seed which shall restore the whole world.

"But the curse or punishment of sin cannot be removed except by the erasure of original sin itself. And the honour of restoring everything that we had lost in paradise pertains not to a man but to the Son of God" (Luther).

So Noah also is not the redeemer. But, like Enoch, he is a witness to the redeemer. Through him after the flood the Lord of heaven and earth makes His covenant with all flesh.

GOD'S COVENANT WITH NOAH (GEN. 6–11)

God decides to destroy all living creatures on the face of the earth
(Gen. 6)

And it came to pass, when men began to multiply upon
the face of the earth,
and daughters were born unto them,
that the sons of God saw the daughters of men
that they were fair,
and they took them wives
of all which they chose (Gen. 6: 1, 2).

89

At the "highly mythological colour" (Schelling) of these verses many readers are offended. Quite rightly. Yet it would be foolish to follow those exegetes who seek to tone down the offence by explaining that "the sons of God" means the descendents of Seth, and "the daughters of men" the Cainites, so that that sin which is here branded is the blending of the godly with the godless. Nothing of this is found in the text; the account is plainly about the union of divine beings with human women. That is of course "a fairly unadulterated piece of heathen mythology", and we have reason to ask how such an account found its way into the Bible and what it has to do in this passage. It is well known that in heathen religions such stories have a large place, and that in Greek and Roman mythology they have become classical. But in the Bible something of this character seems like a foreign body. Yet may it not be that this good heathen mythology stands in this place in the Bible in order to expose the deepest root of paganism? The pagan form corresponds exactly to the pagan content. This event: the lust of the "spirits" for the "flesh", the invasion of the human sphere by metaphysical powers, the demonic impregnation of earthly reality, the pseudomorphic procreation of god-men, which forms this *shameless blasphemous mockery of the birth of the Saviour of the World*—this occurrence is the root of paganism. Without knowledge of this basic fact, this demonizing of life and of the world, the psychology of religion will be unable to understand the "soul" of a "primitive" or "highly developed" man, and Christian missions impotent to proclaim the triumph of their Lord over powers and principalities (Col. 2) and to drive out the demons in His name (Mark 16). At the moment when Jesus appears among men the unclean spirits cried out at His every step from the bodies and souls of those possessed because they knew that the Holy One of God who designs to destroy them had come forth. How can one understand the evangelical records if one will not acknowledge Genesis 6 as their presupposition?

> *And the LORD said,*
> *"My spirit shall not always*
> *rule in men,*
> *for he is also flesh.*
> *So let his days be 120 years!"*(Gen. 6: 3).

Adam's attempt to break down the barriers between God and man is not only followed by Cain's murder of his brother because man could not endure the limitations represented by his fellow-men, but now from above comes the attempt to remove the barrier between the world of spirits and the world of men. Through it man becomes "flesh", not in the good sense of dutiful creatureliness, but in the perverse sense of glorying in his own power. Flesh as "spiritual life-principle"! (*geistiges lebensprinzip*). In such a case the Holy Spirit no longer desires to rule in majesty. His work can no longer be recognized in His directing and creative purity and power, but becomes henceforth transformed into the "creative dynamic" of nature and is experienced as the animation of the vitality of the flesh. In consequence, God withdraws His Spirit to prove the uniqueness of His creative power and the impotence of the creature.

> *There were giants in the earth in those days,*
> *that is, after the sons of God*
> *went in to the daughters of men*
> *they bore them.*
> *These were the heroes of old,*
> *men of renown* (Gen. 6: 4).

This account again resembles similar sagas of many peoples concerning mighty races and giants (it is significant that the Greeks used this word to translate this passage). We think for instance of the account in Hesiod according to which the bronze age was followed by "the heroes of divine race". "In ancient time they were also called demi-gods on the endless earth."

In his book, *Urwelt, Sage und Menschheit*, Edgar Dacqué attempted to reconstruct the gigantic figures of those who lived before Noah from the data provided by myths and sagas and the findings of modern palæontology. Equally valuable for the understanding of this passage is the famous address which Jacob Burkhardt gave without a single note in Basle in the winter of 1870 concerning "historical greatness". In the audience sat the young Nietzsche who, as the one who dared to conceive the idea of the superman, imagined that he alone understood the "profound argument which in its unusual ideas and devious windings approached the fantastic". The "great ones" of world history are individual descendents of the primeval race of giants. The nature of the "great one" remains the same. It is a demonic product, and "great" men are rightly describes as demonic. "Real greatness is a *mystery*", says Jacob Burkhardt. "Time and the man enter into a mysterious compact. History loves to compress itself from time to time into a single man whom the world obeys. These great individuals epitomize whole states, religions, cultures, crises . . . their nature remains truly a mystery of history; their relation to their times is a *hieros gamos* (a holy marriage) seldom realized but in terrible times which provide the single highest measure of greatness, and which alone feel the need for greatness."

These are the giants who make the rest of mankind feel like "dwarfs". And they are tyrants. In their character "there lives above all else a real will to be master of the situation accompanied by an abnormal strength of will which exerts a magical coercion and attracts to itself all elements of power and mastery and makes them subject to itself." . . . The great individual destroys, subdues or uses the wild egotism of other individuals —and suddenly they join together to form a power which leads the process further. In such cases one stands astonished at the rapid and brilliant blossoming of a previously backward culture, which then bears the name of the great man as the century of N.N."

These are the men of renown, "as Napoleon on Elba said: *'mon nom vivra autant que celui de Dieu'*."

> *When the LORD saw*
> *that the wickedness of man was great in the earth,*
> *and that every imagination of the thoughts of his heart*
> *was completely evil every day (radically and totally evil)*
> *it repented the LORD that he had made men*
> *on the earth,*
> *and it grieved him at his heart.*
> *And the LORD said,*
> *"I will destroy man*
> *whom I have created*
> *from the face of the earth;*
> *both man and beast*
> *and creeping thing,*
> *and the fowls of the air;*
> *for it repenteth me that I have made them"* (Gen. 6: 5–7).

Reason may be offended at the statement that God was grieved in His heart, but in the Bible, at the very centre of which stands the passion of Christ, God has revealed Himself not as apathetic "world reason", but as one who is infinitely concerned for His creatures. From nothing He called them all into life that they might rejoice in Him. Now man has ruined everything, and his life has become an unbearable agony in which he tortures himself and others. Yet what is the suffering of the creature compared with the infinite anguish of the Creator? He would prefer an end with horror to this horror without end.

But Noah found grace in the eyes of the LORD (v. 8).

On this thread hangs the whole world. God's grace perceives a point of contact (*Anknüpfungspunkt*) through a single man.

Noah was a man "zaddiq tamim" (v. 9),

says the Hebrew account, so characterizing him as a man whose whole nature is as completely directed towards God's *zedaqa*, i.e. the good will of God which reaches out to him and claims him, as the magnet needle is directed to the polar star.

Noah walked with God (v. 9).

Though we have said that the Holy Spirit of God could no longer guide men, yet here is one who "reacts" to God, in whom the connection, the wire spanning the distance, has not been broken—one who still hears.

What he hears is dreadful: the announcement of the flood in which all flesh, all that breathes, shall be drowned. And the command to build an ark in which Noah's nearest relatives and a pair of each kind of animal shall be saved (Gen. 6: 13–21).

And Noah made it,
exactly as God had commanded him made he it (Gen 6:22).

Such was the obedience of faith by which Noah honoured God when he received the command concerning that which no man yet saw; through which he justified the judgment upon the world of those who ate and drank, married and were married. By this obedience of faith he came safely through the flood to become the bearer and preacher of righteousness through faith, and so the deliverance of eight souls by the ark became the symbol of salvation by baptism in the Church (Heb. 11: 7; 1 Pet. 3: 20–21; 2 Pet. 2: 5).

The Flood (Gen. 7–8: 19)

Many scholars have advanced our understanding of the flood by literary and scientific researches. We can allude here only to the most important points. In the Biblical description itself two traditions can be recognized which recount the same event in diverse ways according to the nature of the countryside in which they originated. Further, many peoples dwelling in districts widely remote from each other—and it may be from all parts of the earth—possess collections of sagas which in their own way recall the great catastrophy. This fact confirms the impression which results from taking the Biblical account seriously, that we are concerned here with a cosmic event and not with the flooding of a certain limited portion of land. "And everything was destroyed which was upon the face of the ground, both man and cattle and the creeping things and the fowl of the heaven: and Noah only remained alive, and they that were with him in the ark." That is unambiguous. Edgar Dacqué has shown in his book *Urwelt, Saga und Menschheit* that the scientific understanding of the flood as a cosmic event is to be sought, following Hörbiger's glacial cosmogony, in the theory that particles of ice or masses of ice dust entered the earth's atmosphere and flooded the earth with waters from space. Such an event must have considerably altered the position and form of our planet. Dacqué believes that this change may be recognized geologically at the point where the mesozoic age ends and the tertiary age begins. The alteration in the appearance of the earth, both in the plant and animal worlds, which marks this geological turning point can be well explained, he considers, by the overflowing waters of the flood. One reason among others why he places the flood at this geological epoch is that the olive tree (Gen. 8: 11) and the vine (9: 20 ff.) are associated with Noah. For both the olive and the vine belong to the plants which we meet for the first time in the last part of the cretaceous period, that is at the end of the mesozoic age.

Students in mythology and natural science must test the accuracy of these researches of Dacqué. Anyone undertaking this task will not only need to be, as Dacqué, master of the pertinent sciences, but like him will require a good ear for the peculiar speech of myth and saga. Such people are apparently few to-day. Dacqué may be right or wrong, and we do not attempt to base confidence in the Biblical account upon the results of his investigations. We have referred to his work rather because what he says is at least powerful evidence of the *reality* of the occurrence of a flood as related in the Bible.

The Covenant of Forbearance (Gen. 8: 20–22 and 9)

And Noah builded an altar unto the LORD;
and took of every clean beast
and of every clean fowl,
and offered burnt offerings on the altar.
And the LORD smelled a sweet savour,

and the LORD said in his heart,
"I will not again curse the ground any more
for man's sake;
for the imagination of man's heart
is evil from his youth;
neither will I again smite any more
every living thing, as I have done.
While the earth remaineth,
seedtime and harvest and cold and heat,
and summer and winter, and day and night
shall not cease" (Gen. 8: 20–22).

Like two pylons driven deep in the earth, supporting an electrical conductor and standing one on each side of a wide valley there precedes and follows the account of the flood the divine affirmation of the radical evil of the human heart, conjoined in each case with an offensive anthropopathic description of the emotion with which God makes this affirmation. This is intended to make the reader realize that the turning of earth's fate from destruction to the new opportunity of life is grounded solely in the movement of God's heart from "No" to "Nevertheless". The expressions of human emotion are indeed most inadequate to describe this transformation, for no human heart, but only God in the supremacy of His divinity is capable of such a change. When in this and similar Biblical passages (cf. for example Hos. 11; Jer. 31: 18–20; Luke 15: 20) the miracle of His mercy is proclaimed in strongly anthropomorphic terms, the picture of God is not degraded to the human—all-too human—but on the contrary, the superhuman (*menschen-unmöglich*) character of the divine graciousness which transcends all that is possible to men is thereby emphasized in a somewhat offensive manner: "I am God and not man". This is perhaps shown most clearly in the words in which the book of Hosea describes the pardoning of Israel:

How shall I give thee up, Ephraim?
How shall I deliver thee, Israel?
Mine heart is turned within me,
My repentings are kindled together.
I will not execute the fierceness of my anger,
I will not return to destroy Ephraim:
for I am God and not man,
the Holy One in the midst of thee,
and no destroyer (Hos. 11: 8–9).

These anthropomorphisms point forward to the one event in

95

which is accomplished the turning of God's heart for all time—from the pardoning of Adam after the fall to the pardoning of the last in the day of judgment—the incarnation and passion of the Son of Man. God's decision to maintain life upon the earth after the fall rather than to destroy it, is founded, too, upon the mercy of God in Christ Jesus. For this reason, and for this reason alone is God ready, despite the fact that the imagination of man's heart is evil from his youth, to sustain the earth perpetually in its majestic order, in the rhythm of life under the sun. The radical evil in man shall not be able to wrench the earth from the invigorating rotation of heaven, for even the chaotic earth must at last become the scene of the glory of her Lord.

Thus God spoke in His heart. And what He speaks in His heart will become manifest as the new legal basis of earthly life in the *covenant* with *Noah.*

And God blessed Noah and his sons, and
said unto them,
"Be fruitful, and multiply
and replenish the earth.
The fear of you and the dread of you
be upon every beast of the earth,
and upon every fowl of the air,
upon all that moveth upon the earth
and upon all the fishes of the sea:
into your hand are they delivered" (Gen. 9: 1–2).

Man receives anew not only the creative blessing upon procreation; but, despite his fatal disobedience, his mastery over the animals is restored. Despite his wickedness he is not humiliated. God dares to clothe him again with full sovereignty. Despite the disgrace he brought upon himself he is still esteemed as the image of God. The slavery of nature and the servitude of vanity into which he fell through his emancipation shall not be final. From now on the creature awaits with anxious expectancy the revelation of the glorious liberty of the sons of God (Rom. 8).

In one respect the original order of creation (*Schöpfungsordnung*) is changed. Whereas at first man and animals were to live upon plants alone (1: 29 f.) they are now allowed to eat also flesh.

Every moving thing that liveth
shall be meat for you;
even as the green herb have I given you all things
(Gen. 9: 3).

Now man lives by taking animal life. The peace of paradise is mutilated until the day when the anointed one of the race of Jesse shall establish His kingdom: "Then the wolf shall be the guest of the lamb, and the panther shall lie down with the kid. The calf and the young lion shall feed together, and a little child shall lead them. The cow and the bear shall be friends and their little ones shall lie down together, and the lion shall eat straw like the ox" (Isa. 11).

Now that killing is allowed for the maintenance of life the two laws which set limits to it become of the greatest importance:

> But flesh with the soul thereof, with the blood thereof,
> shall ye not eat (Gen. 9: 4).

Life itself, the "soul" of the flesh, resides in the blood (Lev. 17: 11).

> And surely your blood of your lives will I require;
> at the hand of every beast will I require it,
> and at the hand of man;
> at the hand of every man for his brother
> will I require the soul of man.
> Whoso sheddeth man's blood,
> by man shall his blood be shed[3],
> for in the image of God made he man (Gen. 9: 5).

If anyone sheds the blood of man, his blood will be shed by man:

"SHOPHÉKH DAM HA-ADAM, BA-ADAM DAMO YISHAPHÉKH."

One should read the sentence in Hebrew aloud in order to feel the magical power which flows from the diction of the divine fiat, which is the basic foundation of human law. It secures the humanity of man by declaring inalienable and inviolable the brotherhood and divine likeness (Gottebenbild-lichkeit) of every single one who bears a human face. The radical evil of man consists in this, that, refusing to belong either to God or to his brother, he seeks to glorify himself. That is his sin and his death. He cannot live in this way in God's creation; he becomes his brother's murderer. If despite this man is to live in God's creation in the fundamental recognition that the imaginations of his heart are evil from his youth up, some limit must be set to the beast which lurks within man's nature. The murderous despotism of men must be met by superior force. God ensures this by charging the other men to

G

kill the murderer. By investing men with authority over the lives of others the divine Judge institutes government (*exusia*), which as the holy servant of God does not bear the sword in vain, and as the avenger executes wrath upon the evildoer (as Paul says in Rom. 13). From the duty of revenge resting upon each member of the clan to the sovereignty of an emperor this superior force assumes a variety of forms. In any case there is no authority which is not of God, and the powers that be are ordained of God (Rom. 13). This rests upon the command to Noah. In all their diversity, the governments of the nations are but variations of one authority, that emergency order (*Notordnung*) by which God in the covenant with Noah gave to men the possibility of living without mutual destruction, and to "be fruitful and multiply, and bring forth abundantly in the earth" (9: 7).

With His promise and command to Noah, the Judge of the world rivets the evil to the earth, so that it becomes in a measure a concern within this world. The judgment upon evil is not thereby annulled; on the contrary it proceeds in God's name with inexorable severity, but is now a judgment among men upon earth and only for time, not as the divine condemnation to eternal damnation. Man continues in the valley of decision in which his life is at stake. And yet his whole existence, including this decision, is encompassed by the goodness of God.[1] In all nature death through its dread function serves life, removing consumed and exhausted life to make way for new possibilities of life. Despite this function of death, or rather precisely because of it, life abides upon the earth "in the hope that the creature itself also shall be delivered from the bondage of corruption into the glorious liberty of the children of God" (Rom. 8: 21).

With this aim in view God sustains the peoples of the earth by giving them in the covenant with Noah their government and political order. He gives to each after its kind, and not simply to the chosen people. In the covenant with Noah all peoples of the world are embraced as well as Israel. It is to be observed that the Mosaic law is not identical in import with the laws given by God to the heathen. Of course it has also this import—as Luther expressed it. "Moses is the *Sachsenspiegel* of the Jews"; but however strongly this might impel us to place the Torah parallel to the nomos of any of the other peoples, we are prevented from doing so by the recollection that Israel

---

[1] Cf. Fr. Gogarten, *Staat und Kirche*, "Zwischen den Zeiten," 1932, Heft 5; Politische Ethik 1932.

is the chosen people whose development of government does not run parallel to world history, but, since Jesus Christ is the King of Israel, forms a prophetic part of *that other* history with which the Redeemer cuts across world history. By the decision at this point of intersection God sustains and leads the heathen through the constitutions (*Verfassungen*) which He gives them on the basis of the covenant with Noah. What He thus gives them are emergency orders by which, despite the evil imaginations of the human heart, He gives them life and sustains them to the day of Jesus Christ. The expression "emergency orders" (*Notordnung*) awakens the thought of need. But where God gives there is no lack. What the heathen have received is of priceless value, and in many respects valuable even to Christians. Concerning worldly government and the way in which corporal and temporal goods should be administered "the heathen have much to say and to teach us". And, to speak the truth, "they are in such matters far more competent than Christians" (Luther). We are amazed when explorers like Bruno Gutman and Ernst Johanssen bring to light the treasures possessed by African tribes in the way of ancient decrees, practical wisdom, political institutions, education and statesmanship. Yet much that is to-day being revealed would appear still more significant and be less likely to lead to false conclusions if it were clearly recognized that what is here in question is gifts of the covenant with Noah. We should also be well advised not to use the expression "ordinances of nature" (*Schöpfungsordnungen*) too recklessly, but to speak rather of "Noahtic ordinances" when we refer to the family, nation (*Volk*), state, society, economic life, etc. In this way we should avoid the misunderstanding that these ordinances as they now are have their origin in the creation concerning which it is written, "And God saw everything that he had made, and behold it was very good". For in reality they are conditioned by that breach in the good creation which is signified by the fall, and form a compromise between the unchanging goodness of the Creator and the radical evil of man. "For the hardness of your heart he wrote you this precept, but in the beginning of creation God ordained it otherwise" (Mark 10: 5 f.). From this it follows that, firstly, all these institutions are ambiguous, being both gifts of God's goodness and products of human wickedness. And secondly it follows that they are neither universal nor final; God will change them according to His will and the human situation, and at length will annul them when His Kingdom comes. Even before this final culmination the command may go forth at any time to those who are called to be the people of God: "Get thee out of thy country, and from thy kindred, and from thy father's house, and become a guest and stranger upon the earth, waiting in faith, and a citizen of the *polis* whose builder and maker is God" (Gen. 12: 1 and Heb. 11: 8–16).

Christian missions know this conflict. All our thinking about state and Church, politics and the gospel must take account of it in the realization that the Noahtic ordinances are given not to conserve eternally the earth as it is, but to maintain it until the coming of Jesus Christ, in anticipation of a new heaven and a new earth wherein dwelleth righteousness (2 Pet. 3: 13).

The Sign of the Covenant

To every divine covenant of the Bible pertains a *"sign"* which carries the significance of a pledge. *Sacramentum* means in the language of Latin law the retaining fee which both parties to a civil law suit deposited as a caution. This sign as a legal custom derives from a time when there existed no written contracts, and such "testimonies" were accordingly necessary (cf. the taking off of the shoe in the Book of Ruth, chap. 4). Like all God's covenants in the Bible, the Noahtic covenant is not an agreement between two equal partners. It originates quite "onesidedly" in the clemency of a perfectly free Lord who has obligations to nobody, and upon whom no one has a legal claim. By grace alone He binds Himself in eternal loyalty, and establishes His sign.

> *And God spake unto Noah, and to his sons with him, saying,*
> *"And I, behold I establish my covenant with you,*
> *and with your seed after you;*
> *and with every living creature that is with you,*
> *of the fowl, of the cattle, and of every beast of the*
> *earth with you;*
> *with all that went out of the ark,*
> *for everything that lives upon the earth.*
> *I will establish my covenant with you;*
> *neither shall all flesh*
> *be cut off any more by the waters of a flood;*
> *neither shall there be any more a flood*
> *to destroy the earth."*
> *And God said,*
> *"This is the token of the covenant which I make*
> *between me and you and every living creature*
> *that is with you for an age of the world:*

I do set my bow in the cloud;
it shall be for a covenant
between me and the earth.
And it shall come to pass, when I bring a cloud over the
earth, that the bow shall be seen in the cloud;
and I will remember my covenant,
which is between me and you
and every living creature of all flesh;
and the waters shall no more become a flood
to destroy all flesh.
And when the bow is in the cloud
and I will look upon it,
that I may remember the age-long covenant
between God and every living creature
of all flesh that is upon the earth."
And God said unto Noah,
"This is the token of the covenant,
which I have established between me
and all flesh that is upon the earth" (Gen. 9: 8–17).

It is the marvellous bow that extends over the earth when the light of the sun is scattered by raindrops, the bow said by many Gentiles—Babylonians, Indians, Arabians, Greeks—to be the bow of the storm god from which he shoots the arrows of lightning and hail, and which he then hangs upon the clouds or places upon earth "when the arrows of his wrath are sped and the sinews of his fury relaxed" (Babylon); the bow, or more precisely *"the bows* which tinted Kronion erects high in the clouds as a sign to mortal men" (Homer). In Egyptian thought the rainbow is the essential part of the otherwise invisible vault of heaven, the marvellous inner framework upon which rests the firmament. The seven colours intimate that seven "faithful ones" stand arched over the earth in protection. When God masses clouds over the earth He lets His bow shine forth in token of His faithfulness: the heavens shall not fall, for grace embraces the earth despite the radical evil of men.

The Creator of heaven and earth looks upon the bow in the cloud to remember His age-long covenant (*Weltzeitbund*). So the sacrament of the Noahtic covenant is, like all Biblical sacraments, a "token" of the faithfulness of God directed towards the goal of redemption. As the apostle says of the Lord's Supper, "As oft as ye eat this bread and drink this cup ye do show the Lord's death till he come", so each appearance of the rainbow is the proclamation of the great salvation by which God will at last redeem His earth. All time since the flood is at every moment a respite of grace. The covenant of grace with Noah guarantees the postponement of the end in the hope of a good end—the establishment of the Kingdom of God instead of catastrophe. It is as it were the divine moratorium with a world encumbered with debt. With it begins the age of God's *anoché*, his "forbearance", during which the sins which are committed remain by divine patience unpunished until the time when God shall show that He is righteous and the justifier of him who lives by faith in Jesus Christ (Rom. 3).

The Noahtic Covenant is thus Sealed in Christ

Through Him and in anticipation of His revelation God sustains the earth despite its corruption. His sacrifice alone provides a basis for, and justifies, God's silent waiting. God's dealings with the heathen, as also the history of the chosen people and evangelical history take place on the soil of the Noahtic covenant. But not only is it true that Jesus grows out of this soil; He is at the same time the foundation of this soil. The covenants of the Bible are so to speak circles of revelation of varying radii, but all have *one* centre. Moreover we do well to reflect that this one centre—Jesus, the Saviour of the World —is the fountain-head of all these circles of revelation and not simply their product. Jesus Christ is God's faithfulness towards the world; in Him alone is the whole present. He is the meaning, the *dynamis*, the possibility and the riches of every revelation.

Noah's Curse and Blessing (Gen. 9: 18–28)

A signpost at once obscure and prophetically clear pointing to this hidden centre of the Noahtic covenant, a suggestion of the particular land and the race of mankind in which these circles of divine revelation will find their centre for this act of revelation which establishes and fulfils all others, is provided by the remarkable story of Noah's drunkenness and the curse and blessing which he spoke as he awakened from the intoxication of the first vintage after the flood.

This is one of the significant Old Testament "legends of the saints" which many people find so offensive that they would be relieved if they could be erased from the Bible. But these Biblical offences are salutary, for they clearly indicate that it is not the purpose of this Book to praise human virtue and to present an assembly of the religious and moral élite of mankind. The kind of men here chosen are not selected on account of their moral excellence, but simply by the will of the Lord who is pleased to glorify His grace through sinners. This people is "holy" only because He who alone is holy has called it to be His own to the end that they might declare the excellence of Him who has called them out of darkness into His marvellous light (I Pet. 2: 9).

Was there really nothing more edifying to relate concerning "the hero of the flood" who is described as "an upright man and blameless" and who "lived a godly life in his time"? And yet Luther is right when under this apparently "foolish and utterly useless story" he writes the words, "Praised and blessed eternally be God, who leads His saints so marvellously (Ps. 4: 4). For though He allows them to be weak and to fall, and to be so filled with unbelief and vexation that the world judges and condemns them, He pardons their weakness and has mercy upon them. And those on the contrary who imagine themselves to be angels He hands over to the devil and casts them off utterly."

This concerns, however, only the general import. The "foolish and utterly useless story" offers other and most important insights.

> *And the sons of Noah, that went forth of the ark,*
> *were Shem, Ham and Japheth:*
> *and Ham is the father of Canaan.*
> *These are the three sons of Noah,*
> *and of them was the whole earth overspread* (Gen. 9: 18–19).

The future of the various races is evidently decided at this point.

> *And as a husbandman Noah planted*
> *for the first time a vineyard* (Gen. 9 : 20).

This statement carries the account of the development of culture which we met in the previous chapters a step further. Agriculture is enriched by the cultivation of the vine. This is more however than a merely cultural matter. From the narrative of the migration of man from the garden to the field and from the progress of the Cainites we have already learned that culture and cultus are most intimately related. This is doubly true of the culture of the vine. The heathen maintain that a god, Dionysos or Osiris, gave directions concerning it, and thereby made a blessed gift to men. For wine not only "cheereth God and man" (Judges 9: 13), but allows man to partake of the delights of divine existence by the intoxication which raises him as upon holy wings above his narrow limitations. From the part which Canaan plays it is clear that the narrative of this chapter has regard to these religious associations. Among the Canaanites the Israelites meet this western Asiatic religion of intoxication which threatens to seduce them. The law and the prophets abhor and forbid it as shamelessness and prostitution. For instead of "maintaining the modesty of this my mortal body (see 3: 21), this Dionysiac religion of intoxication is exhibitionism, i.e. a voluptuous exposure of nakedness. The Israelitic revelation will have nothing to do with such ecstatic conditions in which religion becomes an intoxication of love in which man forgets himself and imagines himself to melt into the ocean of divinity. No; it places man in holy sobriety before God with the petition: "Speak, Lord, Thy servant heareth". Because the indigenous Canaanites have polluted the Holy Land with such customs the land has spewed them out (Lev. 18). That is the meaning of the curse which Noah pronounces when he awakens from his wine and becomes aware of what his youngest son has done to him:

> *Cursed be Canaan;*
> *a servant of servants shall he be univ his brethren* (Gen. 9: 25).

From now onwards the Canaanite becomes to the Hebrew reader *Kna'ani*, a derivation of *kana*, meaning to shrivel, subdue, humiliate.

> *Blessed be Jahweh, the God of Shem;*
> *and Canaan shall be his servant* (Gen. 9: 26).

Noah's first-born son, Shem, is the bearer of the proper revelation—that which the Bible calls the "Name" of the Lord, the shem Jahweh—and is therefore as it were the sealing wax upon which the unknown God sets the stamp of his true nature, in order that he may be thus recognized and known. Noah addresses the blessing in the form of thanksgiving to God Himself, as though he would say, "It is not necessary for me to grant Shem my blessing, for he has already received the spiritual blessing. He is already God's son from whom the Church will proceed and be planted, as it was begotten and planted by Seth before the flood. And it is particularly clear and evident that he brings God and his son Shem into close association and so to speak marries them each to the other" (Luther).

> *Yapht elohim le-yepheth*
> *God enlarge Japheth!*
> *He shall dwell in the tents of Shem,*
> *and Canaan shall be his servant* (Gen. 9: 27).

This is a remarkable prophecy. By it he declares that same mystery which Paul (Rom. 11: 11) and Christ (John 4: 22) touch upon, that salvation is of the Jews and yet the Gentiles will also be partakers of it. For although Shem is the true root and stem, the Gentiles will be grafted on to this stem like a strange twig and will partake of the fat and sap which is in the chosen tree. This light Noah sees by the Holy Spirit, and although he uses obscure words, he none the less prophesies very definitely that the Kingdom of the Lord Christ will be built and planted from the tribe of Shem and not of Japheth.

This prophecy thus pictures the Church of the Gentiles and of the Jews. For Ham is rejected and not allowed to partake of the spiritual blessing of the seed "unless something should happen through limitless free grace" (Luther). It is, however, going too far to say that Ham is rejected. For the remarkable thing is that Ham is not rejected, but only his one son Canaan. For the rest it is left an open question for grace to decide what shall happen to the Hamites. And despite the fact, which we must here recall, that God in examplary fashion manifested his wrath and power upon the Hamitic Egyptians, and slew their firstborn because they would not let his firstborn son Israel go free, yet the Church of Christ has to-day every reason to praise the grace of God for the miracles which He has wrought among the Hamites from eunuch of the queen of Ethiopia to the present day. Where God leaves even a tiny fissure, His grace finds a way of streaming through with the glory of its light. So we bless the God of Shem as we see that not only Japheth but also many children of Ham have found a place in the tents of Shem. "So we Gentiles who are children of Japheth have indeed no promise which is specially given to us, and yet we are included in the promise which is given to the Jews. For we are foreordained for the communion of saints, of the people of God. And these things are not written for Shem and Japheth but for those who come after them.

"This is what Moses secretly declares in saying, "Blessed be the LORD, the God of Shem". For he thereby declares that the promise is only to be found there where the LORD of Shem is. Therefore a Jew is not a partaker of this promise unless he has the God of Shem, i.e. unless he believes. So also Japheth is not a partaker of the promise except he dwells in the tents of Shem, i.e. unless he is included in the communion and society of the same faith which Shem has" (Luther).[1]

"When we consider the three words of Noah which he

[1] Weimar Ed., 51, 242.

uttered when on awaking from his intoxication, he saw the garment which covered him; when we see the numb, drunken man who lay there in all the disgrace of his nakedness suddenly transformed into an angel of light who sees through the centuries into the future, and speaks of God's blessing with enchantment, and decides the fate of nations with his curse and blessing; what human tongue ever embraced in so few words such a stream of knowledge or reposited in one event so apparently simple the import of so many baffling mysteries!"[1]

The Generations of Noah (Gen. 10)

"The Creator, who gives to all life, and breath and all things, has caused all races to be descended from one man, and to dwell upon the face of all the earth, and has determined beforehand their times and the bounds of their habitations, that they might feel after him and find him." Those were the words of Paul to the Athenians upon the Areopagus, as he began with their religion in order to declare to them the name of the unknown God (Acts 17). The same message is embedded in the tenth chapter of Genesis, where, from the root of Noah and his three sons, Shem, Ham and Japheth, there arises the genealogical tree of all peoples with many branches according to their countries, their languages, their races and nations.

The import of this genealogy is universality. It bears witness that there is no race and no nation upon the earth that did not live with God in the Noahtic covenant. This would remain valid even if modern anthropology should prove that the list is incomplete. The gaze of the writer is not limited to his own people or his own race, but "seeks to embrace and arrange the peoples of the whole world" (Gunkel). He thus seeks to include all, for it is the intention of the Noahtic covenant that none should be lost, but that all should be partakers of the same salvation. "Hope's invisible green entwines itself among the dry twigs of this catalogue of nations, the hope that the paths of the nations which diverge so greatly will at length converge upon a goal ordained by the God of revelation" (Franz Delitzsch).

The more closely this list is observed the more is one astonished at the complexity of the race problem—of which most modern men have a remarkably primitive conception—as it is presented by this ancient picture. The three great circles intersect each other at various points. That is partly due to the fact that two different documents (the Priestly code and the Jahwistic tradition) have been worked into each other. The

[1] Hamann, R. A. Bd. 1, S. 71.

very fact that there are various traditions is worthy of attention. Moreover, not only the tradition but the reality is mobile; the races and tribes are all in motion and are constantly running into each other. What belongs to a race depends not only upon the blood but equally upon the language and the countryside. From this results a picture which is perpetually moving and changing.

We shall content ourselves here with these general remarks, and refrain from giving an account of the valuable details which have been worked out by scholars concerning the origin and destiny of the various nations mentioned in the list. But we must draw special attention to verses 8–10.

Cush begat Nimrod (v. 8).

He was the first professional soldier on earth. The word might also be translated "hero" or "violent ruler". The line of development in culture and vocation—gardener, husbandman, herdsman, musician, smith, vine-dresser—which is also a development of settlement and political order, is here carried a step further. Nimrod, who is the first to find his full vocation in waging great wars, is at the same time the first founder of the city and empire.

> *And he was a mighty hunter before the LORD:*
> *wherefore it is said, even as Nimrod, a mighty hunter before the LORD.*
> *And the beginning of his kingdom was Babel,*
> *and Erech, and Accad, and Calneh in the land of Shinar*
> (Gen. 10: 9, 10).

In Nimrod, the violent hunter before the LORD, we recognize unmistakably the prototype of those mighty kings of Babylonia and Assyria, whose passion was the great hunt, and who delighted to have themselves portrayed as mighty hunters in combat with lions and buffaloes, and who drove the nations into alliances and deliberately founded their empires on the basis of power.

The close connection between the hunter and the king with divine nimbus is shown by Schiller in his treatise on the first human community, where, following the line of the Mosaic documents, he describes how after the flood when scarcely any men remained and Asia was falling prey to the wild beasts, the people became so grateful to their deliverers out of this dire distress that they conferred upon those who overcame the beasts immortality and divine honours. So among the Greeks, for instance, Oedipus, Perseus, Hercules, Theseus and others of their descendants gained their apotheosis. Anyone who laboured for the overthrow of these common enemies was the greatest benefactor of mankind. His deeds raised the natural supremacy of his courage and strength to a concentrated power. The leader of the hunt became the commander and judge. Unwittingly he had gathered around him a kind of bodyguard which supported his claims with wild enthusiasm and terrorized by their number any who opposed him. Nothing was wanting to make him king but ceremonial recognition—and how could one deny him this as he stood at the head of his armed and dominant hosts? Since he was the most powerful to ensure the carrying out of his commands, he was the most fitted to rule. Since peace and security from the communal enemy were his gift, he was the general benefactor. He was already in possession of power since the mightiest stood at his command.

So Nimrod, the mighty hunter before the LORD, indicates the direction in which the cultural and political "progress" of mankind after the flood was to proceed.

Babel (Gen. 11: 1–9)

The fact that this account is placed after the genealogy of the nations indicates that the branching of the stem of Noah did not mean inevitably division and confusion. Yet it is precisely the attempt of mankind after the flood to weld into a compact unity divergent forces and thoughts by the realization of a great common idea by their own gigantic efforts which falls under God's judgment and ends in complete confusion.

> Go to, let us build us a city and a tower
> whose top may reach unto heaven.
> So shall we make a shem, "name", for ourselves,
> so that we may not be scattered over the whole face of
> the earth (Gen. 11: 4).

This attempt is the fatal deed, the concentrated effort of humanity after the flood. The plan originates in a technical discovery which is fundamentally a confusion of words. We have spoken already of the close relationship in which word and reality stand. Through his creative Word God created reality. By a "brilliant" exchange of words men begin the work which ends in complete confusion of speech. The story relates how when men entered the plain of Shinar where there was no quarried stone, they invented *lebena leaben* and *hachemar lachomer*, a soft substance which they were able to employ as hard building material. This invention signalizes a creative power of man which opens up limitless possibilities. When this point is reached men living in the culture of Eden and Nod consider themselves so advanced that they are sufficiently mature and powerful to determine their own destiny and to build the *polis* which shall bind together all the diverging tendencies of the human family, and to erect a tower "whose foundations shall rest on the bosom of the underworld" (as Nebopolazzar expresses it in the architectural documents at the restoration of the structure) "and whose top may reach to heaven". With the help of the populace they undertake the same gigantic task which the "giants" before the flood, the men of renown, *anshe ha-shem*, had in their own way set themselves—they are resolved to win for themselves an imperishable name (*shem*) and to impart to human destiny its final form and abiding meaning.

From excavations we are continually learning more about the high culture of the Babylonian lowlands, which owed its existence to "a community founded on common endeavour (*Willensgemeinschaft*) which was held together by a common emotion (*Weltgefühleinheitliches* resting on an intuitive conception of reality (*Wesensschau*)".[1] From this situation much in the account, especially the beginning concerning the "one tongue and one language" receives its distinctive colour. "Sumer exerted its influence over the world with the dynamic of a great creative act, which answered in a definite manner the profoundest questions of spiritual (*geistig*) life concerning the mystery of life and death, sin, fate, God, mutation, eternity, the soul, redemption, and like a diviner's rod by its world-wide expansion awakened and guided the slumbering possibilities in other cultures". It is most remarkable that, so far as eye can scan, the whole of this flowering of the human spirit lies before the historian fully developed and in original freshness and perfection. "The classic age of ancient oriental culture thus lies at the very beginning of our historical knowledge or *before* it."[2] The truest symbol of the Sumerian ideology is the *cicurate*, the many-storied tower whose top reaches to heaven, which has so far been found by the excavators in eighteen Sumerian (i.e. Babylonian) settlements.

Gunkel says, "Only a barbaric foreigner could misunderstand the purpose of the building" as does the Bible. Anyone indigenous to the country knew its meaning—no profane

[1] Alfred Jeremias, *Handbuch der altorientalischen Geisteskultur*, 2 Aufl.
[2] Hugo Winckler, *Die Babylonische Giesteskultur*, 2 Aufl., S. 8 f.

'tower' is it, but a temple of the gods constructed not *against* God, but *for* God". It is equally barbaric, according to Gunkel, to interpret the name "Babel" as "confusion", for it means "Gate of God". This is correct, but then it belongs to the barbarism of the Bible, and indeed of the whole Bible and not merely of this particular narrative, that it condemns as culpable arrogance the highest achievements of human power and effort and the excessive elevation of culture among high religions. Thus every attempt—the old and new Germanic as well as the Sumerian-Babylonian—to erect from beneath a tower whose top shall reach to heaven, is condemned. To the Biblical narrator, and to the Biblical prophets who are to follow him, the tower of Babel is more than an ancient event; in it they see a parable of world history. To them it is at once the deed of the generation of that time and the root which from generation to generation sends out its shoots in repeated new attempts—(With unprecedented technique and new methods which seemed to guarantee success our contemporary world has renewed the ancient attempt. And what catastrophy have we experienced! Yet almost before the structure has collapsed the reconstruction of the old is again begun with redoubled enthusiasm. The conditions and resources for the unifying of mankind and the mastering of fate by men were perhaps never so propitious as to-day. And yet precisely to-day how monstrously do all things seem to part asunder and to work against each other, and how impotent is our generation to solve the simplest problems of life and economics!)—until God at the end of the day shall finally overthrow "Babel" (Rev. 18).

> The LORD said:
> *Go to, let us go down,*
> *and there confound their language,*
> *that they may not understand one another's speech"*
>
> (Gen. 11: 7).

"Moses describes God's zeal to hinder that which men purpose in the very words he uses to express men's zeal. Come . . . let us go down. This is the way whereby we draw near to heaven—the descent of God to the earth; not a tower of reason whose top reaches to heaven, through whose bricks and mortar we propose to make a name for ourselves—and whose banner becomes a token of warning to the erring crowd. God has reserved to Himself the power to unite men in one speech and in one true knowledge. The propagation of the gospel is the means whereby our hearts and thoughts and reason shall be united. The prophets of both the old and new covenants console us that Babel will be destroyed and that the dispersion of the human race, like that of the Jewish people, will have its end. The maintenance and government of the world will remain a continuing miracle until the mystery of God is ended."[1]

Through the vicissitudes of attraction and repugnance and the political action and reaction of internationalism and nationalism God sustains man on the basis of the Noahtic covenant in hope of the promise of His Kingdom, "the *polis* whose maker and builder" (technician and demiurge, Heb. 11: 10) He Himself is. In this city the purpose is not that men should make a name for themselves, but that the LORD should make Himself a name and thus reveal Himself as the One who dwells in their midst and that they might recognize Him and confess Him. The foundation of His Kingdom and the strange kind of politics in which He engages on the earth are concerned with the revelation of His name (*shem*) (Isa. 55: 13).

The Line of the Descendants of Shem's First-born
announces the new movement which God institutes in human history for the revelation of His name. "Shem" is *name*. The line of the descendants of Shem's first-born runs through Terah to Abraham. "My father was a wandering Aramaean" was the customary saying of the Israelite when he placed the first-fruits of the promised land on the altar (Deut. 26). The list in this chapter confirms that his fathers roamed the borders of the great Aramaic-Arabian desert and touched only the periphery of Babylonian culture. Ur, where they settled for a time, is "the only ancient Babylonian city on the west bank of the Euphrates".[2] In the cities east of the Euphrates, however, the Hebraic nomads were quickly absorbed into the Babylonian population dwelling there. From Ur Terah migrated northwards with his family to Haran in Mesopotamia. After Ur Haran is the other famous site of the cult of the moon. The clearest indication of the connection of the Terahites with the cult of the moon is found in the name Laban, which means moon. Elements of the moon cult can still be traced in ancient Israelite religion.[3]

The purpose of the numbers is to fix the date of the event

[1] Hamann, R. A., Bd. 1, S. 72.
[2] Fritz Hommel, *Die altisraelitische Ueberlieferung in inschriftlicher Beleuchtung*, S. 211 f.
[3] Cf. Ditlef Neilsen in the 5th chapter of the 1st volume of the *Handbook of Ancient Arabian Anthropology*, Copenhagen, 1927.

(recorded in the next chapter, 12: 4) towards which the whole line moves. In the 365th year from the first birth after the flood, i.e. a solar year of years, Abram receives the divine call to depart from Haran. For a moment his path touches that circle of Babylonian culture whose centre is the dictum, "Let us make a name for ourselves and build a tower whose top shall reach to heaven", then moves away tangentially in centrifugal motion. *Lêk-leka*, "Get thee out", is the key word for this completely new movement of which the creative impulse is the call from beyond, the call from the mouth of Him who called forth heaven and earth out of nothing. Abram is called forth in order that the promise of salvation decreed in the Noahtic covenant may be fulfilled in that which shall be wrought of God in him and his descendents. God's Abrahamitic covenant serves to fulfil the Noahtic. Abram is to be the father of the chosen-people who call upon the name of the LORD (12: 8) and who as strangers upon the earth hasten expectantly towards the *Polis* of God. Through the life of this father who walks by faith the Creator and Redeemer designs to bless all nations of the earth (12: 3). With the consummation of this company of the elect, the Ecclesia (Church), and only so, will human political and religious history come to rest. Only by the proclamation of the name of the LORD through the evangel will human languages be freed from the curse and placed in the service of understanding.

When at the Pentecostal festival of the New Covenant, which fulfils all divine covenants, the Holy Spirit made known that name of God's revelation which remained unknown in the Old Testament, the name of *Jesus*, as the name of the one ordained of God to be LORD and Christ, to whom the Kingdom was given, so that all who are to be saved must call upon His name, the crowd grew indignant and in astonishment said one to another, "Behold, are not all these who speak Galileans? And how hear we every man in our own tongue wherein we were born? Parthians, and Medes, and Elamites, and dwellers in Mesopotamia, and in Judaea, and Cappadocia, in Pontus and Asia, Phrygia and Pamphilia, in Egypt, and in the parts of Libya about Cyrene, and strangers of Rome, Jews and proselytes, Cretes and Arabians, we do hear them speak in our tongues the wonderful works of God" (Acts 2).

Because Christ Jesus is the Yea and Amen of the Noahtic covenant, His apostle can, in the light of this, say to the un-cultured idolaters in the heart of Asia Minor that "in times past the living God allowed the heathen to walk in their own ways, yet nevertheless left them not without witness to Himself, but showed them great kindness, and sent rain and fruitful seasons from heaven, and filled their hearts with gladness as well as food" (Acts 14: 15–17). To the idolatrous and superstitious Athenians he could proclaim the unknown God as the one whom they ignorantly worshipped. "He is not far from every one of us. For in Him we live and move and have our being; as certain also of your own poets have said, 'We also are His offspring'" (Acts 17: 27–28). These are not declamations of the philosophy or psychology of religion; they are pure evangelical *kerugma*. Speaking strictly as a Christian, one would have to say that the attempt to prove such things by the philosophy of religion is the purest nonsense. But the *missionary* as the messenger of the gospel should and must say to every "heathen" that he belongs to God, and has always belonged to God, in consequence of which God has not left him without witness. It is the proper task of the missionary to seek out these testimonies to the unknown God among the heathen to whom he is sent; to discover what their own poets have said. From this standpoint the legends and fables, the sagas and proverbs merit the attention of the Christian missionary. At the same time he will do well to remember that the apostle designates these voices as "poets", not as prophets (which should be borne in mind also when we cite the *Edda* or other expressions of Germanic religion). Thus every missionary who seeks to discover the attestations of the unknown God among his heathen must continually "remember that this indication that God has concealed His glory from the wise and prudent expresses a law which is always valid. The work of God, in the life of even primitive men, is not easily seen by our natural or scientific vision. For this reason, according to the testimony of Scripture, God has chosen in the human spirit the ignoble and despised in order that on the one hand His footmarks may be undiscovered by the scholar who glories in his academic learning, and in order that on the other hand they may be revealed to him who is not offended at the insignificant and maybe foolish garments which enfold them".[1]

It is not the purpose of the messenger of Jesus to pass judgment on the religious and moral condition of this or that heathen tribe, but, in virtue of the highest authority, to take captive the heathen to whom he is sent for his LORD. Therefore he challenges him with the fact that he belongs to this

[1] Ernst Johanssen, *Geistesleben afrikanischer Völker im Lichte des Evangeliums*, S. 6.

LORD. He speaks to him of Jesus not simply as the Redeemer who freed him from the slavery of idolatry, but as the One who died for him, for the forgiveness of the debt which the heathen owes not to one of the idols, but to the living God. But how can I be concerned about the message of the forgiveness of a God to whom I am not conscious of owing a debt? The apostolic "therefore"—"Therefore thou art inexcusable, O man, whosoever thou art"—is binding only if God's invisible nature, His eternal power and divinity, is really revealed to all (Rom. 2: 1). And the gospel only becomes good news to a man when it tells him he is a sinner before the Father of Jesus Christ whether he was previously as a pagan conscious of such sin or not. The gospel is binding for the pagan only if the Father of Jesus Christ was always the God of the pagan who bound Himself to him in the Noahtic covenant. Then it becomes indeed the call to decision to "all men everywhere". Such is in fact the intention of the Noahtic covenant and of the gospel: God overlooked the times of ignorance in view of the coming "But now" He calls all men to repentance through the word of the evangel. Until this time He held back the *"krisis"* of the world, "because he hath appointed a day, in the which he will judge the world in righteousness by that man whom he hath ordained" (Acts 17: 30 f.). That is the marvel of the *"zedaqa"*, the saving righteousness of God, that He judges the rebellious world only by the One Man who remained obedient to Him even to the death upon the cross. "And He has given assurance unto all men by raising Him from the dead" (Acts 17: 31). The Father's plan of salvation is to judge no one Himself, but to hand over the whole krisis to the Son, that the world might be saved. To Him, because He is the son of man, He gives authority to sit in judgment. Wherever His word sounds forth, there is the *Now* in which judgment is passed on the world: Verily, verily, I say unto you, He that heareth my word, and believeth on Him that sent me, hath everlasting life, and shall not come into condemnation, but is passed from death unto life. Verily, verily, I say unto you, The hour is coming, and now is, when the dead shall hear the voice of the Son of God; and they that hear shall live" (John 5: 24–25).

In anticipation of this saving judgment (*Heilsgericht*) the "krisis" of the world was held back since the making of the covenant with Noah. In anticipation of this judgment, God created by His Word a special history, which though taking place within world history, intersects it and brings it to the point of decision. Thus within the history of the nations, which is itself completely guided by His hand, there occurs the history of His chosen people; that history which is in especial manner revelational history, because it revolves around one Fact, and is in every century nothing but the authoritative witness to that one event which is the only new thing under the sun, and which means the restoration of heaven and earth—the crucifixion of the anointed King among the chosen people, the crucifixion of Christ Jesus and His resurrection from the dead by the power of God for the salvation of the world.

As the promise which God gave to Abraham is the fulfilment of what He had promised to Noah, so His faithfulness to the chosen people despite Israel's infidelity is the Amen to that faithfulness which in the Noahtic covenant He promised to the whole earth. He can no more let unfaithful Israel fall than He can allow the rebellious earth to relapse into chaos (Isa. 45: 18):

> For my name's sake will I defer mine anger,
> and for my praise will I spare thee, Israel,
> so that I do not destroy thee (Isa. 48: 9).
> Such a thing seemeth to me as in the days of Noah,
> when I swore that Noah's water
> should never again sweep over the earth,
> so have I sworn not to be angry with you nor to reproach you.
> For the mountains shall depart,
> and the hills be removed;
> But my kindness shall not depart from thee,
> neither shall the covenant of my peace be removed,
> saith the LORD, that hath mercy upon thee (Isa. 54: 9 f.).

At no time did God so universally declare the vocation of Israel to a world mission as in the years when the last remnants of the faithless people pined in Babylonian captivity (Isa. 40–55). And even after Israel had done its utmost against God in effecting the crucifixion of Christ as of one accursed by the heathen authorities, God in utter faithfulness decreed that "the fall of Israel should be for the salvation of the world, and the loss of Israel the wealth of the heathen". Accordingly the apostle to the Gentiles cannot hide the mystery from his brothers: "Blindness in part is happened to Israel, until the fullness of the Gentiles be come in" (Rom. 11: 25).

That is the mystery of His faithfulness. And His faithfulness is the mystery of the patience with which He postpones the judgment of the world from the days of the flood to the present. That is not, as scoffers presume, the slackness of His promise, but the marvel of His patience with us, for it is not His will that any should be lost, but that every man should repent (2 Pet. 3: 9). All are, by the word of Jesus Christ, to be placed before the decision of faith. In pursuance of this, Christ even "went in the Spirit and preached to the spirits in prison, which were previously unbelieving, when the longsuffering of God waited in the days of Noah" (1 Pet. 3: 18–20). In order that all may be placed in decision before Christ, God holds the earth in the Noahtic covenant—in faithfulness and in hope of awakening faith (*aus Treue und zum Glauben*)—until the *Day of the LORD*. "The day of the LORD will come as a thief in the night; in the which the heavens shall pass away with a great noise, and the elements shall melt with fervent heat, the earth also and the works that are therein shall be burnt up" (2 Pet. 3: 10). In the light of this, how earnestly should all who through the words of prophets and apostles are aware that this fire stands before them "be diligent to be found of him in peace, without spot and blameless, and respect the patience of God for their salvation" (2 Pet. 3: 14–15). But the scoffers who wantonly abuse the patience of God as though this corrupt earth would endure eternally, should be reminded that it was precisely through such presumption on the part of the antediluvians that heaven and earth, which through the Word of God owed their permanence to water, were drowned with water, and that the heaven and earth of to-day are, by that same Word, prepared against the day of judgment (2 Pet. 3: 3–7).

"For as the lightning cometh out of the east, and shineth even unto the west; so shall the coming of the Son of man be" (Matt. 24: 27). Then the rainbow will no longer appear as a sign in the heavens. "The sun shall be darkened, and the moon shall not give her light, and the stars shall fall from heaven, and the powers of the heavens shall be shaken: and then shall appear the sign of the Son of man in heaven: and then shall all the tribes of the earth mourn, and they shall see the Son of man coming in the clouds of heaven with power and great glory. And he shall send forth his angels with a great sound of a trumpet, and they shall gather together his elect from the four winds, from one end of heaven to the other. . . . But as in the days of Noah, so shall also the coming of the Son of man be. For as in the days that were before the flood they were eating and drinking, marrying and giving in marriage, until the day that Noah entered into the ark, and knew not until the flood came, and took them all away; so shall also the coming of the Son of man be.

Watch therefore!" (Matt. 24).

2

THE COVENANT WITH ABRAHAM

GENESIS 12-50

THESE chapters relate the origin of the chosen people and thus lay bare the root from which springs the story of the Church in every age. The God of Abraham, Isaac and Jacob is not only the God of Moses, but also the Father of Jesus Christ. And the witness of the New Testament begins with the "Bible" of the origins of Jesus Christ, with the family tree which demonstrates that the LORD of the Church is "the son of Abraham" (Matt. 1: 1). It is the unanimous witness of prophets and apostles that the Church of God from Abraham to those who live at the time of the last judgment is one Church, comparable to an olive tree—an olive tree, however, from which the Gardener has removed several natural twigs (the Jews who did not believe on the Messiah), and replaced them by grafting in the Gentiles as wild shoots. "And if some of the branches be broken off, and thou, being a wild olive tree, wert grafted in among them, and with them partakest of the root and the fatness of the olive tree, boast not against the branches. But if thou boast, remember that thou bearest not the root, but the root thee. If the firstfruit be holy, the lump is also holy; and if the root be holy, so are the branches" (Rom. 11: 16–18).

The point of this is the unity and wholeness of the Church. The metaphor of the "root" which the apostle employs is characteristic of the "total thinking" (*ganzheitliches Denken*) of Biblical writers.[1] If we would understand a letter of Paul or one of the Gospels or a saga of the patriarchs, we must learn to think in this "total" fashion. This is an original kind of thought to which many moderns, particularly scientists, are strangers, for they imagine that in science only the kind of thought which splits things up into atoms is permissible, i.e. a thing can only be scientifically comprehended when it is severed from its context, and the individual pieces of which it is "composed" isolated. In contradistinction to this, "total" thinking conceives that the living reality can only be comprehended in its entirety. It is, so to speak, genealogical thinking which thinks in

[1] It is the great merit of Johs. Pedersen in his book *Israel* (I–II Sjaeleliv og Samsundsliv, Kobenhavn 1920, Eng. edition 1926) to have demonstrated this "total thinking" (*ganzheitliches Denken*) of the Israelites.

terms of roots and trees, and seeds in the which is planted in the earth, however small it may be, the whole tree. Naturally, the tree is only present as "promise" not as "fulfilment" in the seedling or the root; the plant must have its history before the tree blossoms and bears fruit. Naturally, the tree must have time to become what it is; but it will become precisely that which it is, and what it always was from the beginning, and will never become anything else.

This mode of thought can be well illustrated by the Hebrew language. In Hebrew—as in other languages—the bearer of the concept is "the root". That means that the essential signification of a word is bound up with a particular group of "radicals", usually three consonants. By the insertion of vowels between the consonants, by the repetition or doubling of the consonants, or the addition of consonants as prefix or suffix, the root begins to grow and throw out shoots in such a way that the fundamental conception is enlarged, or more precisely defined, varied or modified, but never abandoned. If, for example, one were in German to join together the three consonants l–b–n with various vowels, there would result quite distinct concepts such as "laben", "leben", "lieben", "loben", which have no relationship with each other. Such a thing would be impossible in Hebrew, for here the root l–b–n is always bound up with the idea of "whiteness", whether I say "laban" = he is white, or "hilbinu" = we have purified, or "yitlabben" = he submits to be purified, or "lebena" = the light brick, "lebona" = the white incense, "libne" = the white poplar, "lebanon" = the snow mountain, "leben" (Arabic) = the milk—everything springs from the root l–b–n, and more may be added, but nothing whose characteristic is not the colour white.

In conformity with this method of building words (*Wortbildung*) is the manner of constructing sentences (*Satzbildung*). In Hebrew a word can constitute a sentence, because a word represents a whole picture, for each Hebrew word is originally and really a self-sufficient and independent concept, so that there exist so to speak not different classes of words, but only nouns, which only by their position in the sentence come to possess superiority or subordination. The same word "can", according to the position assigned to it, be noun or adjective or verb. And since a single word may form a complete sentence a discourse is composed by enlarging and transforming the idea or the picture which lies in this one word by adding others to it—"and . . . and . . . and . . . and". Not only a sentence but a whole story may emerge from a single word at the beginning, and accordingly as this word represents a static or moving picture the narration describes a condition or an event. Many peculiarities of Hebrew syntax which seem impenetrable to our logic become explicable when this is understood. Similarly we begin to see how the art of Hebrew poetry consists in the unfolding of a word which is itself a picture, e.g. in Psalm 121: "The Guardian".

Like the formation of words and sentences, the meaning of Hebrew words is "total" (*ganzheitlich*), both in the realm of psychology and sociology. As we have seen, the Hebrew word for soul does not distinguish the soul from the body. In the Bible man does not *have* a soul; he *is* a soul. Adam "became a living soul". Nephesh ("soul") signifies the whole of his living unity, the whole living creature that he is, spiritual as well as corporeal, from the centre to the outer limits of his life. Division here would mean derangement. And just as man is a living creature only in this totality of his being, so he lives not as a self-contained and self-sufficient individual, but as a scion of his race, a son of his family. He is "a son of man", "*ben ha-adam*". Without using this remarkable expression it is impossible in Hebrew to signify the individual man. "*Adam*" (man) is one of the collective words in which Hebrew abounds ("collective" is an inaccurate word, for "*adam*" and similar words are not collective nouns but root-concepts), and means at one and the same time the first man and the sum total of men. This sum total is an original totality, not a "mankind" which emerges by addition or abstraction. Consequently the life which the individual receives is not a kind of impersonal energy, but rather a life with peculiar characteristics conditioned by the fact that he receives it from such and such a line of ancestors, e.g. that he is a son of Shem, more precisely a son of Abraham, or more precisely a son of Jacob. The life of the fathers and the life of their descendants is one. The sons "fulfil" the life of the fathers, and the fathers are always present in the life of their descendants and gather together, so to speak, the life of their sons.

Certain distinctions which seem to us important become less weighty in the light of this conception, as does also the question which the thoughtful scholar of to-day feels he must put to the patriarchal narratives, viz. whether these relate personal experiences of the three men or whether they form a mythical presentation of the history of Israel. We ask the question in our desire to think clearly on historical issues, but really the question is unhistorical for it does not comprehend the meaning of the Biblical narrator. He would completely fail to understand our question. For to him Abraham and the sons of Abraham, Jacob and Israel, Jacob the man and Jacob the tribe form so completely one unity that they cannot be sundered. One of the children of Israel or several—it does not matter who the narrator is, for he does not present private views or private investigations—recount to the community that which is conserved in tradition and in living memory concerning their own origins. They narrate to the present living generation of the chosen people not the life history of distant men but the story of their own fathers and therefore their own life story; not something which is past, but the life which moves forward with them, which has brought them from yesterday to to-day and will lead them from to-day to to-morrow.

THE CALL OF GOD (GEN. 12: 1–3)

The LORD said to Abram,
"Get thee out
of thy country,
and from thy kindred,
and from thy father's house,
unto a land that I will shew thee;
and I will make of thee a great nation."

This call of God creates a new race. It removes Abram from the land of his birth, from his blood-relations and from his political community ("father's house" is a juristic-sociological idea). His existence from this moment onwards is founded entirely and utterly upon the Word of God. He has a command and a promise and nothing besides. His flesh and blood are not changed; he remains a man like all others. That which makes him and all the "sons of Abraham" distinct is that they have heard a call and followed it, that they have received a promise to which they hold fast in believing trust.

Abram could obey the command to found a new nation only in blind faith, for his wife was barren (Gen. 11: 30).

I will bless thee;
be a blessing (Gen. 12: 2).

The word "bless" occurs five times in these two verses. Evidently it expresses the meaning of God's call, What is a blessing? *"Beraka"* ("blessing") is the energy of life, the capacity for life, the salutary potence which imparts to the life of a "soul" or living creature abounding life. It resembles for example that which is in the berries of a cluster of grapes, so that one says, "Destroy it not; a blessing lies therein". So Abram and his barren wife are to be blessed and become a blessing by which all nations of the earth shall be blessed and saved from corruption. Since Adam all who are born lie under a curse. Adamic humanity is like a plant which thrives in hope, then withers, and is unable to bring forth fruit. In Abram they are to be blessed so that they may bring forth their fruit. Abram is thus not called to the enjoyment of a private bliss but to the salvation of all races upon earth, so that they may truly become that for which they were created. *Pars pro toto*: the Creator and Redeemer chooses a part that He may lead the whole to its goal.

> *And I will make thy name great* (Gen. 12: 2).

The "name" (*shem*) is the meaningful expression of the whole of life, "a form with its own distinctive impress which unfolds itself in life" (Goethe). He who has a great name is famous. But we must consider what that means. A famous man is one who impresses his character upon hundreds and thousands and conditions their life by his life. So Abram's nature is to become determinative for unnumbered hosts. They will call themselves by his name, as they bless themselves in him.

THE HOLY LAND (GEN. 12: 4–9)

In his seventy-fifth year, in the three hundred and sixty-fifth year (i.e. a solar year of years) after the first birth following the Flood, Abram goes forth. He is to occupy a new land which God will show him. He wanders through the whole length of the Holy Land from Sichem to its southernmost borders. He marks it well, and wherever God reveals His presence, he erects, as landmarks of the holy region, altars at which he may call upon the name of the LORD. Not in order to make a name for himself, but in order that the name of the LORD may be hallowed, and His will done on earth as in heaven, Abram enters the land of strangers. In obedience he pursues his way and brings no stone for the tower whose top should reach to heaven. Leaving behind him the precincts of the city where men seek to secure their existence and endeavour to make a name for themselves, he awaits that ordering of events and constitution of society which is absolutely determined by the will of God—the "polis", as the apostle (Heb. 11) says, whose maker and builder is God. In faith he begins to take possession of the Kingdom for God by erecting in Canaan memorials to God's revelation. Here again everything proceeds according to the principle, *pars pro toto*: for by the occupation of one land the whole earth is claimed for the rule of God.

THE FLIGHT INTO EGYPT (GEN. 12: 10–20)

In the third volume of his *Economic Ethics of the World Religions* Max Weber begins his essay on ancient Judaism with the following sentences: "What, sociologically regarded, were the Jews? *A pariah people.* That means, as we know from India, a people living as guests among a community from which they are ritually (either formally or actually) divorced. All the essential characteristics of their relationship to the surrounding world, above all, the life of the ghetto long before they were forcibly interned, and the peculiar dualism of their ethics towards those within and those outside their own group, can be explained by this fact. Yet Judaism differentiates itself from the Indian pariah races in the following ways: 1. The Jews were (or rather became) a pariah people in a surrounding community which was without caste. 2. Their promises of salvation were completely different. Whilst for the Indian pariah castes the system of caste was eternal, just as the world was eternal and had no history, for the Jews the world was neither eternal nor unchangeable, but was rather something created, whose orders were products of history and destined to give way before the conditions willed by God."

Weber answers the question how the Jews became a pariah people with highly developed characteristics by pointing to the peculiar conditions presented to the immigrating Israelites by the geography and politics of the Syro-Palestinian mountain area. The contrasts in economic conditions decreed by nature in Palestine have from the very beginning found their expression in contrasts in the economic and social structure. Weber then directs our attention to a class which proved most important for Israel's beginnings. "We have the settled population on the one hand, consisting of the patricians of the city and the farmers (some residential, some free, others liable to feudal service or tax or rent) who cultivate corn, fruit and wine and herd cattle; on the other hand we have the free Beduin with their camels; and between them there stands the class characteristic of all Mediterranean lands even to modern times—the half-nomadic herdsmen of sheep and goats. The manner of life of this class is in Mediterranean lands everywhere conditioned by the necessity of finding a *change of pastures* (and the comparative ease with which this may be effected for sheep and goats in contrast to cattle) over wide areas—over the Abruzzi to Apulia, or over half of Spain, and over similar distances in North Africa and the Balkan lands. This 'trans-humance', as it is called in Spain, has two results: firstly, a periodic migration of the whole community, and therefore, in contrast to the formless joining together of the Beduin, a more closely-knit and ordered community; secondly, a more orderly relationship to the inhabitants of the regions through which it moves. The relationship of the herdsmen of sheep and goats both to the farming and city community rested normally on definite legal rights of pasture and path defined in contracts. They were *gerim*. The *ger* (*metoikos* or temporary resident), whilst alien to the native race, is legally protected, in contrast to the complete alien, *nokri*, who is without legal rights.

"The migrating herdsmen became subject to universal developmental tendencies. The gradual transition from a semi-nomadic way of life to the herding of sheep and goats, and then to permanent settlement, and at last to residence in a town under the pressure of constraint is reflected both in the sagas and in the historic tradition. According to the saga, Abraham possesses camels as well as sheep, and drinks no wine, but entertains the three men in the divine epiphany with milk. He wanders as a *ger* with a contractual right to pasture from place to place, and only at the end of his life does the saga permit him, after protracted negotiations, to acquire a grave in Hebron. Isaac resides, in virtue of a contract, in the region of Gerar, and digs wells there, but is repeatedly obliged to change his abode. Jacob, in contrast to the farmer Esau, is essentially a herdsman dwelling in tents, but even he settles as a *ger* in Shechem and acquires land (Gen. 33: 19). At the end of his life it is accounted deceit that he presents himself to Pharaoh as nothing but a herdsman in order that he may live as a ritually separated *ger* without mixing with the Egyptians. He pursues agriculture and requires corn for food. The possession of cattle is ascribed to all the patriarchs. Joseph finally, as governor of Egypt, regulates the land tax of the country.

"It is important to note the popular conception of the keepers of sheep and goats presented by tradition in the days of the kingdom. It is a tradition which finds expression in the patriarchal legends. Here the patriarchs are specifically pacifist figures. Their God is the God of the peaceable (Gen. 13: 14 f.). They appear as isolated fathers of families. Tradition knows nothing of political parties among them. They are tolerated as *metoikoi*. They are in the position of shepherds who secure for their families pastoral preserves by peaceful contract with the inhabitants, and, in case of necessity, as with Abraham and Lot, peacefully divide the land among themselves. They display no sign of personal heroism. A mixture of trustful, God-given humility and good-naturedness combined with a subtle cunning which is countenanced by their God, characterizes them. The narrators assume that their public will find it natural that the patriarchs, rather than defend the virtue of their wives, should prefer to pretend that their beautiful and attractive wives are their sisters, and surrender them to their protectors of a day, leaving it to God to set them free again by directing plagues against their possessors. (Then follows the well-known list of similar instances so much discussed in Germany to-day by those who otherwise know nothing of the Old Testament.) This is the customary ethic of a pariah people, which together with a very decided trustful obedience characterizes the general picture of the inner motives of these men as seen by tradition. They are evidently *metoikoi*, herdsmen of sheep and goats, who are settled among citizens possessing powers of defence." Weber immediately, however, safeguards himself against the tendency "to regard the pacifism of these semi-nomads as something inherent in their character. That is distinctly not the case. It is rather simply a result of the defenceless state of the herdsmen when they divide into small groups as they settle in particular places. Whenever they are able to organize themselves into powerful political units it is completely absent. The patriarchs did not always in Israelite consciousness have the attitude which characterizes them in the accepted redaction of the written Torah". Weber then draws attention to certain passages in Genesis where remnants of a warlike picture of the fathers of Israel are found, above all, in "the much-discussed 14th chapter of Genesis, which discloses Abraham as the warlike hero who, with a few hundred followers enters the lists against the alliance of Mesopotamian Kings, including Hammurabi, and victoriously recovers the booty which they had wrested from the Kings of the Canaanite cities". Weber is of the opinion "that the characteristics, so different from those found elsewhere, which are presented by such fragments, evidently became completely overlaid by the pacifist attitude which was consonant with the prevailing conditions of a later age''.

We offer no opinion on the question whether this literary conclusion is correct, because it is our intention to take the Biblical narratives as they are; and here a warlike heroism is to be found alongside the pacific characteristics of the patriarchs. We have cited so much from Weber because his exposition assists our understanding of the patriarchs sociologically, and in particular helps us to realize the peculiar position in which Abram found himself when in the obedience of faith he settled as a *metoikos* (or as the apostle expresses it, a *paroikos*) in the promised land as in a strange country, and with Isaac and Jacob, co-heirs of the same promise, could dwell only in tents and not in immovable houses (Heb. 11: 8 ff.). Weber's moral indignation at the ethics of these *metoikoi* may help us, with some amazement it is true, to understand aright the remark of the apostle that God was not ashamed to be called their God, just as Jesus was not ashamed to be called our Brother (Heb. 11: 16; 2: 11). No harm is done if Weber's words prevent our honouring the patriarchs as moral heroes. The earlier and oftener we are led to feel that the Bible is an offensive book, offensive not least to men of high morality, the better it is. (Let it be said, by the way, that the same people who when they read Genesis are scandalized at the pacifism of the patriarchs are later offended at the bloodthirstiness of the Book of Judges!)

The Kingdom of God, which is the essence of the calling and migrations of Abraham, is most certainly not what we moderns call the kingdom of heroic goodness or of moral and religious values and personalities. The Biblical narrative ruthlessly exposes the patriarchs. Abram is evidently not intended to be understood as the father of faultless personalities, but as the father of those who fall and are raised up again by an invisible hand, who repeatedly fall and repeatedly are raised by Him whose power is mighty in those that are weak. Not to Abraham belongs the glory, but to the guiding and upholding power of Him who alone is good.

Abram is not the founder of a sect of men whose life consists in their being better than others. He and his people live through the grace of Him who has called them, though sinners, into His light. Therefore they can never stand over against the world in self-righteous isolation. They do not condemn others, but intercede for them. When later (Gen. 18) God discloses to Abraham that judgment is decreed upon *Sodom* and *Gomorrah* the patriarch begins to beg and intercede. It is said that Voltaire laughed at this Jew bargaining with God. But Luther with deeper insight writes: "The saints are the true 'atlantes', who bear the whole heavenly structure upon their shoulders, i.e. they restrain and bear the mighty wrath of God, yet even in deepest affliction hold fast their faith in God's grace and mercy, though they see before their very eyes its apparent contradiction."

The destruction of Sodom and Gomorrah holds up to us a dreadful warning. God is not mocked. True, in the Noahtic covenant He swore never again till the day of judgment to drown the earth in a flood; nevertheless He reserves to Himself freedom to consume parts of the earth, festering sores on the body of humanity, with fire. So the example of Sodom and Gomorrah moves like a warning finger through the whole Bible. And, let it be understood, even here there is something more than a mere moral. It shall be more tolerable for Sodom and Gomorrah in the Day of Judgment than for that city which rejects the gospel (Matt. 10: 15). Yet it is the duty neither of the sons of Abraham nor of the disciples of Jesus to call down fire from heaven upon the wicked. On the contrary, in recollection of their own guilt and trusting in the Son of man who came not to destroy men's souls but to sustain them, it is their privilege to step into the breach and to intercede with God to the uttermost like Abraham.

Anyone who has gained a real insight into the life of Abraham and his divine leading, and seen how he was diverted from all familiar prepared paths of men and led into a pathless wilderness where, so to speak, he was led blindfold by an intangible guidance over abyss after abyss, will lose any inclination he may have had to criticize the father of the faithful.[1]

The moralistic standpoint completely fails to comprehend the intention of this narrative. The *denial of his wife*, which, as is well known, is related twice of Abraham and once of Isaac,

[1] He will, if indeed any desire at all remains to appraise the manhood of Abraham and other Biblical figures, rather say with Nietzsche (in the Kröber edition of Nietzsche's *Works*, VII, S. 77): "In that book of divine righteousness, the Old Testament, there are such men, events and endeavours after such high ideals, that the literature of Greece and India has nothing worthy to be placed by its side. It is with awe and reverence that one stands in the presence of these massive remnants of what men once were, an awe which awakens one's own thoughts concerning ancient Asia and its protruding peninsula called Europe, which always seeks pre-eminence over Asia as the soil of 'human progress'. Of course, anyone who himself is but a witless peaceful domestic animal knowing only the needs of domestic animals will neither be astonished nor ashamed—for our taste for the Old Testament is a touchstone of our ability to recognize greatness and pettiness."

has in each case its definite meaning in the context of the whole. In each case far more than the reputation of the patriarch is at stake, namely the Promise, the divine work of salvation. For if anything should happen to the mother of the race in the strange harem the blessing with which God blessed the patriarch becomes ineffectual.

In the 12th chapter this danger is accentuated by its immediate connection with the patriarch's first departure from the holy region. After proceeding from Shechem over the shoulder of the mountain range west of Jordan into the southern valleys, he is driven by hunger into the "foreign country" of Egypt— and after a few weeks of imminent danger chased out again. "Take thy wife, and go!" commands Pharaoh with kingly brevity and indignation. If we have succeeded in making clear the relationship between the father of the race to his people, we cannot fail to realize that Abram here *anticipates prophetically* (not allegorically!) the experiences which his descendents will later have in foreign Egypt. Indeed soon afterwards God revealed to Abram, to his horror, "that his seed shall be a stranger in a land that is not theirs, and shall be slaves, and they shall afflict them four hundred years; and also that nation whom they shall serve will I judge: and afterward they shall come out with great substance" (Gen. 15: 13 f.).

In harmony with this, according to the narrative of Matthew's gospel, the "Son of Abraham" who fulfils all things shall in his "Genesis" (Matt. 2: 13–15) and tenderest childhood recapitulate the early history of Israel and fulfil the word of the prophet: "Out of Egypt have I called my son" (Matt. 2: 13–15, Hosea 11: 1).

GOD'S STEWARD (GEN. 13)

And Abram was very rich in cattle, in silver, and in gold
(Gen. 13: 2).

He was thus as the elect of God, as the holy one, no mendicant monk. "Should we for this reason hold St. Francis in higher honour?" asks Luther, and answers: "No!" It is true that Abram is the servant of God, and that he must therefore be prepared to place all, his possessions and his life-blood, in the service of God and His Kingdom. But then, is not God also the LORD of the earth and its goods? Are not land and cattle, gold and silver His good creations granted us to devote to our own use and the needs of our neighbour and the glory of God? Jesus promised that to those who seek the Kingdom of God and

His righteousness all things shall be added. He calls the meek who decline to contend for the goods of the earth blessed because they shall inherit the earth. This is the meaning of Abraham's life, if man would rightly possess and use the earth and its fullness, he must not grab them like a thief, but receive them thankfully as a trust from the hand of God.

The earth is the LORD's, and the Holy Land is, as it were, the royal domain of the great King. He called Abram to be steward of this royal realm in order that from this beginning and through him He might claim the mastery of the whole earth and expel all who seek to possess it by force. Accordingly Abram, declining to contend with his nephew over the pastures, gives him the choice: "If thou goest to the left, I will go to the right; if thou goest to the right, I will go to the left." When Lot had chosen the attractive, well-watered pastures of the Jordan which lay like a paradise before him, there remained for Abram only the barren highland region. But at God's gracious command he claims it for his own:

> *Lift up now thine eyes,*
> *and survey the place where thou art,*
> *to the northward, to the southward,*
> *and eastward and westward;*
> *for all the land which thou seest, to thee will I give it,*
> *and to thy seed for ever.*
> *And I will make thy seed*
> *as the dust of the earth,*
> *so that if a man can number the dust of the earth,*
> *then shall thy seed also be numbered.*
> *Arise! Walk through the land*
> *in the length of it and in the breadth of it,*
> *for I will give it unto thee."*
> *Then Abram removed his tent, and came and dwelt*
> *by the evergreen oaks of Mamre*
> *near Hebron,*
> *and built there an altar unto the Lord* (Gen. 13: 14-18).

This is probably the place which is still called by the Arabs who inhabit Palestine "the holy terrain of the friend of the merciful".

THE HOLY WAR (GEN. 14)

A powerful gust from the storms of world history greets the reader of this chapter. Possibly it is a part of an ancient epic which has been prosaically revised, like the fragments in Num.

21: 14 ff. or Jos. 10: 12 f. This is not the place to discuss the many literary and historical problems presented to scholars by this strange document. Anyone interested should read the short essay by Franz M. Th. Böhl: "Das Zeitalter Abrahams",[1] in which he will find further information. It used to be customary to identify Amraphel with Hammurapi the great law-giver of the middle east and the founder of a Semitic dynasty in Babylon, and to place the war in the twentieth (or according to another reckoning, in the twenty-first) century before Christ. To-day Böhl and other investigators are inclined to identify Tidal, "King of nations" with a famous Hittite king who ruled in the second half of the sixteenth century. None the less, to us it still seems most natural to think of the time of Hammurapi, when along with the wave of Semites who founded the dynasty in Babylon, the Elamite power increased and other groups of nomads—Semitic, Kassitic, Subaraic—were on the move and attained hegemony.[2] Abram's migration may be connected with these. According to Biblical chronology the war took place in the year 2061 B.C., i.e., on a careful assessment, six years after Hammurapi began his rule in the city of Babylon. Not that we are obliged to accept this of necessity, for it is not essential that the Biblical chronology for this early period should conform strictly to the chronology of the modern historian.

In any case, the campaign, was evidently primarily concerned with the safeguarding of trade routes through the Lebanon and the region west of Jordan to the important harbour on the Elanic Gulf (and thence by sea to upper Egypt and southern Arabia), which is typical for the position of Palestine. Canaan, the narrow strip between the sea on the west and the desert on the east is the bridge for the caravans and armies between north and south and the meeting-place of the great cultures of Mesopotamia, Asia Minor, and the empires of the east on the one hand, and Egypt, the Arabian peninsular and India on the other hand. Small wonder that upon this tiny portion of earth innumerable peoples and races have met and that those who dwelt here were in every age drawn into the struggles for world supremacy. At the same time, the mountains west of Jordan, which Abram the Hebrew made his home, lie like an island of rocks, exalted and difficult to overrun, above the rivers of world history.

Whilst Lot, who had settled among the anarchic minor kings of the Jordan districts, is drawn inevitably into the war and

---

[1] *Der Alte Orient*, Bd. 29, Heft 1.
[2] F. W. König, *Geschichte Elams*, *Der Alte Orient*, 29. 4.

I

carried off with all his goods, Abram remains unmolested. Loyalty and nobility alone lead him to call to arms his three hundred and eighteen "devoted servants" (or "comrades of the oath", as Böhl translates the word in verse 14, which seems to indicate that Abram's men were united with him in a cult community (*kultgenossenschaft*), and to pursue the victors and despoil them of their booty.

When Abram, returning from the fight, entered the valley of kings,

> *Melchizedek king of Salem*
> *brought forth bread and wine* (Gen. 14: 18).
> *He was the priest of the most high God;*
> *and he blessed him and said,*
> *"Blessed, Abram, to the high God,*
> *Maker of heaven and earth.*
> *Blessed be the most high God,*
> *which hath delivered thine enemies into thy hand".*
> *And he gave him tithes of all* (Gen. 14: 18, 19).

A mysterious encounter and an action of the profoundest significance! From the mists of antiquity there gleam here for a moment the golden pinnacles of the holy citadel. Jerusalem, the polar opposite of Babel! Jerusalem: the city of the great king, the focus of God's priestly kingship over all the empires of this world.

> In Salem is His tabernacle,
> and his dwelling place in Zion.
> There he breaks the arrows of the bow,
> shield, sword and battle.
> Thou art more glorious and mighty
> than the mountains of prey.
> The proud must be robbed and fall asleep,
> and the hands of all warriors sink in impotence.
> At thy rebuke, O God of Jacob,
> the horse and chariot subside in sleep.
> Thou art to be feared;
> and who can stand in thy sight when once thou art angry?
> When thou didst cause judgment to be heard from heaven
> the earth feared and was still,
> when God arose in judgment
> to help the poor.
> When men rage against thee
> Thou dost harvest honour;

and when they rage still more furiously
Thou art armed with better panoply.
Pay your vow, and honour it, to the Lord your God;
let all that be round about him
bring presents to him that is to be feared,
who denudes princes of their courage,
and is terrible among the kings of the earth (Psalm 76).

Jerusalem, the city of Christ, where the throne of God's annointed and His steward of the house of David shall stand.

The Lord said unto my Lord,
"Sit thou at my right hand,
until I make thine enemies thy footstool."
The Lord shall send forth from Zion the sceptre of his
    kingdom:
rule thou in the midst of thine enemies.
When thou hast conquered thy people will gladly
sacrifice unto thee in holy attire.
Children shall be born to thee
like the dew of morning hours.
The Lord hath sworn, and will not repent:
"Thou art a priest for ever
after the order of Melchisedek."
The Lord at thy right hand shall strike down
kings in the day of his wrath.
He shall judge among the heathen,
and shall vanquish them;
He shall wound the heads in many lands.
He shall drink of the brook in the way;
therefore shall he lift up his head (Psalm 110).

These two psalms, echoing the metallic notes of the fourteenth
chapter of Genesis, give the clearest indication of the meaning
of the encounter of the patriarch with the priestly king before
the walls of Salem. Once again it is a prophetic event which
the father of God's people experiences. When we consider this
or any other story of Abraham, it is as though we held in our
hand the fruit of a great tree and marvelled to see how the
fruit enfolds the seed from which shall spring the whole tree.
Every word of the ancient narrative becomes transparent, and
through it we see the whole story of the revelation of God's
kingly rule which shall liberate His earth from every foreign
power—from David and Solomon, Isaiah and Jeremiah, Ezra
and Nehemiah, to the presentation of Jesus, the son of Abraham,

in the temple, and His victorious death and resurrection before the gates of Jerusalem, and beyond to the final goal which is unveiled in the closing chapters of the Revelation of John, where we see the Holy City, the new Jerusalem, coming down from God out of heaven, and hear a mighty voice from the throne saying, "Behold, the tabernacle of God with men! And He will dwell with them, and they shall be His people, and God Himself shall be with them, and be their God. And God shall wipe away all tears from their eyes; and there shall be no more death, neither sorrow, nor crying, neither shall there be any more pain: for the former things are passed away."

The Epistle to the Hebrews (Ch. 7) expounds this in the light of the coming of Jesus, showing that in Melchisedek (one who, being without genealogy, and belonging to no order of priests, is accredited directly by the high God) a mighty priesthood (which is at once the ground and completion of the Levitical) meets Abraham and confers on him a blessing which surpasses that revealed in the Israelite cultus. "Melchisedek", which means in English "a king of righteousness" and also "king of Salem", i.e. "king of peace", who is without father, without mother, without descent, having neither beginning of days nor end of life, is compared with the Son of God and abides priest in eternity, when every priesthood ordained for time has been dissolved. "Now consider how great this man was, unto whom even the patriarch Abraham gave a tenth of the spoils. . . . And as I may so say, Levi also, who according to the law of Moses received the tithe from the chosen people, here payed tithes in Abraham; for he was yet in the loins of his father when Abraham met him." In this official act of Melchisedek a priesthood comes into sight which dissolves the limitations of the high priesthood of Israel. It is a priesthood to which Jesus, as the executor of a far better Testament, is called by the special oath of God (Psa. 110). "For such an high priest became us, who is holy, harmless, undefiled, separate from sinners, and made higher than the heavens; who is not subject to death but evermore liveth and in the power of life eternal ruleth and intercedeth for His Church; who needeth not daily, as those high priests, to offer up sacrifice, first for His own sins, and then for the people's: for this He did once when He offered up Himself" (Heb. 7). In Melchisedek's bringing of bread and wine we have a clear allusion to the sacrament of the New Covenant which Jesus instituted for the completion and dissolution of the old.

The name, "the high God", which Abram here invokes and

by which Melchisedek blesses Abram, is, so to speak, inscribed above the name by which God reveals Himself in the Old Testament (Deut. 32: 8; Num. 24: 4). Similarly, directly before God makes His special covenant with Abraham, there is proclaimed in the service of the priestly king of Salem "the office of the Son, who is eternal and perfect" (Heb. 7: 28), which is the indispensable foundation and utmost reach of the Israelite divine service. And so (as Jesus told the Jews—"Before Abraham was, I am" the new covenant which He instituted was before the old, and prepared the ground for the latter. This was the order, not the reverse. "Is not Christianity older than paganism and Judaism, and did not the author and perfecter of our faith Himself say, 'Before Abraham. . . .' "[1]

THE COVENANT RESTING ON LOYALTY AND FAITH (GEN. 15)

The calling of Abraham implies that he is to become the father of a people which shall take possession of the land as a rightful inheritance. Therefore his soul cannot rest simply in personal blessedness. The wonderful promise of God:

> *Fear not, Abram,*
> *I am thy shield and thine exceeding great reward* (Gen. 15: 1).
> is empty if it only touches him personally.
> My Lord, LORD,
> What wilt thou give me?
> My days pass, and I am childless.
> Behold, thou hast given me no seed.
> Behold, the son of my house, Eliezer,
> will become my heir" (Gen. 15: 2).

No, answers God. One who proceeds from thy loins shall be thine heir. And as he showed him outside the tent in the clear Palestinian night air the innumerable glowing stars, and said to him, "So shall thy seed be",

> *He believed the Lord,*
> *and he counted it to him for righteousness* (Gen. 15: 6).

The word "believe" is in Hebrew a Hiphil form of the root "amen", and means literally to account one reliable or faithful or truthful, to trust Him, to rely on His power. Abram believed the Lord's promise of His fatherhood despite

---

[1] Hamann im 4. *Hierophantischen Brief*, R. A. IV, S. 258.
(Aus Treue auf Glauben) i.e. on God's abiding faithfulness and man's response in childlike faith (trans.).

the impossibility of seeing how he could receive a son. He believed in the possibility of God's accomplishing the impossible; of calling into existence that which is not through His Word. And this God reckoned to him for righteousness.

After Abram has believed the mere word, God gives him a sign and pledge that he shall possess the Holy Land. In the manner in which men in those days "cut" a covenant (Jer. 34: 18) with each other, God commands him to prepare a path of blood between the divided animals of sacrifice (these are significantly the five which later Israelite ritual decreed for sacrifice, and the fact that turtle and dove are not cut in pieces is in conformity with this). Vultures descend upon the carcases, and Abram drives them away. And as the sun sinks to rest, amazement grips him and horror and gross darkness. Now God lays upon the heart of the patriarch the burden of the four hundred years during which his descendants shall be brought low by forced labour in a strange land before they can possess the promised land. Yet he is not to be alarmed, for he will find his grave in the land of promise, and his children's children shall return thither. God makes the promise, and in attestation a pillar of smoke and a flame of fire pass between the fragments of sacrifice. These foreshadow the pillar of cloud and the pillar of fire with which God will fulfil His promise and lead back the children of Abraham from the Egyptian house of bondage into the promised land.

So on that day the inconceivable happened; the Lord of the world made a covenant with a man. There the Godhead appeared not as a guarantor of a covenant which men make with one another, but as a partner. The inequality of this partner, whose free and unfathomable will one-sidedly institutes the covenant, is clearly shown by the fact that only He, not Abram, passes between the portions of sacrifice. He gives, and Abram receives. He promises, and Abram believes.

ISHMAEL (GEN. 16)

And what has Abram now? Nothing but the promise that he shall be a father. He is to become the father of the chosen people for whom God has prepared His kingdom to the end that His glory may be revealed to all flesh. He has nothing but faith; he still has no son. Only by a miracle can the promised heir be granted to him. In the chapters which follow all human and natural possibilities of his begetting descendants are exhausted, and the event which is possible only with God is set over against them.

The first attempt to fulfil the promise by natural means is precipitated by Sarai, Abram's wife, when she makes the suggestion:

> Behold now, the Lord hath restrained me from bearing.
> I pray thee, go in unto my maid;
> it may be that I may obtain children by her. (Gen. 16: 2).

So Hagar becomes the mother of Ishmael, the son of Abram according to the flesh. One cannot fail to notice how intensely the narrative endeavours to touch the heart of the hearer or reader by the hopes and disappointments, the varied grievous conflicts emerge from this attempt. How all the threads of our life become tangled through human impatience! Yet God's firm but gentle hand disentangles them. He has mercy on the expelled slave and blesses her son as the ancester of the proud and wild masters of the desert, whose life is strife and freedom. In amazement Hagar praises the "God who sees", who saved her beyond the borders of the Holy Land: "Have I not here looked after Him that seeth me?" Ishmael means "heard of God". "Even for him have I heard thee", God later says to Abraham, "yea, I have blessed him; twelve princes shall he beget. But my covenant will I establish with Isaac, whom Sara shall bear this time next year" (17: 20 f.).

Ishmael is sustained by the Lord; nevertheless he is "outside" like Cain and Esau.

MOAB AND AMMON (GEN. 19: 30–38)

In the birth of Ishmael the natural possibility precedes, and stands in contrast to, the miracle. Now, in Chapter 19, the account of the birth of Moab and Ammon, the children of Lot, presents a still greater contrast. The history of Lot, which began with his departure with Abram, ends with his being made drunk by his daughters in order that they might have seed of him. That is again an attempt, however desperate, to continue the race. The Moabites and Ammonites may be proud of their pure descent from Lot. For the proper sons of Abraham however this possibility does not exist. For them there is only the impossible possibility of Him who calls into being that which is not (Rom. 4: 17), "Is anything too wonderful for the Lord?" (18: 14).

THE COVENANT OF CIRCUMCISION (GEN. 17: 1–14)

When Abram is 99 years old and has still not received the promised heir, the Lord speaks to him:

I will multiply thee exceedingly.
Neither shall thy name any more be called Abram,
but thy name shall be Abraham;
for ab hamon goyim,
father of many virile nations,
shalt thou be (Gen. 17: 2–4).

The name of the patriarch becomes a "prophetic cipher" (Delitzsch). Abraham is the father, utterly and completely father, the "patriarch".

Now, immediately before the procreation of the son of faith, he receives the command to be circumcised in the flesh of his foreskin. The circumcision is the sign of the Abrahamitic covenant by which the LORD binds Himself to be the God of Abraham's sons for the salvation of the world. The account is written with all the formality of priestly-juridical style. If we would understand the meaning of this sacrament, which belongs to the Abrahamitic covenant just as the rainbow belongs to the Noahtic, we need not consult the history of religion and culture. It is well known that not only the Israelites, but about two hundred million people are circumcised. They, however, have the Element without the Word, and only through the Word does the Element become a Biblical sacrament. It is the divine word of command and promise which in the Bible confers upon the sign of circumcision its clear meaning: the sons of Abraham, the father of the faithful, and God's children not by nature but by grace alone—"not from the will or the blood of the flesh (the flesh is circumcised), nor by the will of man, but of God" (John 1: 13).

ISAAC (GEN. 17: 15–18; 15; 20: 1–8; 21: 1–7)

Everything which is recorded concerning Isaac expresses from many aspects this one fact—that his birth is due solely to the power of God. His father Abraham "against hope believed in hope. And being not weak in faith, he considered not his own body now dead, when he was about a hundred years old, neither yet the deadness of Sarah's womb: he staggered not at the promise of God through unbelief, but was strong in faith, giving glory to God; and being fully persuaded that what he had promised he was able also to perform." So the apostle writes to the Romans (4). Nevertheless, according to Genesis, Abraham *laughed* when God in giving him the command of circumcision assured him anew that Sarah would bear him the promised son. That does not contradict Paul. Abraham's laughter was not the fruit of unbelief. Yet the message which the patriarch heard in that hour is so prodigiously mighty that he sinks in adoration to the ground, and so prodigiously para-doxical, so joyous and so impossible, that—he cannot do otherwise—he laughs (*yizchaq*). "It is contrast which makes a thing laughable" (Delitzsch). Astonishingly, God is not offended at his laughter, but says to him, "Good, yizchaq, 'one laughs'—this shall be the name of thy son!'".

Abraham is not the only one who is obliged to laugh. When, soon afterwards, Sarah, playing eavesdropper to the conversation of the mysterious guests, hears that she is to have a son next year, she cannot do other than laugh to herself, for already it had ceased to be with her after the manner of women. To be sure, she at once attempts to deny that she laughed, but the honourable guest expressly affirms, "Nay, but thou didst laugh". It is of no consequence. But her laughter is the clearest proof of the incredibility of this birth.

And when after the whole hope, now so near its goal, had been almost ruined by Abimelek's desire, "in the innocence of his heart", to marry Sarah (Chap. 20), the mother at last joyfully holds the child in her arms, she says,

> *God has made me to laugh,*
> *for all that hear will laugh with me,*
> *yizchaq li!*
> *Who would have said unto Abraham,*
> *that Sarah should have given children suck?"* (Gen. 21: 6–7).

So Abraham called the son, whom Sarah bore to him when he was a hundred years old, Isaac, "he laughs".

BY GRACE ALONE THE INHERITANCE OF ABRAHAM IS PROMISED ALONE TO THE SON OF FAITH (GEN. 21: 8–21)

Only in this way are the true children of Abraham born. Natural descent does not accomplish it. Only the Word of the Creator and Redeemer, which summoned Abraham forth, can engender for him true sons. And only the son of Abraham who lives by faith is true to type. The Jews who had forgotten that, and imagined that they were sons of Abraham because they traced their fleshly ancestry back to him, were told by John the Baptist, "God can of these stones raise up children unto Abraham". And concerning the centurion of Capernaum, in whom He saw a faith such as He had not found in Israel, Jesus says: "Many shall come from the east and from the west, and shall sit down with Abraham, Isaac and Jacob in the Kingdom of Heaven; but the children of the kingdom shall be cast into outer darkness." Paul grounds himself therefore firmly in the text of Genesis when he apparently (Gal. 4) turns everything upside down in writing to the Galatians that the Jews who pride themselves on their legally legitimate connection with Abraham are in reality the children of the slave woman (and thus brothers of Ishmael), whilst the heathen who have been brought in simply by the call of God are the true brothers of Isaac, the children of promise. According to the law of nature and the law of the nation Ishmael had the first claim to the heritage of Abraham (Deut. 21: 15). But what matters here is the ordinance of the free grace of God. That this is hard and grievous to men is made abundantly clear to the reader of the account of the *expulsion of Ishmael and his mother* (Gen. 21). On the festival of the weaning of Isaac, Ishmael "plays" or "mocks" or "jests" (what evil he did does not clearly appear (cf. v. 9); the Hebrew word which expresses this is significantly an intensive form of "yizchaq") and thereby so irritates Sarah that she begs Abraham to "cast out this bondwoman and her son; for the son of this bondwoman shall not be heir with my son, even with Isaac". This was a hard saying in the eyes of Abraham concerning his son. But God said to him, "Let it not be grievous in thy sight because of the lad and because of thy bondwoman. In all that Sarah hath said unto thee, hearken unto her voice; for in Isaac shall thy seed be called. And also of the son of the bondwoman will I make a nation, because he is thy seed." So God hears (*wa-yishma elohim*) the cry of the fainting boy, shows Hagar a spring in the desert, and promises her that her son shall become a great nation.

THE ABRAHAMITIC COVENANT WAS CONFIRMED BEFORE OF GOD IN CHRIST (GAL. 3: 17; John 8)

The texts in Genesis are in this respect clear enough; yet it is understandable that among the Israelites the misunderstanding arose that natural descent from Abraham and the fact of legally belonging to his people conferred on one the heritage of the promise whereby God had blessed the patriarch. But repeatedly God questions this racial claim of Israel. The prophets demand the circumcision of the heart, and, by the proclamation of the pure election of grace reject every legal claim, until at last, when the time is fulfilled, the only-begotten Son of the Father appears, and, as the true son of Abraham, places all the sons of Abraham in the valley of decision. The last prophet, John the Baptist, proclaims it unmistakably: "Now comes the Lord, and will sweep his threshing-floor, dividing the chaff from the wheat. And think not to say within yourselves, 'We have Abraham to our father"; for God is able of these stones to raise up children unto Abraham." Whether any man is of the truth or of the lie, whether he is truly a free son of Abraham or a slave of sin, whether a child of God or a child of the devil, is decided by this—whether or not he realizes and acknowledges that the One in their midst is the son of Abraham, nay more, the eternal Son of God. That is the unprecedented crisis which Jesus thrusts upon the people of the Old Testament. No wonder the Jews from Jerusalem, seeking to protect themselves, cried out to Jesus, "Are we not right in saying that thou art a Samaritan, and hast a devil?" But Jesus maintained His ground, and went further— "If any man will keep my word, he shall not see death for ever". Then answered the Jews, "Art thou greater than our father Abraham, which is dead? And the prophets are dead. Whom makest thou thyself?" Jesus answered, "If I honour Myself, My honour is nothing. It is my Father that honoureth Me; of whom ye say that He is your God; yet ye have not known Him. But I know Him; and if I should say, I know Him not, I should be a liar like unto you. But I know Him, and keep His saying. Your father Abraham rejoiced to see My day; and he saw it and was glad". Then said the Jews, "Thou art not yet fifty years old, and hast thou seen Abraham?". Jesus said unto them, "Verily, verily, I say unto you: Before Abraham was, I am." Then took they up stones to cast at him. But Jesus hid himself, and went out to the temple (John 8).

In using the words, "Abraham your father rejoiced that he should see my day; and he saw it, and was glad", Jesus surely thinks of the laughter from which Isaac received his name. The *Targum Onkelos* translates the "and he laughed" of Gen. 17: 17 with "and he rejoiced". An ancient midrash says, "Much laughter rang through the universe in the night that Isaac was born". And do not the songs and music of Christmas really move gently through the stories of Isaac? Does not the bright radiance of Advent illumine the faces of those who take part? The angels descend to proclaim the glad tidings, and the hearts of those who hear leap for joy. Is there not hidden in the depths of these ancient accounts the paternal joy of God, the joy of the father in heaven over the birth of His own Son as Son of man and Son of Abraham? Do we not perceive in the words of the ancient narrative something of the smile which plays around the mouth of the eternal Word, and upon the face of the Child in the manger? And under the oaks of Hebron and in the tent of Sarah do we not breathe that singular blend of odours of earth and the air of heaven which meets us in the fields of the shepherds and in the manger at Bethlehem?

Franz Delitzsch remarks concerning the reception of the three heavenly guests in the little wood at Mamre: "The converse of Yahweh with the patriarchs takes place on this occasion with greater human intimacy than ever, for the import of their message is the birth of Isaac, which forms the great prototype of the appearance of God in Christ. As the era of the *nomos* begins, which brings the consciousness of the infinite distance between the holy God and the sinful creature, Moses hears the voice out of the burning bush: "Draw not nigh hither: put off thy shoes from off thy feet". But the age of the patriarchs is more evangelical; it is, as the time before the law, a prototype of the time after the law.

THE PACT WITH THE KING OF PHILISTIA (GEN. 21: 22–34)

Transported with joy that the promised heir has now really been given to Abraham, the reader might easily forget that the inheritance itself is still merely a promise. Abraham has, it is true, the word of the *Lord:* "I give to thee and to thy children the land where thou dwellest as a stranger, the land of Canaan, for an everlasting inheritance", but he holds none of this in his hand. By a treaty of settlement with the Amorites of the Hebron area he has secured the right of pasture in this countryside. So far that is all. In the land to the south he is still legally completely unprotected, as the twentieth chapter shows. But the lords of the land are dimly conscious of the mysterious fact that a mighty God is "his shield and exceeding great reward". So one day there comes to him the King of the Philistines, Abimelek, accompanied by Phichol, the commander of his armies, saying:

> *God is with thee in all that thou doest.*
> *Now therefore swear unto me here by God*
> *that thou wilt not deal falsely with me, nor with my children,*
> *nor with their children:*
> *but according to the kindness which I have done unto thee,*
> *thou shall do unto me, and to the land*
> *wherein thou hast sojourned"* (Gen. 21: 22, 23).

A remarkable intuition of the possibility that in future the relationship of Abraham's descendents to the Philistines

of Palestine might be reversed. It gives Abraham the opportunity to point out that Abimelek's people have already seized
by force one of his wells. After Abimelek's apology, he makes
a pact with him in Beer-Sheba, at the "seven wells", and
constrains him to accept seven lambs as a legal witness that
this well was dug by Abraham.

The patriarch is so moved and filled with hope at this small
legal success that for the first time he plants a tree, and there
worships the LORD under the name of "God of ages", "Eternal
God". The man who plants a tree intends to remain. So the
tamarisk on the southern border of Palestine proclaims Abraham's hope that he will abide for ever in the Holy Land. He
plants it in faith. For at the time he is merely a sojourner in
the land of the Philistines, as the last sentence of the chapter
makes clear.

ABRAHAM'S TEMPTATION (GEN. 22)

Abraham's heir, the son of faith, lives only by a miracle of
grace. The word of promise called him out of nothing into life,
and only the word, which raises the dead sustains his life. The
patriarch, as the story relates, still possesses his son only in faith.

"The marvellous simplicity of this narrative possesses
greater power than the most detailed and elaborate tragedy",
remarks Calvin. The manner of the story matches perfectly
the matter: it is indeed no tragedy, but a story of the obedience
of faith to the uttermost and of the confidence of faith to the end.

The tamarisk is planted; Abraham has the promised son in
whom he has a visible, tangible support to which he may secure
the wide net of the promises. Suddenly, by a single word, God
robs him of everything: "Sacrifice him!" By this word God
does more than assail Abraham's human paternal love. He
lays an axe at the root of the patriarch's faith in God. "He tempts
him." What does that mean? Chrysostom expounds it thus:
"God contradicts himself, faith contradicts faith, the command
contradicts the promise." And Luther agrees with him: "God
evidently contradicts Himself. For how can the two sayings be
reconciled; 'In Isaac shall thy seed be called' and 'Take thy
son and sacrifice him'. He does not say that a robber will come
and carry off his son; for then Abraham could always have
hoped that his son would live and that he would at last have
him again. No; he commands him to kill him himself, so that
he can have no doubt whatever that he is dead.

"Human reason would infer either that the promise is
deceptive or that this cannot be God's command, but the

instigation of the devil. For if Isaac is slain the promise is null and void; and if the promise stands firm this cannot be the command of God. Human reason, I say, cannot conclude otherwise."

"All the more gloriously does Abraham's faith shine forth when he obeys God with a willing heart. In this he departs not from the promise—the promise so stern and contradictory. Between life and death there is no middle course, yet he believes that his son, though he die, shall have seed. In this way Abraham holds fast to the promise, and ascribes to divine majesty the power to raise his dead son again. Already he had seen how he was born of a withered body and a barren mother, and now he believes that even after he has been buried and turned to ashes, he shall be raised from the dead, to the end that through him he might have seed. He accounted, as Heb. 11. 19 says, that God can raise from the dead and make alive.

Thus Abraham well understood the article of the resurrection of the dead, and by it resolved the contradiction which otherwise cannot be resolved. Therefore is his faith praised by the prophets and apostles. For thus he reasoned: To-day I have still my son; to-morrow I shall have nothing but ashes; how long these will lie scattered about I know not; but this I know, that they will again become alive, whether during my life or more than a thousand years after my death. For the Word says that of this Isaac who is to become ashes I shall have seed" (Luther).

So Abraham "reckoned" in faith, as the Epistle to the Hebrews expresses it. And this reckoning of faith is the counterpart of the reckoning of God by which Abraham was righteous in God's eyes (Heb. 15: 6).

The temptation of Abraham is written for our comfort and admonition, yet it would be a mistake to link it too closely with the problems of our life of faith. We need to remember, as Luther says, that here we have a truly patriarchal temptation which could be withstood only by the father of the faithful. More is here at stake than personal matters, even the noblest and dearest. What is really at stake is the whole divine promise, the whole expectation, the complete salvation of the world that was promised Abraham in Isaac.

Can we not see how this path of sacrifice is overhung with the darkness of Good Friday, and how this dark cloud itself is tinged with the radiance of the Easter sun?[1] As the stories of the anticipation and birth of Isaac become transparent

[1] Cf. Gerhard Schmidt, *Evang. Schulblatt*, 1934, Heft 1, S. 14.

pictures of Christmas when the light of the gospel is placed behind them, in similar manner the words of this chapter become transparent: " . . . Take thy son, thine only son whom thou lovest . . . Moriah . . . offer[1] him there for a burnt offering upon one of the mountains . . . after three days . . . he spoke to his servants, 'abide ye here with the ass' . . . he took the wood of the burnt offering, and laid it upon his son . . . my father . . . my son." Can we read that, and especially the ambiguous "God will provide himself a lamb for a burnt offering", so reminiscent of Johannine speech (and so important, as verse 14 shows, for the narrative, because thereby the name of the sacred place, "Moriah" or rather "Ariel" (Isa. 29) is signified), without as it were looking through a window into the far distance to see the only begotten Son whom the Father loved following the path of the passion from the Mount of Olives through Gethsemane as the Lamb who bears the sin of the world?

And he took the ram, and offered him up for a burnt offering
(Gen. 22: 13).

The sacrifice which God spared his "friend" (James 2: 23), the patriarch of the people of faith, He made Himself; the eternal Father did not spare His own son, but delivered Him up for us all (Rom. 8: 32).

Directly following the account of Abraham's deliverance, his blessing is confirmed by the messenger of God, and the promise repeated that his descendents shall be as numerous as the stars of heaven and as the sand upon the sea shore, and that they shall inherit the "high gate" of their enemies. The sons of Abraham, that is to say, who are still more or less *metoikoi* unprotected by law, shall rule as lords, sitting in the gate of the cities of the Holy Land, i.e., sitting in the place where justice is administered and the government meets in conference. (In the old Turkish empire the seat of government was still called "the high gate".) For the kingdom is destined for the sons of Abraham.

The story of Abraham and his blessing is concerned not with religious speculations but with the occupation of a kingdom upon earth. Its prevailing conception is "the high gate of God" upon the earth, the absolute supremacy of God's government over men—"Thy Kingdom come. Thy will be done on earth as it is done in heaven". That is the parole of the people of

---

[1] The German expression conveys the sense of "raising up" the sacrificial offering.

Abraham, of all who are born of the Word and who through the command of the Word are summoned to overthrow the gates of the enemy. Like Abraham, in blind obedience (verse 18), they follow the voice of their Lord, and serve the politics of the Kingdom of God, which stands in contrast to the politics of the kingdoms of this world and the "art of the possible", as the art of the impossible.

The chapter concludes with a brief account of the increase of the family from Abraham's brother Nahor to Rebecca. The reader becomes dimly aware of something, and can test in Chapter 24 whether he is on the right track. So far as we are acquainted with the tribes who are here named as descendants of Nahor, they resided or wandered along the borders of the Syro-Arabian desert. The name Uz at the end of the chapter is like an outstretched finger pointing to the *"man in the land of Uz, whose name was Job"* and his temptations. Even if there remains some ethnological uncertainty about identifying the two Uz, there is no doubt that the wise men of the book of Job are sons of the east (the fourth opponent, Elihu, is described as a descendent of the Bus of Gen. 22: 21), and, what is more important, their wisdom has its roots outside the region of the mosaic Torah in the soil of the earliest fathers and patriarchs mentioned in Genesis. The Book of Job is, as Delitzsch said, "the Melchisedek of Old Testament books".

THE PURCHASE OF THE SEPULCHRE (GEN. 23)

Now Sarah dies, 127 years old. And Abraham is still a stranger and sojourner, though doubtless highly esteemed, for the lords of the city call him a "prince of God". They perceive the nobility and integrity of this stranger who is the "friend of God". But they fear also lest he should outstrip them, and they have little inclination to grant him a legal right to their land. What is Abraham to do? Where shall he bury the body of his wife, the original mother of the people of promise? He is firmly resolved to bury her in the Holy Land, for he believes the promise that he and his children shall abide there for ever. And he desires to bury her not in foreign soil, but in the soil of his own land. Therefore he is prepared to participate in the protracted and typically oriental negotiations with the owners of the land for the lawful purchase of the field with the vault. He will accept it neither as a loan nor a gift, but gladly pays an exorbitant price and weighs out the silver to the full weight of commercial exchange, as the account expressly states.

This purchase is so important to the narrator that he cites the whole document of purchase, according to which "Abraham procured of Ephron the field including the vault and all the trees which are upon the field and on all its borders". The purchase is important because it legally secured the first and only piece of land which the patriarch possessed in the Holy Land—his own grave!

ISAAC SEEKS A WIFE (GEN. 24)

One last task awaits the patriarch: to seek a wife for the heir of the promise. It is so important that the right one, the one whom God has chosen for him, be found; for it is through her that the sanctified life which lives solely by God's faithfulness is to be transmitted, and the glorious blessing handed on. Only by obeying the guidance of God in that complete trust which follows to the smallest detail can the right maiden be found. Therefore the narrator, who when he chooses can write with the utmost brevity, here goes into such apparently trivial details that the scoffer may well ask whether the Holy Spirit has nothing else to teach and recount than camels and nose rings and arm rings and all the graceful characteristics of a young girl. But everything is essential.

Abraham, being himself too old to undertake the journey, sends his major domus, "the eldest servant of his house, that ruled over all that he had". This is evidently the man of whom Abraham many years earlier had said "he will in the end be my heir". Now he sends him with a commission to his relatives in the old homeland. There, most probably, is to be found the one ordained of God. Yet even this is not certain; in this case again may not God have a plan suspected by no one? One thing only is certain—in no case should Isaac leave the promised land for the sake of a wife. And behold, the God of Abraham leads the servant by "the way of faithfulness" (Gen. 24: 48), and the aged patriarch has the joy of seeing Isaac bring his young wife to the tent of his mother Sarah. And Isaac "loves her".

THE DEATH OF ABRAHAM (GEN. 25)

Before he dies, Abraham gives to the sons of his concubines their inheritance and sends them forth to the east. Only the one is to remain in Palestine. And the inheritance which he leaves to this one is, apart from the movable possessions and a few rights as *metoikos*, only the field with the sepulchre and —the great promise.

Then the patriarch sinks to rest, "an old man, and full of years; and was gathered to his people. And his sons Isaac and Ishmael buried him in the field which he had purchased from the sons of Heth".

"Behold, even this great man, the father of promise, of faith, and of the children of God, dies as we do. The death of these most holy patriarchs and most loving fathers, beside whom we are nothing, is in no way different from our death, but is equally dreadful and ignominious. Their bodies are buried and consumed of worms. They are unceremoniously buried to prevent putrid odours, as though they had never been such holy men's bodies. And yet they were very holy people, and truly continue to live in Christ" (Luther).

For Abraham and his sons "died in faith" (Heb. 11). In arguing against the Sadducees for the resurrection on the basis of Scripture, Jesus uses the words spoken to Moses by God from the burning bush: "I am the God of Abraham, of Isaac and of Jacob". From this it follows that they live to God; for God is not a God of the dead, but of the living. "I am your God"— that was His word to them, and they had believed Him. And there it remains, in spite of death and sin.

Therefore Abraham lives—and, indeed, the whole Abraham. "If anyone says: '*Anima Abrahae vivit apud Deum, corpus hic jacet mortuum* (the soul of Abraham lives to God; his body lies here dead): the *distinctio* is mud. I repudiate it. The sentence must run: *Totus Abraham*, the whole man shall live. But in your way you tear off a piece of Abraham and say, this lives. So speak the *philosophi*" (Luther).[1] The Bible however says that the whole Abraham lives. "He was gathered to his people," assuredly not only backwards to those who died before him, but also forwards to the coming generations. And if the patriarch lives, even after his death, then he lives not in the isolation of some private blessedness, but in the totality of his people, as the "root", the father of the community which lives by the word of life and waits in anticipation of the resurrection of the dead. If Abraham died in faith, then it was the faith that from his descendants there would emerge a people inheriting the promise and possessing the land. This is why the purchase of the sepulchre in the Holy Land seemed to him so important.

[1] *Table Talk* 5534

JACOB (GEN. 25: 19–50; end)

The Election of Grace

Through Isaac and Rebecca the holy tribe of Abraham must be continued and the promise handed on. How can that be? How will the people of inheritance be born? The story of Jacob is the answer to these questions. And the answer is—by the free election of grace! (*Gnadenwahl*). For not only is Isaac's wife as barren by nature as his mother was, so that it is at once apparent that the members of the Abrahamitic tribe are still born only by the free grace of God, but the situation is further aggravated by the fact that, after a remarkable answer to prayer, Rebecca becomes pregnant. Twins are the result and they struggle together within her. And the LORD says to her:

> *Two nations are in thy womb,*
> *and two manner of people shall be separated from thy bowels;*
> *and the one people shall be stronger than the other people,*
> *and the elder shall serve the younger* (Gen. 25: 23).

That is the decree of the Lord of the Covenant, against which there is no appeal. "This is a choice and outstanding text which is treated so gloriously by St. Paul in the Epistle to the Romans, chap. 9: 10–13, where he says: 'when Rebecca had conceived by one, even by our father Isaac: (for the children being not yet born, neither having done any good or evil, that the purpose of God according to election might stand, not of works, but of Him that calleth) it was said unto her, "the elder shall serve the younger", as it is written, Jacob have I loved, but Esau have I hated.' Willingly do we stand before St. Paul to honour him for the masterly way in which he alone was able to expound and explain this text in a manner worthy of it. He has here manifested and taught us a very acute and powerful dialectic by making clear the difference between the birth and the vocation. Where there is only the birth, there is damnation; for what is born of flesh is flesh. St. Paulus speaks of something more—'by the grace of Him who calls'—i.e. God's Word and promise are added. Above our creatures one must hear Him who desires to rule there and be Son of God, *non ut creantem Deum, sed ut vocantem* (not that we should seek God's work in our creatureliness, but in His calling). If the *prima Nativitas*, our natural birth, were sufficient, why should we have need of God?" (Luther).

Nothing but the divine decree resting on election (determined neither by our natural endowments nor our works, but simply by the One who calls), has power to decide who shall belong to the people of the promise and who shall not. This is proclaimed by the narratives of Jacob from the first to the last word. They relate how every possible weapon was used in the struggle for the blessing of Abraham, and one perceives step by step that between the visible contestants there stands an invisible One who drives them forward, repeatedly effecting a reversal of fortunes and deciding the outcome. A decisive power is at work, controlled by none of those taking part, which disposes of all as it pleases and plays havoc with all our anticipations.

JACOB THE DECEIVER

In the very name "Jacob" everything is said; for *ya aqob* means "he deceives", "he gains by stealth", "he tricks into a fall", and the crown of the stories of Jacob is, so to speak, a fugue on this theme "of the special kingly grace" which is "executed in the presence of the highest, and then made known to the world" (if we may use by way of comparison Bach's *Musikalisches Opfer* and his words of dedication as a comparison).

At his very birth Jacob holds his brother by the heel (*ba aqeb*), evidently because he tries to be born first; therefore he is called "ya aqob". But his attempt to be the first-born fails, and by human reckoning he has lost for ever the expectancy of the blessing of the first-born. Nevertheless he does not abandon hope, but essays every possible means to reverse his fate. We may be filled with moral indignation at the methods he adopts —scripture nowhere maintains that they were good (the account in Genesis hides nothing and the prophet Hosea (Chapter 12) brands him in the sharpest manner)—but we are none the less amazed to see how from his very birth the whole motive of his life is concentrated with utter ruthlessness upon this one point which possesses so little attraction for his brother whose feelings are those of the common herd. Esau missed the grace of God, says the Epistle to the Hebrews (12: 15–17), because he was "common", i.e. ordinary, profane, not captivated by God; he lived in the enjoyment of the moment and was not concerned about his share in the promise of a distant future: "I am at the point to die: and what profit shall this birthright do to me?" (Gen. 25: 32). So in a weak moment he sold his birthright for a mess of pottage.

Should the matter be thus finally settled? Does not the

father still possess authority and power to give the blessing to him to whom it unquestionably belongs, both in his own judgment and by the judgment of providence which caused him to be born first? Isaac thinks so. When he feels his powers fail he resolves to satisfy himself once more with the power and joy of life in order that he may transmit to his favourite son the blessing of Abraham. Therefore he orders Esau to the chase: "Make me savoury meat such as I love, that my soul may bless thee before I die". But Isaac is just a tool in the hand of One above: not by the will of the flesh nor by the will of man was he born; and only by the interposition of a higher power was he saved from the knife which would have sacrificed him. He was married without any effort on his part—and now he must bless *blindly*.

If God chooses to cut across the destiny and decision of the patriarch, he has the freedom—whether we like it or not—to make use of the intrigues of Rebecca. The mother takes advantage of the moment to slip her favourite son beneath the hands held out in blessing. Jacob is not eager to participate in this dangerous deceit: "My father will observe it, and I shall bring a curse upon me, and not a blessing". But his mother constrains him: "The curse be upon me". So he enters his father's tent, clad in the distinctive garments of Esau and with his hands and smooth neck covered with the skins of kids, and plays the game of deceit so well that it succeeds, and upon his head is laid a blessing laden with the dew of heaven and the fatness of the earth, with corn and wine, securing to him mastery over the nations and over his brother.

Esau comes too late. When he realizes what he has done, the aged man trembles with horror. The cry of Esau is terrible, "unendurably bitter":

> *Barakeni gam ani, Abi.*
> *Bless me, even me also, O my father!*
> *Is he not rightly named Jacob, supplanter?*
> *for he hath supplanted me these two times.*
> *Hast thou but one blessing, my father?* (Gen. 27: 34–38).

"Bless me, even me also, O my father!" And Esau begins to cry aloud. But the blessing cannot be nullified: the odour of the Holy Land enfolds the younger brother, and the promise of the kingdom rests upon him. The elder brother remains outside, like Cain and Ishmael, his dwelling far from the rich fields of earth and the dew of heaven; out in the mountains of Seir and in the fields of Edom he dwells, like an eagle in the clefts of the rocks (Gen. 32: 4; 33: 15; Jer. 49: 16). Nevertheless, the God of Jacob is the God of Esau, and the bitter cry of Esau-Edom rings through the whole Bible as the rankling and bravely despairing wisdom of the "deposed, who exalted themselves as the eagle, and made their nests among the stars" (Obadiah 4). The voice of those "whose life draweth nigh unto the grave, and who cry unto God their Saviour day and night" (Ps. 88), from the depths; of those whose "way is hid, and whom God hath hedged in" (Job 3: 23). The stifled cry of the hopeless who "lie deserted among the dead as those who are slain", and hope for the miracle that "the shadows will be raised and even in the grave men will recount the goodness of God and acknowledge his marvels in darkness" (Ps. 88). The despairing assurance of "those afflicted of God, that their avenger lives and shall raise himself from the dust" (Job 19). The cry of those tormented of God throughout their life, who take God to task and would blaspheme Him, but who are overthrown, or rather overcome by His majesty, and "laying their hand upon their mouth and covering themselves with dust and ashes" are constrained to give the glory to Him alone (Job 40: 4). The wisdom which has attempted to recognize the Holy One and to understand His judgments, "which has attempted, O God, and is confounded; which can no longer see God clearly" (Prov. 30), and teaches now but one thing as the beginning and end of all human wisdom, namely to fear God, the Hidden One. The wisdom of Heman, Ethan, Agur, Job and Koheleth. Such is the voice of Esau-Edom in the Bible, the yearning complaint of one in the darkness of exile: "Watchman, what of the night? Watchman, what of the night?" (Isa. 21: 11 f.).

A profound word in the book of Sohar runs: "Those tears which Esau wept brought Israel into exile. When those tears are exhausted and Israel cries, he shall be delivered from exile".[1]

Will Jacob really through the blessing gained by stealth, possess the Holy Land? That is the question which leads us back to the story of Genesis.

If he is to be allowed to remain in the Holy Land, then it can be only by grace. Would anyone dare to maintain that he had earned it? And the narrative shows how, immediately after having surreptitiously secured the blessing, fear of Esau's revenge drives him far away. Will he later return and inherit the Holy Land? Or has not his deed robbed him of all hope?

During his flight in the northern part of the mountainous Holy Land he camps for the night with a stone under his head.

[1] M. Buber, *Die chassidischen Bücher*, S. 689.

Whilst he sleeps something marvellous occurs—he sees in his dream a ladder standing upright upon the earth and reaching to heaven, and behold the angels of God ascend and descend upon it. God stands above him, promises him the blessing of Abraham and says, "I am with thee, and will keep thee where-ever thou shall go, and will bring thee back into this land. I will not desert thee until I have fulfilled all My promise to thee." Can that be true? Is it not merely deceptive? Jacob resolves to test whether the LORD is really so gracious to him: if the LORD really sustains him in the foreign land and brings him back to the Holy Land, it is clear that the LORD is willing to be his God as He was the God of his father. He leaves behind him as a pledge a memorial stone in this most awful place. It is a firm thread which binds him invisibly to the Holy Land in all his journeyings through strange countries until the day when he shall return to this very spot.

His mother's relatives receive him. But the hand of God which guides him chastises him none the less. He enters a hard school. As he was deceived, so he is now deceived. On the wedding night his father-in-law gives him the wrong bride— instead of his beloved Rachel, her elder sister Leah who pos-sessed no attractions for him. Ten times he is defrauded con-cerning his wages, but repeatedly succeeds by skilful cattle breeding and with the help of God in turning the litter of sheep to his advantage. At last he flees with his wives and children and herds towards Canaan, but is overtaken east of Jordan in the mountains of Gilead by Laban. If God had not intervened and Rachel saved the situation by a trick Jacob would not have escaped unharmed. But he succeeds on the borders of the Holy Land in making a treaty with his Aramaic kinsmen and in erecting a wall. "I will not pass over this heap to thee, and thou shalt not pass over this heap and this pillar to me, for harm. The God of Abraham and the God of Nahor judge between us." And Jacob swore by the "fear" of his father Isaac, i.e. by the Godhead whose appearing had set Isaac in fear and thereby bound him for ever to him.[1]

As Jacob pursues his way he stumbles upon a double encamp-ment of angels. They are evidently the divine guardians of the frontier of the Holy Land. Will these hosts of the LORD guide and protect him, or will they bar his entry?

[1] A. Alt, *Der Gott der Väter*, Stuttgart, 1929.

ISRAEL, GOD'S WARRIOR (GEN. 32)

In fear and trembling Jacob prepares to cross the frontier. To appease his brother whom he defrauded of the blessing of the first-born, he sends rich presents ahead. Then in the night he conveys his wives and children and maids over the Jabbok river, but returns himself and remains on the opposite bank.

And there wrestled a man with him until the approach of dawn.

Who is this man? Is it his own conscience which bars his way? Does his guilty life arise against him? The Biblical account makes manifest that this is a most dreadful contest—a contest of which perhaps we know nothing, but with which God, according to the testimony of Scripture, has tested more than one of His chosen. The patriarch wrestles not merely against flesh and blood; it is as though he wrestled with the devil, yet in reality he struggles with God. God falls upon him like an enemy.

How can Jacob stand? As a man he fights against God with a weapon which the Almighty Himself has put into his hand— the Word of promise. God has bound Himself by His promise: "Thou shall be the heir of blessing". With this Jacob charges Him: "I will not let thee go, except thou bless me". God has given His Word. Jacob has that—that alone. But he holds fast to it despite everything. And thereby he holds the Almighty fast—the creature the Creator, the sinner the Holy One. Such power lies in the weapon that the Deity even by most violent means cannot overcome the man who wields this weapon against his wrath. When he sees that he cannot overthrow Jacob, "the man" strikes him on the hip so that the joint is dislocated. Despite this he remains in Jacob's power, and must at last make the request: "Let me go, for the day breaketh".

At this point of the story we again become somewhat sceptical. Is this "man" really God? Is he not clearly a ghost of the night who is startled at the light of day? Is it a demon of the river? Is it Jacob's fantasy? Are these the children of his fevered mind which arise before him.?

That Jacob is in a condition of extreme excitement is quite certain in any case. His mental balance is obviously disturbed. But that tells us nothing about the reality of the apparition. It certainly does not mean that "the man" is nothing but the creation of his fevered brain. It means only that there, where a man wrestles with God in profoundest temptation the limits of reason are transcended. In a normal frame of mind, except there be a dreadful temptation, no man would enter upon such a contest, far less prevail. "For no man, when he is healthy and in his senses, can do that which nature accomplishes when she stands in need and is under pressure. When nature is weak and worked to death, she can overcome all burdens which she otherwise could not endure" (Luther).

No; it was really God. The "man" himself admits it: "Thou hast wrestled with God and man, and hast prevailed . . . Thy name shall be called no more Jacob, but Israel, God's warrior."

The patriarch, it is true, goes from this arena of contest limping and with a maimed hip, and yet he can call the place Peniel and confess: "I have seen God face to face, and my life is healed". "Art Thou He," he thinks, "my dear heavenly Father and Lord; I thought it was some ghost or perhaps a man. And now Thou art my antagonist, who hast blessed me and my father Isaac and my grandfather Abraham" (Luther).

But is this revelation of God, the form in which He here appears, not too fantastic? We cannot help asking, with Jacob, "Tell me, who art thou?" And we read that Jacob received no answer. "Wherefore is it that thou dost ask after my name?" replied the Unknown, then blessed him, and vanished. So the patriarch did not discover the name. But he does hold fast to the new name which he himself received, "Israel, God's warrior, for thou hast wrestled with God and man".

And now we are able with Luther to say, "without the slightest contradiction this man was not an angel, but our Lord Jesus Christ, who is the eternal God and yet was to become a man whom the Jews would crucify. He was well known to the holy patriarchs, for He often appeared to them and spoke with them. Therefore He showed Himself to the fathers in such form as would indicate that He would sometime dwell with us on earth in the flesh and in human form". Jesus Christ is therefore the undeclared name of this man. And with Luther we are constrained to say further: Jesus Christ in that night when He fell upon the patriarch in his solitude, wore a "Larve", and mask.

Fantastic though the interpretation may appear, it is in fact conclusive. That is the central miracle attested by all the stories and words of the Bible, that Jesus Christ appeared as a man upon earth to wrestle with men, and to be overcome of them. In Jesus, and only in Him, does the inconceivable happen, that the Almighty gives Himself into the power of men. However fiercely reason may revolt against this, this and nothing else is the message of Jesus, the Crucified. Wherever this message is preached, there is Israel, there men are summoned to wrestle with the Maker of heaven and earth, that His wrath may be averted and His blessing given to those to whom He has promised it in His word. "God was in Christ reconciling the world unto Himself" (2 Cor. 5: 19). It is the "marvellous war"[1] in which God in Christ overcomes His holy wrath, and turns the crisis of His sinful people to victory.

Where Christ is, there is Israel, there begins God's fight. His gospel summons all who hear it to wrestle for the blessing of Abraham, for the mercy of God upon all races of the earth. Despite all terror and guilt they hold fast to the promise of salvation for the world; they will not let God go except He bless them. One weapon only have they in this struggle—Jacob's good weapon, the word of divine promise. As those who are assaulted, believing in the Word, they wrestle in the holy fight to which He has summoned and equipped them, and in which He is at once their antagonist and their protector, "fighting against them with the left, and for them with the right" (Calvin). That is the significance of Israel.

In the Holy Land (Gen. 33–35)

To escape the attentions of Esau who comes forth to meet him in Palestine. Jacob is obliged to make lavish use of his powers of persuasion. At length he succeeds; Esau returns to Seir, and Jacob, after remaining a short time in Succoth, enters peaceably the region of the city of Sichem. Here wide possibilities apparently open before him, for he is able to secure part of a field on those plains destined by nature and history to be the focal point of Canaan. "Sichem lies in the very heart of Palestine, i.e. roughly at the intersection of lines running north-south and east-west across the land. And it seems as though the geological past itself had seen to it that precisely here the historical centre of Palestine should develop. A deep declivity in the backbone of the range between Ebal and Gerizim forms a natural pass from west to east only 500 metres above sea level, and less than 800 metres above the Jordan valley, and in this pass a whole network of good paths from all directions intersect. Sichem is, in fact, the uncrowned queen of Palestine."[2] (Jerusalem has by no means so good a claim to this dignity, and it was only through the peculiar history of the children of Israel and David that Jerusalem became the capital

---

[1] The phrase is borrowed from Luther's *Easter Hymn*, "*Christ lag in Todesbanden*" (trans.).

[2] A. Alt, "Jerusalems Aufstieg," Zeitschr. d. *Deutschen Morgenländischen Gesellschaft*, 1925.

of Palestine). How propitious it was therefore that Jacob and his sons should firmly set foot on this place. From here more easily than from any other point they could traverse the whole land which stretched before them on every side, as Hamor said as he pleaded in the city council for an alliance with the family of Jacob which would secure to them Connubium and Commercium —marriage and commerce (34: 21).

That which had been promised, and which Abraham in his life-time had beheld in faith from afar, seemed now to fall suddenly into the lap of Jacob like ripe fruit. The son of the most influential man of the city, Hamor, fell in love with Jacob's daughter Dinah, and desired her as his wife. Dinah's brothers set forth the condition that all the citizens of Sichem should be circumcised. The sons of Jacob did this with the cunning motive of revenging themselves for the pregnancy which Sichem had brought upon their sister. And when the citizens of Sichem three days later were unfit for battle they unleashed a frightful blood bath. In despair Jacob cried: "Ye have troubled me to make me stink among the inhabitants of the land, and I have so few men. When they gather themselves together against me they will slay me; and I shall be destroyed, I and my house". In his last will (Gen. 49: 5–7) Jacob cursed and cast out these two sons because of their shameful deed.

As in all the stories of Jacob, the human and divine motives are here intertwined. Passion and cunning set the play in motion, but the Lord of the promise has clearly a hand in it. A great promise was awakened when Jacob bought a portion of land in the centre of Palestine. As by this act the claim of his descendants to the whole of the Holy Land was documented, so similarly "God bought the Jewish nation as a strip of the earth with the intention of winning over all nations, so that each should be as dear to him, and lie as near His heart as this one. The right of all nations in relation to Israel's resembles the right of the Jewish nation to the whole land in relation to Jacob's right to this particular portion".[1]

That is true. In God's taking possession of Jacob, and in the gaining of a field in Palestine there lies God's claim to rule all nations of the earth: *pars pro toto*. But the divine goal will not be attained by the methods at that time employed in Sichem. Assuredly the fence separating the chosen people from the nations of the world shall be broken down—but not by the moods of a lover. And assuredly the day will come when men from all points of the compass shall again come and sit with

[1] Hamann, R. A., Bd. 1, S. 75.

Abraham, Isaac and Jacob at table in one Kingdom, and strangers shall become citizens; but it must not seem as though by cunning the citizens of a heathen city could be received into the covenant of circumcision, and in this way "One People" of God (Gen. 34: 22) be formed from the two. The knitting in of the "heathen", the nations, the gathering in of the "world" can never mean a secularizing of God's claim to rule. The people of God, the fellowship of the Lord, the *"kyriake"* (Church) is in the world and for the world, but it must never lose its own proper nature and distinctive character through admixture and secularization.

God in no case tolerates this "peaceful" mixing (the word "peaceful" is repeatedly emphasized in this story). The events in Sichem bring Jacob into the gravest danger, and entail a stern purification of his tribe: the strange gods which had been brought along, and the ornaments, must be handed over and buried; and the fear of God falls upon the surrounding cities. Then the patriarch leads his people in holy procession to Bethel, and receives there, in the place where the God of his fathers appeared to him in a dream as he fled from Palestine, the confirmation of the great promise (35: 1–15).

On the way south from Bethel the heart of Jacob is stricken with a deep and irremediable wound—his darling wife, Rachel, dies in giving birth to her second son.

In Hebron he finds his aged father still alive. Isaac is 180 years old. He dies in a strange country, and is laid to rest, like Abraham, in the family grave, by his two sons, the elected one and the rejected one.

The Genealogy of Esau-Edom (Gen. 36) and the list of the Edomite kings, show clearly that in continuing this line, the God of Jacob says to any who receives the blessing: "Thou standest by faith. Be not highminded, but fear". If thou become arrogant, God could reverse the relationship of those who are within and those who are without (Rom. 11: 20).

Joseph

The narratives of Joseph form the protracted concluding portion of the story of Jacob. Many a reader who was repelled by what preceded finds himself pleasantly delighted with the story which now unfolds. He recounts it gladly to children, for he finds it easy to draw from the stories of Joseph a good moral. And in fact they read like an exemplary lesson to one of the proverbs of Solomon's collection—among which there is a number which were taught in the Egyptian schools of wisdom. How much easier it is to adapt this material than the barbaric themes of the stories of Jacob which centre in the doctrine of predestination!

But let no one be deceived. The key in which the stories of Joseph are set is undoubtedly different, but the themes remain the same as in the story of Jacob—the partiality of love, deceiving and being deceived, thwarted, used and directed by the will of God for the education of the elect in accordance with His purpose and aim. God manifestly has His hand in the passionate struggle of the sons of Jacob for the pre-eminence, and purifies all who take part by distress and grief of heart.

From the deception concerning the blood-stained coat, which broke Jacob's heart, to the moment when Joseph revealed his identity to his brothers—how much imposture, how much purification!

> Ye thought evil against me;
> but God meant it unto good,
> to bring to pass, as it is this day,
> to invigorate a great people.

This word, uttered by Joseph at the conclusion (Gen. 50: 20), expresses the meaning of the whole story.

The same characteristic which during his lifetime became evident in Jacob, manifests itself also in Joseph: he is beloved of God, and all things therefore work together for his good. Nothing can separate him from God, neither his own guilt nor the wickedness of others.

"The Lord was with Joseph, and he was a prosperous man" (Gen. 39: 2). It is true, he is cast into the pit and into prison, but every time he comes out again. He has the blessing, and upon everything he does the blessing rests. And from the story of his life it becomes clear that this blessing is not given to make him and his family happy. It is rather in very truth the great blessing of Abraham, through which the Creator and Redeemer will bless all nations of the earth and redeem them from corruption. Joseph, sold by his brothers' hatred and envy into a strange land, saves not only Israel but Egypt also. That is a prophetic prelude to the salvation of the world by the suffering of the servant of God, Israel, which is grounded and fulfilled in the One Brother who rejected by all the sons of Israel and sold for thirty pieces of silver, Christ Jesus.

The Blessing with Crossed Arms (Gen. 48)

From his first to last breath, Jacob's life is a story of contest by all available means for the inheritance of the blessing of Abraham. From the divine utterance concerning the twins to Jacob's last action on his death bed it is manifest that God promises His blessing to whomsoever He chooses, not on account of some natural or ethical-religious prerogative or merit, but by His free choice, according to the decision of His grace. This is the truth which the patriarch confesses in his last act of faith "by faith Jacob, when he was a dying, blessed both the sons of Joseph" (Heb. 11: 21). He called Ephraim and Manasseh to his bedside so that he might adopt them and give them their share as sons in the blessing. Joseph leads the two boys to their grandfather in such a way that his right hand should rest on the head of the elder and his left hand on the head of the younger. Jacob however, crosses his arms so that he might bless the younger with his right hand. "Not so, my father", cries Joseph, and takes his father's right hand to lay it on Ephraim. But Jacob declines, saying, "I know, my son, I know well".

Jacob have I Loved but Esau have I Hated

The reader cannot fail to observe in the story of Jacob how passionately the characters take sides in love and hate. "Isaac loved Esau, but Rebecca loved Jacob." From this arises a fearful conflict until in the end Isaac, against his own heart-felt wish, gives his blessing blindly "in faith" to Jacob. In a foreign land Jacob comes to love Rachel, whereas Leah is odious to him. For Rachel he serves seven years, "and they seemed unto him but a few days, for the love he had to her" (Gen. 29: 20). But contrary to the ardent desire of his heart, Leah is given him first in marriage. In passionate jealousy the two women strive against each other for the love of their husband. And it is precisely the favourite wife who remains childless. She cannot endure it—"she envied her sister, and said to Jacob, 'Give me children, for otherwise I die' ". The jealousy of love of these two women determines, by a strange interweaving of divine grace, the order of birth of the fathers of the twelve tribes of Israel. On his return to the Holy Land Jacob has to lay his dearest wife in the grave; but he loves her two sons more than his other children. What anguish of heart is his through this partisanship!

Do we not see reflected in all this the heart of Him who called himself a "jealous God" and said "Jacob have I loved, but Esau have I hated"? the heart of the God of Jacob who is assuredly no God of the philosophers and jurists, but is clearly the God of love, of true, irrational love, which can give no *ratio*, no reason why it loves, or why it loves thus and not otherwise; which loves whom it pleases and simply because it pleases.

The Blessing of the Twelve Sons of Israel (Gen. 49)

Before his death the tribal father gathers his sons together so that he may transmit to them his vital power (*Lebenskraft*) —which is no mere natural vitality, but the divine promise. By his blessing he stamps each tribe with its own characteristics. Judah is characterized as a young lion, Issachar as a bony ass, Dan as a serpent by the way, Naphtali as a fleeing hind, Joseph as a young fruit tree by a well, Benjamin as a devouring wolf.[1] The Hebrew, who finds such difficulty in expressing abstractions, is able in a few words to throw the salient features into relief by a picture.

By his blessing the patriarch at the same time defines the future of each tribe till "the end of the days" (Gen 49: 1). This he does principally by assigning to each one its portion in the promised land: to Judah the luxuriant vineyards; to Zebulon the sea shore towards Sidon; to Issachar the charming plain where, however, the Canaanite barons long remain; Dan will tenaciously contest his right to his dwelling-place, and under no less pressure Gad will have to repel foreign claims. By his father's blessings, Joseph enjoys the abundant blessing of the eternal hills. Asser's land, abounding in olives, will provide him with rich food.

Besides his blessing, Jacob utters a curse—Reuben, who as the first-born had a natural claim to a blessing, is rejected because of the incest which he had committed. Simeon and Levi are scattered abroad in Israel because of the outrage which they perpetrated in anger, and to them is allocated no particular part of the Holy Land. That Levi's punishment is later transformed into a holy vocation, and his puritanical fanaticism (which in struggling to maintain the purity of the chosen people ignores humane considerations) placed in the service of the sanctuary (Deut. 33: 9; Ex. 32: 25–29), is to be ascribed to "the incredible kindness of God which unexpectedly shines forth"

---

[1] "In the morning he shall devour the prey,
and at even he shall divide the spoil" (Gen. 49: 27).
"This is a terse blessing, admirably understood by the apostle Paul, who gives it an allegorical and esoteric interpretation which indeed is not far removed from its literal meaning. For after he had devoured Holy Stephen like a wolf, he gave the spoil to the whole world through his work as apostle and leader of the Church and his propagation of the gospel in many lands" (Luther).

(Calvin). Jacob's reproach however reveals no indication of this transmutation of Levi's calling whereby his being scattered among the other tribes becomes instinct with redemptive significance.

The Ruler from the Tribe of Judah

The biggest surprise of Jacob's last words is provided by the pronouncement upon Judah.

> *Judah,*
> *Thy brethren acclaim thee.*
> *The sceptre departs not from Judah,*
> *nor the judge's staff from between his feet*
> *until the ruler comes*
> *to whom the nations pay homage.*
> *He tethers his foal to a vine,*
> *and his colt to a branch of the red vine.*
> *He washes his garments in wine,*
> *his robe in the juice of grapes.*
> *His eyes are heavy with wine,*
> *his teeth are white with milk* (Gen. 49: 8–12).

Whereas the other pronouncements allot to each tribe its portion in the promised land, the saying about Judah proclaims the power of the Kingdom with a distinct messianic purpose. That the allusion is really to the King of salvation who is annointed by God "is evident not only from the eschatological limiting time (the designation 'at the end of the days' in verse I refers mainly to this saying), but also from the extent of the Kingdom whose Messiah brings into subjection the nations of the world. A third token is the paradisaic fertility—wine is so abundant that the King washes his garments in it, and binds his regal steed, the ass, to the branches of grapes which are normally so carefully preserved."[1]

We see indeed the fertile vineyards in the heart of the Judean highlands, but at the same time there unfolds before us a vista "of the earth wondrously renewed, where the chosen people shall at last dwell in the midst of the other nations who live together in peace and happiness"[2] (cf. Joel 4: 18; Amos 9: 13; Zech. 9: 9 f.).

In the tribe of Judah there is raised up the dynasty of the representative of the Saviour-King, the ruling house which supplies by the faithfulness of God, through all the centuries the

---

[1] Hugo Gressmann, *Der Messias*, S. 223.
[2] Karl Barth, *Vorlesung Dogmatik* II.

line of precursory caliphs of the Messiah. In this utterance the monarchic culmination of the promise of salvation becomes clear. The chosen people is to have a chosen ruling house from which will come the Prince in whose hand is the consummation of the blessing conferred on Abraham. An attentive scrutiny cannot fail to observe this messianic tendency even in the words of God in His merciful curse after the Fall and later in His words concerning the "seed" of Abraham. But in the words of the dying Jacob it becomes unmistakably clear. It shines forth again in the phrase "star of Jacob" in Bileam's last speech (Num. 24: 17) and later (to mention only the most outstanding passages) in Hannah's song of thanksgiving (1 Sam. 2); in God's promise for David (2 Sam. 7: 12–16); in David's closing words in 2 Sam. 23: 1–7; in Psalm 2, Psalm 110 and Psalm 72; in Isaiah's announcement of the birth of Immanuel; the rod of the stem of Jesse (Isa. 7–11); in Micah 5: 1–5; in Amos 9: 11–15; in the promises of the good shepherd after the manner of David (Jer. 23: 1–8; 30: 18–21; 33: 14–17; Ezra 34: 23 f.; 17: 22–24); in the songs of the suffering servant of the LORD (Ps. 22; Isa. 42: 49; 50; 53); in the prophecies of Haggai and Zechariah (Hag. 2: 20–23; Zech. 3: 1–9; 4: 1–14; 6: 9–15; 9: 9 f.; 12: 9–14): in Malachi 3; and finally in the announcement of the Son of Man in Daniel 7. "Not only was the whole history of the Jews a prophecy, but their spirit was captivated beyond that of all other nations (who perhaps undeniably had by way of analogy a similar dim intuition and premonition) by the ideal of a Knight, a Saviour, a potent miracle-working figure, a *goël* who, descended according the flesh from the tribe of Judah, should proceed from above, from the bosom of the Father. The Pentateuch, the Psalms and the Prophets abound in indications and glimpses of the appearing of this meteor above the pillars of cloud and fire, of this star of Jacob, of this sun of righteousness, with healing in His wings; of the sign of contradiction in the ambiguous figure of one person; of His message of peace and joy and His work and sorrows; of His obedience unto death, even the death of the cross; of His resurrection from the worm-eaten earth to the throne of immovable glory; of the kingdom of heaven which this David, Solomon, Son of Man would plant and bring to completion as a city whose maker and builder is God, a heavenly Jerusalem which is free and the mother of all, a new heaven and a new earth wherein is neither sea nor temple. . . ."[1]

Messianic prophecy is by no means limited to the so-called

[1] Hamann, *Golgatha und Scheblimini!* R. A. VII, S. 56 f.

messianic passages. The establishment of the messianic throne of the house of David is also the centre of the mighty historical work which comprises the Pentateuch, and the books of Joshua, Judges, Samuel, Kings.

The surprising indication in the utterance of Jacob that the Messiah should come of the tribe of *Judah* is corroborated by the special rôle which Judah plays in the story of Joseph as guarantor for Benjamin, and particularly by the remarkable narrative of Chapter 38.

Genesis Chapter 38 breaks into the story of Joseph and is only understandable in the light of Jacob's blessing upon Judah. This story of the experience of Judah with his daughter-in-law, Tamar, who disguised herself as a sacred prostitute in order to have children, displays the peculiarities of the stories of Jacob once again in their most obnoxious form. In order that the first-born of the tribe of Judah may not remain without heir the widowed daughter in-law disguises herself and commits a deed for which Judah resolves to have her burned. But later he must confess, "She is more righteous than I". Like Rebecca, Tamar bears twins, and at the birth the second violently prevents the first who had already stretched out his hand. She said, "How thou hast torn me!" And he was given the name Pharez, "a tear". After him came forth his brother having on his hand the red thread by which the midwife had marked him as the first-born.

Through this Pharez, Tamar became the maternal ancestor and Jacob the paternal ancestor of David and of the promised Son of David, as is shown by the genealogy of Jesus Christ in Matt. 1: 3.

According to the New Testament, in Jesus the Messiah is fulfilled that which dying Jacob saw and proclaimed in his words concerning Judah. He, who at His birth in the manger at Bethlehem was inscribed on the list of the descendents of David, is the conquering hero who by His life and—this is not mentioned in Jacob's words—by His death gained God's victory of salvation. He is referred to in the words which John heard in Revelation (chap. 5):

> Behold the lion of the tribe of Judah,
> the root of David, hath prevailed to open the book,
> and to loose the seven seals thereof.

"The seven seals are the legally prescribed sign of a Testament not yet opened."[1] When the scroll is opened the last will of God concerning the world and its peoples will be not merely made known, but executed. None can loose the seals and execute the testament except the Lion of the tribe of Judah. Who is this?

> And I beheld, and lo,
> in the midst of the throne and the four beasts,
> and in the midst of the elders,
> stood a lamb, as it had been slain.
> And He came and took the book
> out of the right hand of Him that sat upon the throne.
> And the four beasts and four and twenty elders
> fell down before the Lamb and they sung a new song;
> "Thou art worthy to take the book,
> and to open the seals thereof:
> for Thou wast slain,
> and hast redeemed us to God by Thy blood
> out of every kindred and tongue and people and nation;
> and hast made us unto our God kings and priests,
> and we shall be kings upon the earth."
> And I beheld, and I heard the voice of many angels:
> "Worthy is the lamb that was slain
> to receive power and riches
> and wisdom and strength and honour and glory and
>   blessing."
> And every creature which is in heaven and on the earth,
> and under the earth, and such as are in the sea,
> heard I saying,
> "Blessing and honour and glory and power,
> be unto Him that sitteth upon the throne,
> and unto the Lamb for ever and ever."
> And the four beasts said, "Amen".
> And the four and twenty elders fell down,
> and worshipped Him
> that liveth for ever and ever.

The Fathers Died in Faith (Gen. 50)

Jacob dies, and his mummy is carried with solemn ceremonies of grief to the sepulchre in the Holy Land.

Joseph returns with his brothers to Egypt. When he realizes that his hour has come he says to them:

---

[1] Wilhelm Heitmüller, "Auslegung der Off. Joh." in den *Schriften des N,T.*, neu übers. und für die Gegenwart erklärt, 3 Aufl.

"I die,
and God will surely visit you,
and bring you out of this land unto the land
which he sware to Abraham, to Isaac, and to Jacob."
And Joseph took an oath of the children of Israel, saying,
"When God shall visit you,
ye shall carry my bones from hence".
So Joseph died, being an hundred and ten years old;
and they embalmed him,
and laid him in a coffin in Egypt (Gen. 50: 24–26).

A coffin stands ready in Egypt—in hope. So closes the first book of the Torah. "Israel is still in Egypt, growing rapidly into a nation which awaits the promised departure from Egypt. When at last, free from bondage, Israel enters Canaan, two *aronoth* enter with it—the shrine of the One who lives for ever, and Joseph's shrine of death" (Delitzsch).

"By faith Joseph, when he died, made mention of the departing of the children of Israel; and gave commandment concerning his bones" (Heb. 11: 22).

The patriarchs all "died in faith", having nothing in their hand and everything in hope, "not having received the promises, but having seen and greeted them afar off" (Heb. 11: 13). When uttering his parting words of blessing to his sons, Jacob suddenly cried out (49: 18): "I have waited for thy salvation, O Lord". He and his fathers and the faithful who have followed him through the centuries have all "obtained a good report through faith, but have not received the promise". Why not? Because "God has provided some better thing for us, that they without us should not be made perfect". That is the fundamental truth of organic totality (Ganzheit) which applies to every one who belongs to this people, even of the patriarchs and apostles, that none shall attain a solitary perfection without the others. "The individual cannot attain it until the totality of mankind experiences it", as the younger Blumhardt once said. And in the Epistle to the Hebrews the history of the people of faith is portrayed as a mighty relay race which is run from generation to generation through the centuries. The first receives in his hand the staff of life, runs with all the strength of his soul to the place where the second stands, and, dying, hands on the staff to him. The second now runs, then the third, and so the whole line, each one in the full exertion of his life and with the whole staff. None gains the victory for himself—that is the peculiar and exciting thing about a relay—but each is victor with the others, and all have an equal share in the victory when the last one reaches the goal.

"Wherefore seeing we also are compassed about with so great a cloud of witnesses, let us lay aside every weight, and the sin that doth so easily beset us, and let us run with patience the race that is set before us, looking unto the author and finisher of our faith—'*Jesus*'."

Jesus is the guarantee that this whole race is no prancing of fools. He is the Finisher who guides the race to its goal. But He is also the Beginner, the ἀρχηγός, the primal leader of the whole race. All the time He is there; as He was with the first, so shall He be with the last, invisibly present with every generation. He, recognized but by a minority when He appeared for a brief time in the flesh, and cast out by the "sons of Abraham", is the head of the *mia katholike Ekklesia*, the one "total community" (*ganzheitliche Gemeinde*) of those who are summoned by the Word, of whom the patriarchs are Abraham, Isaac and Jacob.

Therefore let us remember the fathers who first obediently heard the divine word of command and in dying passed it on until at last it reached us. "Consider their end, and follow their faith. Jesus Christ is the same yesterday, to-day and for ever."

3
THE COVENANT AT SINAI

EXODUS

FROM this point, the God of Abraham, Isaac and Jacob reveals His divinity and His sole sovereignty in the arena of world history. The history of a family becomes the history of a people. The opening sentences of the book indicate this by stating that the number of the sons of Israel who had come into Egypt amounted to seventy souls; for as twelve is the number of the chosen tribes, seventy is the number of the nations of the world. (The saga that seventy translators rendered the Old Testament into Greek, and the sending out of the seventy apostles besides the twelve (Luke 10) is of a piece with this idea.) Jacob's children have now become, as God had promised (Gen. 35: 11), a *Qehal goyim*, a national community or national Church.

After these seventy had ominously increased in Egypt, with the rapidity of the lower animals ("They increased abundantly" says Exod. 1: 7), a Pharaoh who is restrained by no sense of thankfulness for the services (so soon forgotten) of the Hebrew governor Joseph attempts to render the menacing guest nation harmless by forced labour and by the edict that every new born male among the Hebrews is to be killed. The narrator here is not concerned with moral indignation at these measures of the Egyptian government. The nations of the world and the great powers employ such political devices in order to maintain themselves and to increase their power. God however follows an altogether different "power politics":

"He hath shewed strength with His arm
   and scattered the proud in the imagination of their hearts"

sings the mother of the "wonderful counsellor and mighty prince" of the divine imperial politics.

He hath put down the mighty from their seats,
and exalted them of low degree.
He hath filled the hungry with good things,
and the rich He hath sent empty away.
He hath holpen His servant Israel
in remembrance of his mercy,
as He spake to our fathers,
to Abraham and to his seed for ever" (Luke 1: 46 ff.).

MOSES (EXOD. 2: 1–10)

A mother offers a challenge to the mighty power of God. She commits her lovely little boy, whom for three months she concealed, but can no longer hide from the murderers, in a little tarred box of bulrushes (a Noah's ark in miniature, as the Hebrew expressions show) to the Nile, and thus to the mercy of the heavenly Creator and Father. And, amazing event, the almighty Lord of the world cares for the helpless infant, and begins to reverse the balance of power among men. For He is the Eternal Father (Isa. 9: 5) and does not leave His earth for ever in the hands of ruthless power politicians. Secretly He deploys His power and overcomes by the gentlest means the harshness of the world's great powers. The story of this little child in the ark whom He had chosen to be the saviour of Israel is a symbol of the childhood of the Saviour of the world, who, because there was otherwise no room for Him on the earth, was born in a manger, and whom neither Herod could murder nor the seven-headed dragon (which with its tail swept a third of the stars from heaven) could devour (Matt. 2: Rev. 12).

Like a child at play God executes His plan, and precisely with those who are His antagonists. "Pharaoh, who planned to drown and destroy Moses and all the children of the Hebrews, is obliged to bring up Moses at his daughter's hand. Pharaoh is slapped over the mouth and nose. This daughter of the great king becomes the maidservant of the Lord God." (Luther).[1] The princess adopts the foundling, and calls it "Moshe" saying, "From the water (meshitihu) I took him". That is an interpretation of the name which is not only a scandal to Egyptians and Egyptologists, but a profound degradation of a name which was borne by more than one of the proud "sons" of the sun god (in Egyptian Moses means "son") who sat on the throne of Pharaoh—Kemose, Ahmose, Tutmose. Israel's redeemer is "one taken from the water". "God assuredly brought forth Moses, the future redeemer of his people, as it were from the grave, to show that the beginning of the salvation of the Church is like a creation out of nothing" (Calvin).

THE REPROACH OF CHRIST (EXOD. 2: 11–22)

Almost more wonderful than his deliverance is the fact that Moses "when he was come to years, refused to be called the

[1] The quotations from Luther concerning Exodus are, unless another context is indicated, taken from Luther's *Sermons on Exodus*, 1527, Weimar Ed., Bd. 16.

son of Pharaoh's daughter; choosing rather to suffer affliction with the people of God, than to enjoy the pleasures of sin for a season; esteeming the reproach of Christ greater riches than the treasures of Egypt" (Heb. 11: 24 f.). He renounces the brilliant future which beckons to him at court, and enters into solidarity with the misery of his humiliated and tormented brothers. This leads him to the bitter experience that at the very moment when he tries to establish brotherhood among them, they reject him: "Who made thee a prince and a judge over us?" He is obliged to relinquish his attempt to help his compatriots, and leaves Egypt "relying in faith on him who is invisible as though he saw him" (Heb. 11: 27). In an alien land it becomes manifest that this passion for justice on the part of Israel's future lawgiver was rooted in something deeper than blood relationship and national solidarity. Is it his business, a foreign refugee, that Midianite girls are driven from the wells by shepherds? Has he not learned by experience the futility of upholding the oppressed? No! His blood boils whenever a person suffers injustice. He arises and chivalrously helps the girls and waters their sheep. It might easily have cost him his life; but this time the result is propitious. He wins shelter and employment with the priest of Midian, and in the end one of his daughters as his wife. The son whom she bears he names Gershom, saying: "Ger, a guest have I become in a strange land". "He desires in the name of his son to have a perpetual symbol before his eyes that shall stimulate him to hope in the promise given to him" (Calvin).

THE BURNING BUSH (EXOD. 3: 1–12)

"A long time afterwards" (Exod. 2: 23), when the King of Egypt is dead and Moses old, God hears the groaning of the oppressed Israelites, and remembers His covenant with Abraham, Isaac and Jacob. One day when Moses had led his father-in-law's sheep beyond the pastures to the mountain of God, he sees suddenly a burning bush which is not consumed. And as he endeavours to approach in order to examine the "phenomenon" he hears from the bush the command: "Put off thy shoes from off thy feet; for the place whereon thou standest is holy ground".

The burning bush, "Sené", is a parable and symbol of God's revelation at Sinai where "the whole mountain was altogether on a smoke, because the Lord descended upon it in fire" (Exod. 19: 18), "and the sight of the glory of the LORD was like devouring fire on the top of the mount in the eyes of the children of Israel" (24: 17).[1] In these epiphanies in fire it becomes clear that "the Lord thy God is a consuming fire, even a jealous God" (Deut. 4: 24; Heb. 12: 29).

> Who among us shall dwell with the devouring fire?
> Who among us shall dwell with everlasting burnings?
> (Isa. 33: 14).

Not simply the ardour of his own heart, but an infinitely greater passion, the zeal of the Lord of hosts (Isa. 9: 7), which is not itself consumed, drives Moses to liberate his brothers and commands him now: "Bring forth my people, the children of Israel, out of Egypt". And the man who once was ready to devote the fiery energy of his heart to the task of liberating his compatriots now seeks with all his powers to escape the responsibility of instigating the holy rebellion in Egypt. "My Lord, I cannot do it", he says, "Send whom thou wilt" (4: 13). Nevertheless he *must* do it, because God wills it, because God is resolved to cast down all alien rule upon the earth and to establish His Kingdom, the complete sovereignty of His will. "I am come to send fire on the earth, and what could delight me more than that it were already kindled" (Luke 12: 49).

THE "I AM" (EXOD. 3: 13–14)

Before Moses accepts the commission, he asks the Deity who here speaks to him as the God of Abraham on the mountain of God in the foreign desert, "What shall I say to the Israelites when I approach them in the service of the God of their fathers, and they ask me what is His name?" He receives the answer:

> *ehyeh asher ehyeh.*
> *Say unto the children of Israel,*
> *'Ehyeh hath sent me unto you.*

In this manner God reveals to him the new name "Yahweh" (or however the four holy characters should be pronounced), which is no name such as the other gods have, for it is neither a conception of God (*Gottesbegriff*) nor an idea of God (*Gottesidee*) nor a name by which men can comprehend or lay hold of Him. In this way He reserves to Himself freedom to be and reveal Himself as and when and where He chooses. "I am that I am", or simply, "I am I". It is an utterance in the first person in which the subject does not become an object but remains

---

[1] "In the nursery the mountain becomes a bush, just as the magic flame of the German myth becomes a rose hedge with thorns," says Bernhard Duhm, *Israels Propheten*, S. 33.

subject. It is thus never possible from the actual presence of God to abstract and objectify a conception. The utterance is made in the Hebrew imperfect which expresses an incompleted action, so that it might be equally well translated, "I shall exist as I shall exist". When He is present He is so only as the Coming One; in His coming, never as the One who has been (*der Gewesene*); only in His action, never as a fact of the past; only in His self-revelation, never in His having been revealed (*Offenbartheit*). Yet even so, in the full freedom of His godhead, He promises His people here and now, there and then, to be present with them in living converse.

The narratives strongly emphasize that the new revelation which is given to Moses is no revelation of a new God. Moses is in no sense the founder of a new religion. "I am the God of thy fathers, the God of Abraham, Isaac and Jacob" (Exod. 3: 6). "I am the LORD. I appeared unto Abraham, Isaac and Jacob as El Shaddai, as "the almighty God", but by my name LORD I was not known to them. I have made my covenant with them to give them the land of Canaan, the land in which they were guests, and I have heard the groaning of the children of Israel, whom the Egyptians kept in bondage, and I remember my covenant" (Exod. 6: 2–5; 2: 24). The revelation of God to Moses, and the new elements it contains, and everything new which Moses is to do according to God's commission, serves to fulfil the ancient promise which God gave the fathers in His covenant.[1]

THE SIGNIFICANCE OF THE OBSCURE PASSAGE (EXOD. 4: 24–26) is to be sought in the intimate relation of the Mosaic service with the Abrahamitic covenant. Unquestionably a very

[1] Albrecht Alt has demonstrated the historic relation between the patriarchs' worship of God and the Mosaic religion of the covenant, and has indicated the basic resemblances on which it rests. (*Der Gott der Väter. Ein Beitrag zur Vorgeschichte der Israelitischen Religion.* Stuttgart, 1929.) "According to our hypothesis, there pertained to the tribes even during the days of their existence outside Palestine (as is evidenced by the God of Abraham and other similar deities) a type of religion which embraced essential features of the later religion of Jahweh—a religion whose main emphasis fell on the relation between God and man (and between God and a human community), without a rigid fixation to any particular place, a religion therefore sufficiently flexible to meet all changes of fortune on the part of the worshippers. Within the limits of small companies there was already operative the same fundamental relation between God and man which was later to bring into subjection the whole nation in the Israelite religion of Jahweh. So the question of the inner disposition of the tribes towards their union around Jahweh receives a satisfying answer—the gods of the patriarchs were the *paidagogoi* leading to the greater God who took their place." S. 67 f.

different meaning can be educed from the story if it is isolated from its context. But we are concerned with the question why (to speak with Luther) the Holy Spirit should mingle such mad extravagant stuff with mighty and noble affairs; the question what the event signifies in its present context. Moses is on the way from Midian to Egypt to execute God's command there, when the LORD suddenly attacks him at the inn near the Egyptian border and seeks to kill him. Zippora, Moses' wife, takes a sharp stone, cuts off her son's foreskin and lets it touch his (her husband's) foot, saying, "Thou art a husband of blood to me". Immediately He (God) lets him (Moses) go. Then she said "husband of blood" because of the circumcision. One is reminded of the sudden attack at night which a certain "man" made on Jacob when he was preparing to cross the Jabbok and so pass the frontier to the holy land. In both cases the issue is raised whether the one who is assaulted will really enter upon the inheritance of Abraham. When He established the Abrahamitic covenant, God said, "The uncircumcised man child whose flesh of his foreskin is not circumcised, that soul shall be cut off from his people; he hath broken my covenant". The present narrative evidently assumes that this is the case with Moses—probably not only because he had not circumcised his son, but because he himself had not received the Abrahamitic circumcision. Zippora thus circumcises her son vicariously for his father. The plausible objection that we should rather assume that Moses had been circumcised as an Egyptian is the product of a world of thought utterly alien to the writer. For him an Egyptian circumcision (if one were really to be presumed in the case of Moses) would in no way fulfil the Abrahamitic command of circumcision. The other objection, that his levitic parents, who for three months had Moses with them, had circumcised him on the eighth day, is equally untenable. For this certainly cannot be assumed in view of the conditions under which they had to keep the young child hidden from the murderers. In any case, the narrative does not hint with a single word that they had circumcised him. And that is the decisive point. For if the intimate connection between the Abrahamitic and Sinaitic covenants is to be secured, there must be no doubt that the mediator of the Sinaitic covenant is invested with genuine membership of the Abrahamitic covenant. For the same reason, the circumcising of the Mediator of the New Covenant is expressly related (Luke 2: 21).

THE STRONG HAND OF GOD AND PHARAOH'S OBSTINACY
(EXOD. 3: 15–11: 10)

Moses is commanded to lead out Israel three day's journey into the desert, in order to celebrate a festival for their God. "I am sure", says God, "that the King of Egypt will not let you go, no, not by a mighty hand. And I will stretch out my hand, and smite Egypt with all my wonders which I will do in the midst thereof: and after that he will let you go" (3: 19 f.). The miracle which Moses performs before Pharaoh, and the plagues which he brings upon Egypt are signs of the superior power of the God of Israel, and that He alone is God. The struggle is fundamentally not against Pharaoh or the Egyptian nation, but against the gods of Egypt, against the demons of the Egyptian empire (Exod. 12: 12; 15: 11; 18: 11). The world is full of gods and religions. When God reveals that He alone is divine by that which He does in and through Israel in the arena of world history, He does not enter into competition with the demons. As the Sovereign, as the absolute Ruler, He divests nature and history of divinity. He who is about to reveal Himself as the sole and free Lord of history, vindicates Himself as the Lord of creation who orders her in freedom and is not bound by "laws of nature". That is the purpose of the miracles and plagues; the more they are heightened, the more clearly must the finger of God be recognized by all whom they touch (8: 15). "If I with the finger of God cast out devils, no doubt the Kingdom of God is come upon you", said Jesus (Luke 11: 20). Nevertheless, neither the miracles of Jesus nor those of Moses form a conclusive proof of God for anyone who does not believe. The obstinate can always say, "By the lord of devils He casts out devils" (Luke 11: 15).

It seems incomprehensible in regard to the plagues of Egypt that God Himself should strengthen and harden His antagonist. For a long time Moses achieves no success. The oppression of Israel only becomes worse. "I have uncircumcised lips", says Moses, turning away from God's further commands. By this expression he means, "My lips are manifestly unhallowed; my word possesses no authority with Pharaoh, and is in vain even with the Israelites who will not listen to me" (Exod. 6: 12; 6: 30). But God replies to him, "I myself have hardened Pharaoh's heart; I will multiply my signs and wonders in the land of Egypt". God chooses to reveal Himself as the Lord of all Lords, as the mightiest of the mighty. Therefore His antagonist must confront Him with his final resistance in order that the power of God may come to its fullest expansion. All the troops of the enemy must be placed in the field and overthrown before God leads forth His "armies" (Exod. 7: 4).

Since the liberation of Israel is bound up not only with the unfolding of the full power of God, but also with the revelation of His intrinsic freedom, it is repeatedly emphasized in these narratives that God hardened Pharaoh. Not as one executing a moral law for the world, nor because Israel is better, or more willing or nobler, does God perform His wonders in Israel, but alone of the grace which flows from His divine mercy. He says to Moses, "I will be gracious to whom I will be gracious, and will show mercy on whom I will show mercy" (Exod. 33: 19). Completely free, in kingly sovereignty. The absolute glory of His person is nowhere and never so luminously manifest as when He shows mercy to whom He will show mercy. "Who hath first given to Him, and it shall be recompensed unto him again?" (Rom. 11: 35). He acts not as arbiter over good and evil, but simply from His own utterly free impulse. So all rests not on anyone's willing or acting but on God's grace. Therefore the scripture says to Pharaoh, "I have roused thee in order to manifest my power upon thee, that my name may be declared in every land". So He has mercy on whom He will show mercy, and hardens whom He will harden (Rom. 9: 14 ff.).

THE PASSOVER (EXOD. 12–13)

The tenth and last plague by which God achieves the liberation of Israel is connected in this narrative with the establishment of the passover-mazzoth festival and the command to sanctify all the firstborn.

The fatal day of the Egyptians is the birth of Israel to the freedom of the people of God. Therefore the month Abib in which this decisive turning-point was reached is to mark the beginning of the Israelite year, and all sons of Israel in the garments and attitude of emigrants are to eat unleavened cakes and bitter herbs at every recurrence of this season "unto eternity" (so long as the world endures) to keep the mighty act of salvation in lively memory. "In every age", says Rabbi Gamaliel, Paul's teacher, "it is the duty of everyone to imagine that he himself fled from Egypt, for it is written (Exod. 13: 8): 'Thou shalt shew thy son in that day, saying, This is done because of that which the LORD did unto *me* when *I* came forth out of Egypt'. Therefore we are bound to give thanks, to extol, to praise, to glorify, to exalt, to honour, to laud, to elevate and pay homage to Him who has done these wonders for our fathers and for us all, who led us from bondage to freedom, from sorrow to joy, from sadness to festivity, from darkness to the great light, from slavery to redemption. Before Him let us all say Hallelujah!".[1]

It may be possible to interpret the feast of passover and the feast of unleavened bread as rites of nature among shepherds and farmers. However that may be, these chapters portray its origin purely historically as the remembrance and present representation (*Vergegenwärtigung*) of the act of salvation whereby God liberated Israel for divine service. From its very beginning, the attack on Egypt and the extraordinary and revolutionary intervention of God in world history which it involved, aimed at liberating the oppressed people of Israel as "the firstborn of the LORD" for the divine service. "Thou shalt say unto Pharaoh", so ran the command which Moses received in Midian, "Thus saith the LORD, Israel is my son, even my firstborn: and I say unto thee, let my son go, that he may serve me: and if thou refuse to let him go behold I will slay thy son, even thy firstborn" (Exod. 4: 22 f.). Therefore at last, after all other displays of power, this final stage is reached, that the LORD slays at midnight all the firstborn in the land of Egypt from the crown prince to the firstborn of the most wretched prisoner or the lowest maidservant, and the firstborn of all cattle. But over the houses in which the Israelite families eat the Easter lamb and over the doors whose posts and lintels are smeared with the blood of the slain animal the LORD passes protectingly by. At dawn all the hosts of Israel depart from Egypt. And the night in which the turning-point was reached becomes for Israel a sacred night celebrated from generation to generation by the holy watch of the Easter vigil (12: 42). Girded with sandals on their feet and the staff in their hand, they are to gather together on passover night as those ready to hasten away (12: 11). The passover is the sacrament of those who have escaped from an alien land to make their journey to their fatherland, wanderers between two empires, summoned and expelled from the kingdom of the world to watch and to wait and to hasten towards the Kingdom of God.

"The passover is the most messianic of all Israelite festivals",[2] and most clearly expresses the historical separation of the people of Israel for their salvation (*heilsgeschichtliche Aussonderung*). Through the life, death and resurrection of Christ Jesus, and in special manner through the institution of the

---

[1] *Babylonian Talmud*, "Tractate Pesachim" X, v.
[2] Georg Beer in his *Erklärung des Mischnatraktates Pesachim*, S. 196.

Lord's Supper, it is ended and fulfilled. At the very beginning of his gospel Matthew says that by the flight of the child Jesus and His sojourn in Egypt the word of the prophet Hosea is fulfilled: "Out of Egypt have I called my son". In His childhood Jesus recapitulates the early history of Israel, for He is the firstborn of the Father, and on Him is grounded the fact that God called Israel His firstborn son and fashioned its distinctive history. The sacrifice of His life is the ground and justification of God's passing protectively over Israel, and the blood of the passover lamb points to the redemption through His blood. "As our passover, Christ is sacrificed", says Paul (1 Cor. 5: 7[1]). And John recounts how Jesus is sacrificed as the true passover lamb. On the tenth of the month of Nizan He enters Jerusalem in fulfilment of the ancient decree (Exod. 12: 3–6) that on this day the passover lamb should be taken into the house and kept until the 14th. On the 14th Nizan, Jesus is crucified, and the soldiers do not break his legs as in the case of the two male-factors. "This occurred", says the evangelist, "that the scripture might be fulfilled: no bone of his shall be broken" (Exod. 12: 46). One of the soldiers, however, thrust a lance into His side, and immediately there came out blood and water. This reveals the source of the two Christian sacraments of the Lord's Supper and Baptism (1 John 5: 6 ff.) which now fulfil and replace the Israelite passover. In dying as the true passover lamb, Jesus the Messiah brings to an end the limitation of salvation to Israel. "Behold, the Lamb of God, which takes away the sins of the world" declares John the Baptist at the very outset.

According to the account of the first three evangelists, Jesus was crucified on the 15th Nizan after having celebrated on the preceding sacred night the passover as the father of the house in the fellowship of His disciples and having replaced it by the supper of the New Covenant in His body and blood. At the beginning of the celebration He said to the twelve apostles, "With desire have I desired to eat this passover with you before I suffer: for I say unto you, I will not any more eat thereof until it be fulfilled in the kingdom of God" (Luke 22: 15 f.).

From that evening all who believe in Jesus Christ celebrate

---

[1] "This laudable Easter lamb, so long before ordained, is renewed for us who have the gospel and Christ, in that we eat, drink, and are nourished by that true Easter lamb which is Christ. In this faith the children of Israel partook of the Easter lamb, and were saved by this faith, the difference being only that, having a veil before their eyes, their perception was dim, and they saw only the outward corporeal lamb. But since they had the word of God, they recognized Christ and were comforted and reminded of His benefits by the Easter lamb, and thus they lived and found salvation in the same faith as we." Luther, Weimar Ed. XVI, S. 240.

no more the supper in memory of the exodus from Egypt but partake of the supper in memory of the fulfilment of redemption, and as often as they eat the bread and drink the cup proclaim the Lord's death until He come (1 Cor. 11). So also they, and indeed they above all others, are ready to hasten forward in expectation as servants with girded loins ready for departure and under the word of command: Watch! (Mark 13: 28–37).

THE CROSSING OF THE RED SEA (EXOD. 13: 17–15; 21)

Once more the Lord hardens the heart of Pharaoh in order to demonstrate finally, in his case, the infinite superiority of divine power over a human "Great Power". At the head of his six hundred chosen chariots, the terror of the battlefield, the ruler of Egypt pursues the departing slaves. Several pictures are preserved in which the Pharaohs of that age sought to immortalize their divine invincibility: there stands the king, the son of the sun god, highly exalted, with tensed bow, in his chariot, riding with the furious gallop of his stallions over the ant heaps of his contemptible antagonists. Could such a power fail to prevail over the miserable Hebrews? In despair the Israelites cry out against Moses who has betrayed them to certain death, "Were there no graves in Egypt, that thou must lead us forth to die in the wilderness?" But he holds fast to the One whom he does not see as though he saw Him. He is assured that the hand which once drew him from the Nile can by a gentle motion provide for his people a dry way through the Red Sea. Therefore he says

> *Fear ye not.*
> *Stand still and see*
> *the salvation of the LORD*
> *which he will shew to you this day.*
> *For the Egyptians whom ye see to-day,*
> *ye shall see them again no more for ever.*
> *The Lord shall fight for you,*
> *and ye shall hold your peace"* (Exod. 14: 13–14).

That is what the Bible means by "faith". The people whom God has chosen that He might reveal through them His unique power and bring to nought the powers of this world, is always utterly powerless and defenceless in the crises of its history. Only "in quietness and confidence" can they be strong, as Isaiah said several centuries after Moses in a similar situation (Isa. 30: 15). God is their confederate. Trusting in Him alone can they withstand every enemy. But God is their only ally and cannot suffer them to seek safety through an alliance with another power. And as in the days of Moses they need have no fear of Egypt, so later when faced with the menace of Syria they are not to put their trust in Egypt:

> Therefore shall the strength of Pharaoh be your shame,
> and the trust in the shadow of Egypt your confusion.
> The Egyptians are men and not God;
> and their horses flesh and not spirit (Isa. 30: 3; 31: 3).

As a signal visible from afar of this infinite qualitative difference between God's holy power and all powers and dominions of this world the miracle at the Red Sea opens the history of Israel:

> *Thou didst blow with thy wind,*
> *the sea covered them:*
> *they sank as lead*
> *in the mighty waters.*
> *Who is like unto thee, O Lord, among the gods?*
> *who is like unto thee, glorious in holiness,*
> *fearful in praises,*
> *doing wonders?* (Exod. 15: 10, 11).

Israel understood the signal; it saw "the mighty hand" of the LORD, the proof and indication of His power. "And the people feared the LORD, and they believed on the LORD and His servant Moses" (Exod. 31: 14).

The apostle Paul expresses the sacramental significance of the sign when he says that all the fathers were "baptized" unto Moses through the cloud and through the sea (1 Cor. 10: 1 ff.). By this he means, as the context discloses, more than that by this event the people were bound to the leadership of Moses. The crossing of the Red Sea was the seal that Israel had been led by God from death to life, from slavery to liberty, from the servitude of the world to the service of God. It symbolizes therefore, under Mosaic conditions and limitations, for the generation of the Old Covenant, that very thing which the sacrament of baptism symbolizes for the generation of the New Covenant, viz., that men are liberated from slavery to the elements and demons of the world by baptism and burial into the death of Christ, so that, as Christ was raised from the dead by the glory of the Father, so now they may walk in newness of life (Rom. 6). The same is embodied in the passover sacrament, which was ordained as a meal to recall the memory of the "exodus".

Those baptized through the cloud and the sea are one with those who live by the death of the passover lamb.[1]

It may be that this analogy of the passage of the Red Sea with Christian baptism seems to many readers inappropriate. Is it true that the catastrophe of the Egyptians and the deliverance of the Hebrews possesses more than a purely earthly and this-wordly significance? Do we not perhaps claim too much even in conferring upon it a significance for world history? And can it have anything at all to do with the Kingdom of God revealed by Jesus? Is the "man of war" extolled in the song of Moses (15: 3) the same God who is the Father of Jesus Christ? Maybe we cannot withstand the power of the "Song of Moses" and perhaps in the antiphonal song to which Miriam dances with the women overlooking the sea which still casts up the corpses of the Egyptians on the shore, we are so vividly aware of the racing pulse of the saved that we no longer have any doubt about the reality of the miracle:

Shiru le Yahweh	*Sing ye to the LORD,*
ki ga'o ga'a	*who, sublimely exalted,*
sus wrokebo	*horse and rider*
rama bayyam	*thrust into the sea*

(Exod. 15: 21).

And yet we must ask ourselves whether this does not express essentially the same as the picture of the conquering Pharaoh with the stretched bow. Can a disciple of Jesus join in this pæan of victory? "In a midrash it is written: When the children of Israel had crossed the sea and the waves had retreated to cover and drown Pharaoh and all his hosts, the angels began their song and the seraphim and ophanim flew through the seven heavens rejoicing at the wondrous good news. The stars and constellations began to dance. You can imagine what joy there was at the news that Pharaoh and the Egyptians were

---

[1] In a sermon of May 28, 1525, on Exodus 14, Luther maintains that the word of Paul, 1 Cor. 10: 1, is not intended to be an allegory. "St. Paul uses it as an example and historical event in itself, as though he would say, 'Our fathers were baptized in the sea just as we are, that is, they also had the word of God that they should die and through Christ enter into eternal life, that is, that they were saved by the word and faith in Christ. Thus by faith in the word they attained the same righteousness which we have. By the word of God in Christ, Abraham entered into eternal life and was baptized. It is clear that in this and many other passages of scripture (Matt. 20: 22) to be baptized signifies and comprehends every danger, struggle and work which God commands and lays upon one. For he has the word of God, and though he be led into all manner of calamities, God delivers him from them by the word, and all his sufferings and temptations become his baptism." Weimar Ed. XVII, 275.

drowned. But the Creator of the world commanded peace and said from His elevated throne, 'My children drown in the sea, and you are dancing and singing?' For Pharaoh and all his hosts and his whole abomination are the creatures of God . . . 'and the Lord had compassion upon His creation'—so it is written."[1] Is this Jewish voice not more "Christian" than the voice of Miriam and Moses?

It is all to the good that we should become aware of the difference between the way God makes known His sovereign claims in the Old Covenant and that which He employs in the New. But we then realize all the more clearly that both in Old and New it is the same Lord who reveals the triumph of *His* Kingdom over the kingdoms of this world. When His conquering hero, Jesus the Christ, appears in the flesh to live, suffer, die and rise again, this in no way signalizes the retreat of the Kingdom of God to an inner citadel involving the surrender of earthly reality to the powers of this world; rather, it then becomes clearly manifest that all the victorious deeds of the LORD recounted in the Old Testament are not, as it might seem, signs of the relative superiority of one racial god over other racial gods, of the Israelite power over the Egyptian, but proofs of the absolute superiority of the one true God over all idols, and deeds whereby nature and history were divested of divinity and robbed of their power, and "the principalities and powers were spoiled and brought forth as a public spectacle in His victorious progress" (Col. 2: 15). "Against all the gods of Egypt will I execute judgment, I, the LORD" (Exod. 12: 12) said God to Moses. And the incomparability of the LORD with all celestial powers is lauded in the song of Moses. But here at the beginning of Israelite history one thing has not yet emerged so clearly as it later will—that the Kingdom of God, to which all the kingdoms of the world are to become subject, is not *of* this world; that its superiority is so absolute that it enters into no competition with the powers of men or of demons, but that rather by the "divine weakness" the energies of revolt are disarmed and the balance of power in the world completely reversed. The LORD Sebaoth will place His government on the shoulders of a defenceless child (Isa. 7–9), and cause the daughter of Zion to proclaim that her king shall come unto her not as a brutal world conqueror, but meek, riding upon the foal of a serviceful ass (Zech. 9: 9). The Lion of Judah who has conquered, stands there as a Lamb that is slain. (Rev. 5). And not those who draw the sword are blessed, but the poor, the

[1] J. L. Perez, *Chassidische Geschichten* (deutsch v. Eliasberg, S. 150.

sufferers, the merciful, the peacemakers, the meek, for theirs is the Kingdom of God, and they shall inherit the earth. (Matt. 5). The story of the exodus from Egypt directs our thought to this by the slaughter of the passover lamb and by emphasizing the utter defencelessness of the Israelites and the complete incommensurability of the power of God. And an ancient midrash records the dream of the Egyptian Pharaoh: "Sitting upon his royal throne he lifted up his eyes, and behold an old man stood before him, holding in his hand scales such as tradesmen use. These he suspended before Pharaoh, and, taking all the elders of Egypt, all the princes and mighty men, bound them together and placed them in one pan of the scales; in the other pan he placed a single little lamb, and the lamb weighed more than they all. Pharaoh was amazed at this potent vision in which a milk lamb weighed more than all the mighty men of Egypt. And Pharaoh awoke, and it was a dream."[1]

The prophetic singers of Israel place the miracle at the Red Sea in a special relationship to the creation of the world:

> Awake, awake,
> put on strength, O arm of the LORD.
> Awake, as in the ancient days,
> in the generations of old.
> Art thou not he that hath cut the serpent of the underworld
> and wounded the dragon?
> Art thou not it which hath dried the sea,
> the waters of the great deep;
> that hath made the depths of the sea a way
> for the ransomed to pass over?
> Therefore the redeemed of the LORD shall return,
> and come with singing unto Zion,
> and everlasting joy shall be upon their head"
>
> (Isa. 51: 9–11; cf. Ps. 74: 13; 89: 10).

The special guidance in the history of the chosen people serves to bring the fallen world once again under the sway of its Maker, and to awaken a general recognition of the glory of His divinity.

The miracle of the Red Sea is thus a landmark on the way to the salvation of the world. The priestly system of dating emphasizes this in its own way: "On the self-same day that Israel had dwelt 430 years in Egypt, all the hosts of the LORD went out from the land of Egypt" (Exod. 12: 41). We saw

[1] Bin Gorion, *Sagen der Juden*, Mose, S. 36.

earlier (Gen. 5) that this figure belongs to a chronological system which estimates the duration of the world at 4000 years and computes the date of the exodus from Egypt to be 2666 years after the creation of the world, so that with this event the last third of the time between the creation and redemption of the world begins. The figures of this chronology at the same time recount the history of redemption to the building of the temple, reckoning twelve centuries from the birth of Abraham to the erection of Solomon's temple (Gen. 21: 5; 25: 26; 47: 9; Exod. 12: 40; 1 Kings 6: 1), and twelve generations of forty years from the exodus to the building of the temple. So the history of redemption moves with measured steps towards its *place of rest*, where not only does the chosen people find rest after long wanderings and strife (1 Kings 8: 56), but God's revelation on earth also enters its resting place (2 Chron. 6: 41). The round figure of four centuries for Israel's sojourn in Egypt had already been intimated to Abraham, and he had already seen in a dream the pillars of cloud and fire by which the LORD led His hosts from an alien land to their home (Gen. 15).

So the baptism of Israel under the cloud at the Red Sea and the slaughter of the passover lamb receive their appointed significance. And at no time, either under the Old or New Covenant, does the mouth of the liberated cease to extol the holy and august conquering hero, the "man of war, the LORD by name" (Exod. 15: 3), until at the end of the days the seven angels pour the last plagues (foreshadowed by the plagues of Egypt) from the seven horns of wrath over the world, and the redeemed stand on the shore of the glassy sea with the harps of God and sing the *song of Moses*, the servant of God, and the *song of the Lamb:*

> Great and marvellous are thy works,
> Lord God Almighty;
> just and true are thy ways,
> thou king of the nations.
> Who shall not fear Thee, O Lord,
> and glorify Thy name?
> for thou *only art holy:*
> for all nations shall come and worship before thee;
> for thy judgments are made manifest" (Rev. 15: 3-4).

IN THE WILDERNESS (EXOD. 15: 22–17: 16)

Israel is called in order that God's name may be "hallowed"

and the true nature and action of His Deity made manifest in distinction from all gods (*Göttlichkeiten*). The special guidance granted to this one people is intended to prosper the coming of God's Kingdom and the fulfilment of His will on earth as in heaven. To this end Israel must learn in the first place to eat its daily bread from the hand of God Himself. Instead of pursuing the struggle for existence as the natural man does by uniting the potence of his own culture with the "divine" powers of nature, it must learn to live by every word that proceedeth out of the mouth of God (Deut. 8). Therefore it is led by the Redeemer into the wilderness, into a "barren land" where all other possibilities are removed and it is utterly dependent on His direct help. The years in the wilderness are thus, as Hosea and Jeremiah declare, the years of childhood in which Israel learnt a childlike trust in the care of its heavenly father, or the years of betrothal when it learnt that faith is a "being betrothed" and means living from hour to hour in the love of the One. It was moreover a time of *"temptation"*, of testing and discipline as these chapters repeatedly emphasize. The people withstood the temptation badly, and even themselves "tempted" God, "murmuring" and "wrangling" and longing again for the fleshpots of Egypt. But God revealed every day anew the inexhaustible resources of His grace. The bitter waters He made sweet by a staff which thereby became a sign of His marvellous alchemy of salvation, saying, "I am the LORD, thy physician". He breathed quails to the people and let manna descend from heaven like dew, thereby showing them how grace is given and received: for each day He provides the day's requirements (literally, "the day's word for the day"), and none can gather more than he needs for the day. "And when they did mete it with an omer, he that had gathered much had nothing over, and he that had gathered little had no lack; they gathered every man according to his eating" (Exod. 16: 18).[1] Also it is impossible to preserve it for the coming day. "Some of them left it until the morning, and it bred worms and stank." On the sixth day there fell a double

---

[1] "In the name of Christ none should be ashamed of another, and none think he is better than another. For the one Christ was given for me and for thee. As Mary and the prophets and all the saints had their experience of Him, so have I had mine. And since I believe in the One in whom they trusted, I have as much right to Him as they. We are all alike; my measure contains as much as theirs, being the equivalent of theirs. And though those who are weak in distresses and temptations seem to possess a contemptible measure and those who make confession a more honourable one, yet in terms of Christ they are exactly alike and possess the same treasure—the entire Christ." (Luther, Weimar Ed. XVI, 311.)

portion, and when some sought to gather some in the field on the Sabbath, they found nothing. He causes a spring of water to break forth from the rock for Moses and confers on His people victory over their principal enemy Amalek when Moses raises hands of prayer. "The LORD is my banner" is the name of the altar that was erected as a memorial.

Paul writes to the Corinthians (1 Cor. 10) that these things happened as examples for us and that the life of the generation in the wilderness was sustained by Christ. "Our fathers who were baptized in the cloud and in the sea all partook of the same spiritual food and drank of the same spiritual drink; for they drank of that spiritual Rock that followed them, and that Rock was Christ." Luther rightly opposes those who hold this to be an allegory. "An example is not called a mystery! That was no figure of speech, but a great and solemn reality, the Word of God which makes alive, and the true faith was there present. Therefore it did not happen to them merely in appearance, but the fact itself was there. Though all the stories have their interpretation whereby they signify Christ, yet they are in themselves most serious, presenting not merely the shell, but also the kernel. St. Paul says, they had the same drink as we, that is, the same faith in Christ that we have. How could they then have pursued a mere interpretation and not have imbibed Christ himself? Indeed!"[1] Similarly Calvin sees in the Pauline words a refutation of the scholastic dogma which teaches that grace was first imparted to us in the New Covenant, and only figuratively represented in the sacraments of the Old Covenant. "The word of the apostle testifies that the substance (Inhalt) of the sacraments was offered to the ancient people no less than to us. There is merely a difference of degree between them and us. Naturally the question then arises: if we now in the Lord's Supper eat the body of Christ and drink His blood, how could the Jews share in the same spiritual food at a time when there was no flesh of Christ which they could eat? I reply: the flesh which did not yet exist was none the less their food. And that is no empty and cavilling statement. For their salvation depended on the virtue of the death and resurrection of Christ, that is on His flesh and blood. So they must have partaken of the flesh and blood of Christ if they had communion with the benefits of redemption. This partaking was a mysterious work of the Holy Spirit whereby the flesh of Christ, as yet uncreated, imparted to them its virtue. Yet of course they ate in their way which was different from ours."[2]

[1] Weimar Ed. XVI, 276. [2] *Kommentar zu* 1 *Cor.* 10, 1 ff.

"That our doctrine be better received I will speak of it clearly and crudely. We treat of the forgiveness of sin in two ways. Firstly, how it is achieved and earned; secondly, how it is dispensed and given. Christ earned it on the cross, not in the sacrament or Lord's Supper. Yet in the sacrament He dispensed and gave it through the Word, as also in the gospel wherever it is preached. The winning of it took place once for all on the cross; the dispensing of it happened often, both before and after, from the beginning of the world to its end. For because He had resolved to win it sometime, it was all the same to Him whether He dispensed it before or afterwards by His Word . . . When one considers the events by which He won forgiveness, it had not yet happened at the Last Supper; now it has happened and is past. So when we consider the dispensation of forgiveness, time is of no account, but it happened from the foundation of the world, as John says in Rev. 13: 8, that the Lamb of God is slain from the foundation of the world."[1]

Does this annul the distinction between the Old Testament and the New? In no way. But it does take seriously the recognition that the Jesus proclaimed by the apostles is really the Christ of Israel, "so that the blessed and joyful estate of the Church ever reposes in the person of Christ" (Calvin).[2] The generation in the wilderness enjoyed living intercourse only by God's impartation of Himself, which He revealed in the incarnation and crucifixion of His Son. The accounts of the experiences of that time are thus for us a testimony to that which God accomplishes through Jesus Christ—and at the same time an example of the obstinacy of those that are called! In their journey through the wilderness the children of Israel were brought into a typical "temptation"—to believe in the possibility and necessity of committing themselves utterly to God. They stood the test badly, becoming covetous, murmuring, and "tempting" the LORD. Thereby they brought judgment upon them and became guilty with the others of the death of Christ. It is this "testing", the critical situation in which everything hangs on faith, which the ancient account emphasizes, and concerning which the apostle declares that it has "typical" significance for Christians, because by the preaching of the Christ who appeared in the flesh and suffered crucifixion they are placed in the same critical situation as the fathers. Only for them the decision of faith has become incomparably more serious by the lateness of the hour. "Now all these things

[1] Luther, *Wider die himmlischen Propheten* . . . Weimar Ed. XVIII, 203–5.
[2] *Inst.* II, 6: 2.

happened unto them for ensamples: and they are written for our admonition, upon whom the ends of the world are come" (1 Cor. 10: 11).

It is the *rejected One*, the Messiah afflicted and at last crucified by the grumbling people, sometimes dimly perceived, sometimes clearly apprehended, who directs the history of Israel with threats and promises, like the pillar of cloud by day and the pillar of fire by night. Jesus the Christ is the goal, the telos and the crisis of Israel. Therefore the deepest significance of the events of the Old Testament is not to be found in themselves. The events are not "complete", but are prophecies of the one event—the human birth, the death, and the resurrection of Jesus Christ. That is what Jesus told the Jews (John 6) on the day after the feeding of the five thousand. They demand of Him a sign in order that they may believe that He is the bread of life, and make reference to the miracle whereby "bread from heaven" (Ps. 78: 24) was given to the fathers in the wilderness. Jesus answers them: "Verily, verily, I say unto you, Moses gave you not that bread from heaven; but my Father giveth you the true bread from heaven. For the bread of God is He that cometh down from heaven, and giveth life unto the world. I am the bread of life. He that cometh to me shall never hunger, and he that believeth on me shall never thirst."

THE SERVICE OF THE PRIEST OF MIDIAN (EXOD. 18)

Moses has now led his people to the mountain in the wilderness where once as he guarded his father-in-law's sheep the LORD appeared to him in the flaming bush with the commission to liberate Israel. "The token that I have sent thee", so ran the word of God to him at that time, "shall be this, that after the exodus from Egypt ye shall worship me in this mountain" (3: 12). This mountain of God was evidently regarded as sacred by the Midianite peoples among whom Moses had spent the major part of his life as a guest, and Moses' father-in-law Jethro served the deity of the mountain according to ancient rites. Now, while the Israelites encamp at the foot of the mountain before the LORD has made His covenant with them, Jethro approaches, leading Moses' wife and children. Moses tells him what the LORD has done to Pharaoh and the Egyptians. The Midianite, overjoyed, cries out, *"Blessed be Yahweh who has delivered you out of the hand of the Egyptians. Now I know that Yahweh is greater than all gods"*. That does not mean that the heathen Jethro has been converted to Yahweh. On the contrary, he rejoices that Yahweh, his God, whom he has always served as priest of Midian, has proved Himself mightier than all gods by His victory over the Egyptians.

Since Yahweh by this deed has also clearly shown His desire to be the God of Israel, the priest of Midian at once orders burnt offerings and sacrifices to be made so that together with Aaron and the elders of Israel he may partake of the meal. By this act he receives Israel into the community of the cult of Yahweh. It is Jethro who does this, not Moses. The latter takes no part in the feast of initiation, evidently because as son-in-law of the priest of Yahweh and as a sojourner among the Midianites who worshipped Yahweh he had already been received into the community of the cult of Yahweh. The next morning the priest of Midian renders the Israelites one further momentous service by inducing Moses to transfer to other shoulders part of the burden of leadership, the judging of the people. He counsels him to stand before God on behalf of the people; to receive God's commandments and to bring before God the cause of the people; to expound to them the decrees and laws, and to teach them the way they should go and the works they should do. But for the smaller cases of law he is to seek out God-fearing men and make them rulers of thousands and hundreds and fifties and tens, "*So Moses hearkened to the voice of his father-in-law, and did all that he had said.*"

This account shows that Israel took over from the Midianites important aspects of their "religion"—admission into the community of the cult of Yahweh and leading characteristics of legal practice. That which later occurs on Sinai when God admits the nation into His covenant, inviting Aaron and the elders to a *feast on the mountain* (Exod. 24: 9–11), and giving Israel the law by Moses is revealed by this narrative as a phantasmagoria of religious history. As we read, it seems as though we were sitting in a darkened room and watching upon the white cloth stretched above the door the shadows of the figures which move to and fro in the light. On the basis of this chapter and other passages in the Old Testament the comparative study of religion may perhaps venture the statement that the deity of Sinai was worshipped by the Midianites (that is, in effect, the Kenites) earlier than by the Israelites.[1] It belongs to the incarnation of the divine revelation that it should assume the forms of religion—in order to disrupt them! The relationship between the worship of the Israelites and Midianites is not of such a kind as would warrant us in saying that the Israelites

[1] Cf. W. Vischer, *Jahweh, der Gott Kains*, München, 1929.

under Moses had merely accepted the religion of the Midianites or Kenites. When the tribal God of the Midianites revealed Himself as the God of Israel by leading the Israelites out of Egypt to Palestine this was, regarded simply from the stand-point of the comparative study of religion, such a completely new revelation that it was bound to break the bonds of every previous faith in Yahweh. The miracle whereby Moses at a stroke releases water from the hard rock in the wilderness is like a parable of the Mosaic revelation. For the God of the desert mountain and His cult were a dry rock from which the streams of living waters first flowed by the miracle of the revelation through Moses-Israel.

THE LAST PREPARATIONS FOR THE RECEPTION OF THE WORD OF GOD (EXOD. 19)

Neither by nature nor by historical development did Israel become the people of God. The LORD is neither the natural God of the Hebrews nor the epitome of their racial energy, nor the idea of their historical mission, nor the demon of their fate. He is the "Holy One", and Israel's communion with Him rests upon a *covenant* which in the whole field of religious history has no peer; for in this covenant the Deity is not merely a guarantor but a partner. A partner however of such a nature that the other partner, Israel, stands in no relationship of equality and is of itself in no way capable of entering into the covenant. In a completely one-sided fashion the LORD is the founder of the covenant, Israel's union with Him rests entirely upon *His choice*, upon His free will. He looks with favour upon Israel (as the recurrent expression runs), He chooses him, He desires him for Himself and wishes him to desire Him. Therefore the purport of the covenant is that God should reveal His will to His people in the law and the commandments. The Law is thus in no way the presupposition of the covenant, but its content, not that which makes it possible but that which makes it real. The presupposition is the act of God, His gracious dealings with Israel. That was the message of the preceding narrative and the nineteenth chapter vividly re-emphasizes it: "*Ye have seen what I did unto the Egyptians, and how I bare you on angels' wings, and brought you unto myself*". The fact that the Israelites had seen and experienced this act of God is the requisite preliminary to the fact that God now confronts them with the choice, as He had confronted the fathers, whether they are prepared to enter upon a responsible dialogue with Him, whether they will henceforth so live that their life is a hearing and answering of His Word. Of His own accord He begins the dialogue (just as in the beginning out of nothing He called the world into being by His Word) and thus affords them the opportunity of answering Him. This responsible hearing of the Word of God in the ὑπακοὴ πιστεῶς, the obedience of faith, raises Israel's experience as history, i.e. as the deed of one who stands in responsible freedom, far above that endurance of, and rebellion against, fate, which one is otherwise accustomed to call history. *"Now therefore, if ye will obey my voice indeed, and keep my covenant, then ye shall be a peculiar treasure ("royal realm") unto me in distinction from all other nations."* That does not mean, as is immediately clear from the addition of "for all the earth is mine", that the other nations do not belong to God but rather that, through the special guidance of Israel, God will validate His right to possess all nations. *Pars pro toto* is again the import. The notion that God's covenant with Israel signifies the surrender of the other nations or that it founds an Israelite empire at the expense of the other nations is a gross misconception. God chooses Israel not to rule but to serve, and indeed to fulfil a priestly service: *"Ye shall be to me a priestly kingdom"*. It is no duty of a priest to seek his own and to rule over human souls. His personal happiness is utterly secondary to his duty to stand before God in intercession for all the members of his community. So Israel is called to be a priest among mankind and only thus to a royal freedom and dominion. When it takes upon itself the yoke of Christ it is freed from the yoke of the world, and exactly in the measure that it seeks to serve as a priest will it exert a royal sovereignty. By its calling it is separated for exclusively divine functions and thus removed from the profane customs of the world and wordly powers. That is what God means when He goes on to say: *"Ye shall be a holy nation"*. A holy nation from the sociological standpoint means "sociologically regarded a pariah people, a people living as guests and ritually, formally, or factually different from their environment".[1] And this again in the sense of *pars pro toto*: God separates Israel to sanctify His name before all flesh and to liberate all His creatures from bondage to the elements of this world for His Kingdom. As those who receive the promise and the laws of God Israel is separated from all peoples *for* all peoples.

In the preparations for making the covenant the utmost emphasis is laid on the fencing around of the mountain from

[1] Max Weber, a.a.O., S. 1–6.

which God is to speak to His people. This is evidently to
guard against the misunderstanding, so near to hand, that the
covenant would lead to the effacement of the boundary between
God and man and so to that "blessed union" which forms the
summit of religious yearnings. We have seen that it is precisely
this desire which is the sin and the death of man. The deification
of man, the promise "ye shall be as God" is the satanic temptation. Redemption therefore for man consists essentially in this,
that his limits are clearly drawn and that he learns to stand at
a distance in reverence before God. In sharpest contrast to the
attempts of the religious man to overstep his boundaries the
command is issued to Moses: *"Thou shalt set bounds to the
people round about, saying, Take heed to yourselves that ye go
not up into the mount, or touch the border of it: whosoever toucheth
the mount shall be surely put to death. There shall not a hand
touch it, but he shall surely be stoned or shot through; whether it
be beast or man, it shall not live"*. In the most impressive manner
the people must be made to realize that it stands in the presence
of an Other who even when He speaks to them, and precisely
then, remains Other and Holy. Then only are His words good
news, then only have they power to end man's godlessness
which makes him more wretched than a masterless dog, when
they are truly words of God, words which man could not speak
to himself. Therefore God's words are preceded and accompanied by thunder and lightning, by the smoking and quaking
of the mountain to the end that Israel may unmistakably
realize that the words which are now directed to him do
not arise from his own soul (*Gemüt*) or spring from the religious
genius of his leader, but are words of the LORD, and that
Moses serves only as mediator.

The Church (*Gemeinde*) of the New Covenant stands no
longer before a mountain which can be touched with the hand
and which quakes and burns under the Word of the LORD. It
has entered upon the festive gathering and company of the
firstborn whose names are written in heaven and to the mediator
Jesus. For the Church the words "take heed" have now an even
graver import. Woe betide her if she does not listen in fear and
trembling to the voice which addresses her from heaven as to
the voice of the holy God. "For if they escaped not who refused
him that spake on earth, how much more shall not we escape,
if we turn away from him that speaketh from heaven: whose
voice then shook the earth: but now he hath promised, saying:
Yet once more I shake not the earth only, but also heaven. And
this word, Yet once more, signifieth the removing of those

things that are shaken, as of things that are made, that those things which cannot be shaken may remain. Wherefore, since we receive a kingdom which cannot be moved, let us display thankfulness, whereby we may serve God acceptably with reverence and godly fear: for our God is a consuming fire" (Heb. 12: 25–29).

I, THE LORD, AM THY GOD (EXOD. 20)

This is the message of salvation, unutterably joyful and inexhaustibly rich:

"I, I, am thy God".

Just this is the miracle of His love, that God reveals His eternal power and glory, Himself, His I, when He says to Israel: I am thine. That is the profoundest mystery of His being, that He desires not to abide alone, but to have a "Thou". We saw this in the narrative of creation. Now at a specific moment of world history He restores the ruined "I–Thou" relationship. Here He takes a nation just as it is upon earth, raises it from its lost condition, releases it from all its false bonds, and sets it in a living relationship to Himself. In becoming its Lord He liberates it. And in a perfectly concrete fashion: *"I, the LORD, am thy God, which have brought thee out of the land of Egypt, out of the house of bondage"*. Whoever belongs to God utterly and only, whoever subjects himself to the "I Am" can no longer be the slave of his own Ego and therefore can no longer be the slave of foreign rulers or powers whether visible or invisible, human or demonic. The one who was lost and sold has been found by his rightful lord, the one who was obstinate and despairing has again his master (*Gebieter*). No longer is he the plaything of blind fate and his own still more blind passions, of his laziness and lusts. His life stands under the word of command. The problem of the meaning of existence, the question, "What ought I do?" is answered by the single word that can give an answer, by the divine command:

"Thou shalt" ("*Du sollst*").

I am the LORD thy God, *therefore:* thou shalt! How could God be Israel's ruler if He did not command? The good news, the whole of salvation, is contained in this, that God says thou shalt. The "thou shalt" is the existential corollary of "thou art mine. I desire you and your will for myself, and that you should desire me and me alone".

"Thou shalt have no other gods before Me." For those whose
God He is, He desires to be everything. They are to fear, love
and trust Him above all (Luther). How otherwise could He be
really their God? Of gods, idols, ideals, principalities and
powers there may be many, indeed they can only be conceived
in the plural. But the living God is One, and beside Him there
is none other. Whoever knows Him can acknowledge none
beside Him. His revelation empties the world of gods, and the
one "Yes" to His revelation means a thousand "Nos" to all
other "revelations".

When He says "Here am I," He is Himself present, and all
pictures and concepts of "God" vanish. Every comparison or
analogy with created things ceases. *"Thou shalt not make unto
thee any image of God, or any likeness of any thing that is in
heaven above, or that is in the earth beneath, or that is in the
water under the earth. Thou shalt not worship them nor serve
them."* It is of the essence of the fall of man that he has oblitera-
ted the infinite difference between Creator and creature.
"Although they knew who God is, they glorified Him not as
God, neither were thankful; but became vain in their imaginations, and their foolish heart was darkened. They changed the
glory of the uncorruptible God into an image made like to
corruptible man, and to birds, and to four-footed beasts, and
creeping things. They worshipped and served the creature more
than the Creator, who is blessed for ever. Amen" (Rom. 1).
Therefore God gave them over to the lusts of their own hearts:
"Man's natural spiritual inclination (*ingenium*) is a factory of
gods which is always at work. The spirit (*Gemüt*) begets the
god, the hand bears it" (Calvin).[1] It is God's mighty act of
salvation that He at a particular point (*pars pro toto!*)
liberates them from bondage to the lusts of their own hearts.
He confronts this nation with the fullness of His incomparable
Otherness, and reveals to it His eternal power and godhead. In
this moment all conceptions of God are shattered; all ideas and
symbols of God which arise from the depths of the soul (*seelen-
grund*) are plucked up by the roots. When He Himself, the Living
One, chooses to have intercourse with these people, they dare
no longer confuse Him with pictures of God which are nothing
more than the idealized reflection of their own Ego or the
product of their fears and yearnings. However incomprehensible
it may seem, He, the eternal God, chooses here to love men.
Therefore He cannot suffer them to place themselves in an
æsthetic relationship to Him. They must either love Him or

[1] *Inst.* I, 11. 8.

hate Him! There is no other way, and no middle way; and only he who loves Him completely and loves Him alone really loves Him at all. *"For I the LORD thy God am a jealous God, visiting the iniquity of the fathers upon the children unto the third and fourth generation of them that hate me, and showing mercy to the thousandth generation of them that love Me."* The command which God gives to Israel and which He unfolds in the Law is the command and the law of His love. How could Israel live under this commandment if the graciousness of God's love did not a thousand times outweigh the severity of His love?

"Thou shalt not misuse the name of the LORD thy God (literally, use as empty, vain). *For the LORD will not hold him guiltless that misuseth His name."* Instead of a picture of God, Israel has the name of the LORD, which God Himself gives in order that His people may know Him and confess Him. In the Bible, God's "name" is God's self-revelation—Himself as He presents Himself to those who are privileged to know Him. Israel "has" the name only in so far as it listens to Him. In the beginning God created heaven and earth and all their hosts to make known His name that it might be adored: "Here am I". But man seeks to make a name for himself, and "empties" the name of God. No word has been so emptied of its meaning (and more by those who confessed it than by those who denied it!) as the word "God". The name of God is emptied when it is removed from the person of God like the purple robe from the regal shoulder, and used as a cloak for the vanity and despotism of man. By the name of God the heathen gains power over Him, and gets Him to a degree into his own hands. Thus it is that the attempt to master one's fate is usually undertaken "in the name of God". The name of God then becomes an instrument of terrorism and magic, and soon (when the trick has become transparent) "sound and smoke and an overclouded glow"[1] or an empty nothing shrouded in mist. But this mischief must cease when the LORD reveals His name and begins the dialogue with His people as the "I am". There, from Abraham to the last of his line, the first petition, embracing all others, upon the lips of all who know the LORD and call upon His name is: "Hallowed be thy name."

"Remember the Sabbath day, to keep it holy." As the rainbow is the sign of the Noahtic covenant and circumcision the sign of the Abrahamitic covenant, so the Sabbath is the *covenant sign* of the Sinaitic covenant. On the seventh day everyone who belongs to the people called of God, man and woman,

[1] *"Schall und Rauch, umnebelnd Himmelsglut"* (Goethe) Trans.

parents and children, master and slave, even cattle and the sojourner, must leave his own work. Why? Not simply for social reasons (to this there is no reference in this passage), but because the LORD finished His work of creation in six days and rested the seventh. *"Wherefore He blessed the seventh day, and hallowed it."* We saw that, according to the account in the opening chapters of the Bible, the work of creation moved towards the world Sabbath. Heaven and earth and all their host were called into being to extol God in reverence and exalted joy. But man who was placed at the very head of the exulting choirs departed from the holy service in the effort to invest his life and the world with meaning, i.e. to convert into its opposite the purpose to which its Creator had destined it. A hopeless beginning, for, as the experience of centuries teaches, he is unable of himself to add one particle to the work of the Creator. He succeeds only in destroying the holy consecration of the world, and rendering both it and himself profane. He has lost the liberty of the child of God, and has become the slave of his instinct of self-preservation. In him the creature is subjected to vanity and aimless wanderings (*Kreisläufigkeit*), and all would have perished long ago in utter weariness had not the Creator kept His creatures, including man, alive in hope. He desires again to liberate them from their own "activism" (*Werkerei*) that they may be free to adore His marvellous works. To achieve this goal He separates Israel to a priestly service. To remind them of the origin and purpose of creation, and to switch the empty movement (*Leerlauf*) of time at a certain point back to the line of fulfilment, He commands Israel to sanctify every seventh day as a Sabbath. So Israel's Sabbath days and Sabbath years are as it were the points on a line of promise which runs through all time and points to the eternal Sabbath when at last at the end of the days the stress and struggle of the world shall find its peace in God the LORD.

"Honour thy father and thy mother: that thy days may be long upon the land which the LORD thy God giveth thee." That the eternal God desires to be a father is the reason why He called into being this world with all its creatures and man as His child. And in refusing to remain a child of God, man has forsaken the fountain of life and thus deranged the orderly life of man with man at its most vital point. For the Creator designed this filial love as the governing principle of all human conditions and relationships. For without the veneration of children for their parents human life is wounded at the heart and cannot

permanently be so maintained. And now "the Father of our Lord Jesus Christ, of whom the whole πατριά in heaven and earth is named" (Eph. 3: 14 f.) restores at a certain point of human history the relation of fatherhood between himself and a human tribe, and within this tribe itself. If the Israelites are ready to know and acknowledge God as their Father, they will be able to regulate their relationships with each other in a childlike manner and be *brothers* to one another. When they have heard the voice of the "I am" in such a way that they become His "Thou", they will be in a position to become "thou" once again to their neighbours. "I, the LORD, am thy God", *therefore:*

> *Thou shalt honour thy father and thy mother.*
> *Thou shalt not kill.*
> *Thou shalt not commit adultery.*
> *Thou shalt not steal.*
> *Thou shalt not bear false witness against thy neighbour.*
> *Thou shalt not covet anything that is thy neighbour's.*

The inviolable unity of the two tables, i.e. the necessary deduction of love of neighbour from love of God, is in no way a self-evident truth. It is rather grounded solely in the gracious will of the God whose will it is that he who loves Him love his brother also. So through its covenant with God, Israel becomes a united people of brothers and a living witness of the truth that the fear of the LORD is the fountain of life for His creatures among themselves and that only from the reality of "Glory to God in the highest" does true peace descend to earth.

THE MIRROR OF THE LAW: JUSTICE (EXOD. 20: 22–23: 33)

God is Israel's Covenant Lord (*Bundesherr*). The people belong completely, body and soul, to Him. The living will of the LORD, not some principle of the good, governs the life of the people and of each individual here and now. The ten commandments are the fundamental witness of this appropriation of human life upon earth by the will of God. To understand them as general ethical truths of reason (*sittliche Vernunftwahr-heiten*) is to misunderstand them completely. Besides the ten commandments there is in the Bible a wealth of laws and statutes, ordinances and precepts, which taken together form no book of carefully worked out juristic subtilties, and indeed occasionally contradict each other. They do, however, in their multifarious agility and in their being publicly related to particular situations conditioned by time and culture, bear *witness* to the will of the exalted and invisible Ruler (*Gebieter*), who here and now claims the lives of those who belong to Him. His command meets them exactly where they stand, and directs their steps, in this situation which will never return, to Him. So Israel, just as he is, belongs to Him. So he is liberated by the LORD from the slavery of his own or foreign decrees and redeemed from the schism of good and evil because God in His goodness chooses him and declares that he shall be His, and how this is to be. But commands become transformed into their opposite so soon as they are severed from Him who commands and turned into a "Law", which is, as it were, a substitute for the living presence of the Lawgiver. Their intent is in reality to bind Israel not to a "Law", but to a Personal Will. The source of law is the mouth of the Lord, from which are derived, from time to time and as need arises, the particular precepts whether of Moses or of the priests or of the prophets. With all their variety and occasional contradiction, they are nothing but the thousandfold expression of the glad news that the LORD is Israel's God, and that in consequence every Israelite should love Him with his whole being, and his neighbour as himself. But true love, if anything at all, is never something universal, but something distinctly particular, something which happens here and now in the encounter between I and Thou. It is for this reason that the Biblical commandments and laws are inextricably interwoven with Biblical history. Historical criticism is able at many points to show how the historical development and cultural conditions find their reflection in them. But, just because it is not concerned with the historical development of a principle, the Biblical tradition makes no attempt to keep distinct the various stages of development. Later precepts are found alongside quite ancient ones, yet all are shoots on the same living tree. And since they all proceed from the mouth of the LORD, it matters little who precisely the herald was who at a certain time and place transmitted a particular command to the people. Everything which appears in the books of Moses is ascribed to Moses, since he is the mediator of the covenant from which flow the latest as well as the oldest commandments. Modern research is apt to conclude too readily that any passage which can be shown to be "non-Mosaic" must be a forgery. Such historical distinctions are the outcome of a mode of thought which is utterly alien to the Biblical tradition. So also is the modern apologetic which seeks to prove that Moses was after all the author. Even if no single commandment, as we read it to-day, was spoken or written by Moses, for Biblical thought they all have their origin in the service to which Moses was called, as the mediator of the covenant between the LORD and Israel. Since it was essential that the people should realize that God had really called Moses to this service, God demonstrates His authenticity by the thunder of His voice: "that the people may hear when I speak with thee, and believe thee for ever" (Exod. 19: 9; cf. John 12: 28–30). That certainly does not mean that only those commands are binding which are "historically genuinely Mosaic". The authority of the law is mediated to us solely by the Author, the Giver, of the law, and only he obeys His commands who hears in them the voice of the LORD, and in them encounters not Moses but God.

How this encounter of God with His people takes place upon the soil of earth and within the sphere of time becomes clear as soon as we begin to read the so-called "Book of the Covenant" which follows the publication of the ten commandments. It is an ancient mirror of the law, compacted of divers elements, with certain mutilated passages and others added later, dating from a time when the Israelites were still exclusively a people of herdsmen and husbandmen. Its close resemblance to the legal customs of the ancient orient, as documented in the Code of Hammurapi and also in an Egyptian and Hittite collection, is unmistakable. When we compare them we are astounded at the extent to which God unites His chosen people with the nations around them by a common mode of life. In the realm of law, Israel manifestly learned much from the Canaanites who occupied the land of Canaan before them.[1] In the book of the covenant this is seen in the so-called *mishpatim*, the casuistically formulated statutes which commence with "if the case be such" (*ki*) and "if" (*'im*) and aim at a just settlement of the claims of one man upon another. But in several passages of the book of the covenant these casuistic laws are interrupted by apodictic precepts, so that (in the words of Alt) "a most surprising change of form occurs: the vocative 'thou', so foreign to casuistic legality, appears (Exod. 20: 22–26), and, still more surprising, to "thou" is added in Exodus 21: 13 the "I" of Him who commands." These sentences, occurring between the "*mishpatim*", are the "*dibre yahweh*" (the Words of the LORD) which are charac-

[1] Cf. Albrecht Alt, *Die Ursprünge des israelitischen Rechts* (Verlag von S. Hirzel in Leipzig, 1934), from whom the citations of this section are taken. Further, W. Eichrodt, *Theologie des AT*. I, S. 28 ff.

terized by gravity of expression and the brevity and metrical perfection of their style. They relate everything to the absolute will of the LORD, and assign to every trespass the severest punishment, the personal extermination of the perpetrator. "Religion, morals and law are here inextricably intertwined", and we cannot separate the *mishpatim* from the *debarim* in such a fashion that the one were merely a human duty and the other a divine imperative. In Old Testament tradition they stand inseparably side by side. Indeed for Israel there was as a matter of principle no distinction between spiritual and mundane law, either in the book of the covenant or in any other collection. "Moses appropriately writes that his book is a picture and example of government and life. For so it is, when all is in full swing, that now this work, now that, must be done, and no man can so fashion his life (if it is to be at all godly) so that to-day he obeys nothing but the spiritual law and to-morrow nothing but the mundane law. Rather does God govern all the several laws, as He does the stars of heaven and the flowers of the field, so that man must be ready at every moment to do that which comes to hand. Thus the book of Moses compounds its various parts" (Luther, *Preface to the Old Testament*). All Israel's acts of commission and omission should be done simply as a divine service, for these are people who belong body and soul to God.

The ceremonial decrees which are found at the beginning and end of the "book of the covenant" show that the Israelites are the rural vassals of the divine Lord of the realm. Of him alone are they to accept commands and petition blessings (Exod. 20: 23; 23: 13). He determines the places in the land where "His name shall be remembered", and where He will meet His people in blessing. Here sacrificial altars are to be constructed of earth or unhewed stones of the field which have not been desecrated. No steps are to lead to these, for it would denote impropriety before the LORD if the worshipper, who in his simple peasant's garb wore no covering for the legs, were obliged to mount steps (Exod. 20: 24–26). Six years shall the farmer sow and reap his land, but shall in the seventh year grant it complete rest and leave anything it may bring forth to the poor and the beasts of the field (Exod. 23: 10–11). Similarly a holiday shall follow every six days of work, so that the ox and ass may rest and the son of the maidservant and the sojourner may be refreshed. The regular and ponderous course of the year is to be enlivened by the triple rhythm of the festal roundelay; literally, "Three feet shalt thou dance in the year".

The feast of unleavened bread is celebrated in the month when the grain ripens, the second feast when the corn is ready for the sickle, and at the end of the year the feast of ingathering. So thrice a year every male appears before the face of the LORD, but none with empty hands (Exod. 23: 14–17). The only instruction concerning the gifts and the manner of their presentation is that the first fruits of the field are to be brought into the house of the LORD: "Thou shalt not delay to offer the first of thy ripe fruits, and of thy liquors (literally tears). The firstborn of thy sons shalt thou give unto me. Likewise shalt thou do with thine oxen, and with thy sheep: seven days it shall be with his dam; on the eighth day thou shalt give it me" (Exod. 22: 28–29). Sacrificial blood is to be uncontaminated with leaven; the fat of the sacrifice is not to be kept till the morning; and a kid is not to be seethed in its mother's milk (Exod. 23: 18–19). All slaughter of animals, even for one's own needs, is a sacrificial act. Flesh torn from beasts in the field is not to be eaten, but to be cast to the dogs (Exod. 22: 31).

Thus the LORD's free herdsmen and farmers serve Him with the work of their hands and the joy of their hearts. Their relation to creation, as their relation to the Creator, must be pure; perverse relationships with invisible powers or with other creatures are severely punished: a witch shall not be suffered to live, and whoever lieth with a beast shall be put to death (Exod. 22: 18–19).

In the "Book of the Covenant" the direct decrees concerning the duties of divine service are far more numerous than the indirect, i.e. the precepts which govern the relationship of those living under the divine covenant to one another. Both flow from the same source, for it is the will of the Covenant-Lord to have a people peculiarly His own, and it is this will, and not their natural and accidental characteristics, which makes of the children of Israel a people which on earth and in history is the people of God. The fact that He is their Covenant-Lord determines their constitution and all relationships of the people under the covenant to one another. The Hebrew tribes which the LORD delivered from the house of bondage and claimed for His own possession cannot be other than a free people of free men, and their government is the complete opposite of the pyramid of Egyptian absolutism. One could almost say of the Israel of the book of the covenant what Wellhausen said of certain Arabian tribes, that they are "constituted as a community without official authorities" (*ein Gemeinwesen ohne Obrigkeit*). When in one passage (Exod. 22: 28) a "ruler" is mentioned: no commander is meant, far less a dictator, but simply one of the elders of the tribe or community (cf. 18: 21). There are not even official judges: "jurisdiction is in the hands of free men with the elders (i.e. the representatives of leading tribes) at the head. The priests of the sanctuary are invited to co-operate in the administration of justice only and in so far as a case must be referred to the deity for decision." The legal council sitting at the gate must always bear in mind that "the judgment is God's" (Deut. 1: 17). Every Israelite stands under His protection and under His judgment. The judges, as the mirror of justice (Exod. 23: 1–9) shows, are entirely His instruments. Their sense of justice must be determined by His nature and will, and they must not allow themselves to be influenced by popular opinion or bribery, or even by a prejudice in favour of the poor. Everyone who is involved in a case, whether as witness or plaintiff or as defendant, must keep to the facts. No enmity is to destroy brotherhood: "If thou meet thine enemy's ox or his ass going astray, thou shalt surely bring it back to him again. And if thou see the ass of him that hateth thee lying under his burden, leave him not without help, but help him up again" (Exod. 23: 4 f.).

All Israelites belong to the LORD. Therefore Israelite law cannot be based on class distinction or social standing. The book of the covenant makes only one distinction—between free men and slaves—and even here it is ordained that a "Hebrew" in Israel may be held as a slave only for six years. Only if, because of his love to his master and his wife and family, he deliberately so chooses, can he remain perpetually a slave. The case of an Israelite female slave is somewhat different: normally she cannot be liberated, because she enters a marital relationship with him who buys her, and this relationship can only be dissolved if her master fails to fulfil the duties of husband or father-in-law towards her, in which case it must be dissolved (Exod. 21: 1–11). To describe these regulations governing the rights of the Israelite female slave as "the Israelite law of marriage"[1] is scarcely in order. Albrecht Alt conjectures that Deuteronomy 22: 13–29 contains in slightly altered form marriage decrees which belong to the book of the covenant. The latter as it stands adds only the statement that anyone seducing an unbetrothed virgin shall endow her and make her his wife; even if her father refuse to give her to him, he must still pay the customary fee for a wife (Deut. 22: 16, 17).

[1] Hugo Gressman, *Die Schriften des AT.*, Bd. II, 1, S. 231.

Most of the legal decrees of the book of the covenant are directed to the protection of life and property. It becomes at once apparent, especially in comparison with the code of Hammurapi, how much greater store is set upon life than upon things. For murder (though the distinction is made whether it took place by malicious intent or divine juxtaposition of events) and theft, the penalty is death. Similarly anyone who smites or curses his father or mother shall be put to death. Bodily injuries are punished according to the *jus talionis* ("an eye for an eye . . ."). A domestic animal which slays a man is treated as guilty, and its flesh is not to be eaten (cf. the Noahitic commandment, Gen. 9: 5).

For theft, for damage to neighbours through cattle wandering abroad or fire which spreads to his property, for embezzlement of goods entrusted to one, for loss or injury of animals which should have been watched or were borrowed, restitution must be made, one- to five-fold, unless an accident for which no one was responsible can be proved. Penalties involving loss of freedom, prison or penal servitude do not exist. But a thief who is unable to make restitution may be sold for the price of that which he stole. He is however not to be killed. If, being caught in the act of theft, he is slain in the darkness, the one so slaying him is not guilty of his blood; if however the sun had risen, he is guilty of his blood (21: 37–22; 14). In any case the life of the thief is of more importance than the stolen goods.

Similarly God protects men against ruthless distraint, e.g. a coat taken in pledge must be returned to the poor before sunset: "for it is his only covering, his raiment for his skin: wherein can he otherwise sleep? And it shall come to pass, when he crieth unto me, that I will hear; for I am gracious" (Exod. 22: 25–27). The strongest expression of the superiority of human life over possessions is found in the prohibition of interest and usury (Exod. 22: 24). Even later, when they lived no longer in nomadic tribal companies, the Israelites, despite the introduction of a monetary economy, held faithfully to this prohibition, in sharpest contrast to the ruthless usury of Assyria and Egypt, and only relaxed it in their dealings with aliens (Deut. 23: 21). But this modification in regard to aliens is never made in the book of the covenant, either in this or any other passage. On the contrary, it is twice expressly forbidden to treat the alien in a worse manner. Israel has been redeemed by God out of an alien land: "Ye know how the alien feeleth. I will hear his cry" (Exod. 22: 20–22; 23: 9). In the election of Israel the LORD condescended to the oppressed and impotent. Therefore the weak and those without legal rights, the widows and the orphans, all enjoy His personal protection: "If thou afflict them in any wise, and they cry at all unto me, I will surely hear their cry; and my wrath shall wax hot, and I will kill you with the sword; and your wives shall be widows, and your children fatherless" (22; 22–24).

PROMISE (EXOD. 23: 20–33)

All the laws of Israel are invested with divine promises and point forward to a particular future epoch on the earth. So there belongs to the precepts of the book of the covenant the promise that the LORD by the hand of His angel will bring the Israelites into the promised land and drive out the previous inhabitants—not indeed in one year will He drive them out, for then the land would become desolate and a prey to wild animals, since Israel could not so rapidly make their home in the land and farm it efficiently. Everything depends on Israel's refraining from all relationships with other gods. For the goal of all paths which the LORD treads with His people is that He should reveal Himself as the one sole God.

THE MAKING OF THE COVENANT (EXOD. 24)

After Israel has responded with a unanimous "yes" to the words of God, which, however many they were, portended but one thing: "I, the Lord, am thy God. Thine it is to be my own. Art thou willing?", the making of the covenant takes place, as is appropriate, in a double sacramental act, on earth and in heaven. At the foot of Sinai are erected an altar, the sign of God's presence, and twelve pillars according to the number of the tribes of Israel. Then Moses, as the mediator, sprinkles half the sacrificial blood on the altar of the LORD and the other half on the people, thus consummating the sacramental union of the two partners to the covenant. For the sprinkling with blood, like the walking between the bleeding halves of the sacrificed animals (Gen. 15: 9 ff.; Jer. 34: 18 ff.), is a sign of the uniting of the two parties into an indissoluble life fellowship (*Lebensgemeinschaft*). Immediately following this, Moses along with Aaron, Nadab, Abihu and the seventy elders of Israel ascend the mountain, so to speak, into heaven. There they behold the God of Israel, or, more precisely expressed, the purest brightness of heaven which lies beneath their feet like paving stones of sapphire. The "corner pillars of the sons of Israel" are not consumed by God's nearness. The exalted

Master of the house allows them to eat and drink at His feet and thus receives them to the fellowship of His table. By this holy meal He sanctifies and fortifies His fellowship (*Lebensgemeinschaft*) with His people (cf. Gen. 26: 30; 31: 44, 54).

Now, as the consummation, comes the documentation of the covenant. Once again in the clearest manner the astounding fact becomes manifest that God Himself is the Partner who establishes the covenant, for the "çovenant letter" of this confederacy (*Eidgenossenschaft*), the imperial charter of these herdsmen and farmers who are direct subjects of His empire, is written by God Himself with His own finger on two tablets of stone. To this end the glory of God descends upon Mount Sinai and dwells there encompassed with clouds. Six days Moses waits, six days which are, so to speak, a repetition of the week of creation, for God's present action is a confirmation and restoration of His work of creation. On the seventh day Moses is summoned to ascend into the cloud to receive the documents in stone. The relation of this to the week of creation is clearly emphasized by the fact that before delivering the tables to Moses, God describes *the festival of the Sabbath as the characteristic token of the Sinaitic covenant* (Exod. 31: 12–17).

That the Sinaitic covenant is directed to the renewal of creation is further revealed by the fact that on the mount, in addition to the documents of the covenant, Moses receives also

THE PATTERN OF THE TABERNACLE OF GOD AND ITS FURNISHINGS (EXOD. 25–31: 11)

For the holy tabernacle among the tents of Israel is merely a copy of God's heavenly abode in a small earthly form and is erected in order to demonstrate that His will is to dwell in the midst of His people upon earth. At the same time it expresses symbolically the truth that the world is the temple in which His glory dwells—a truth which men had lost and replaced by the myth of their own divinity. By this act they had made God a kind of alien in His own world, "a wayfaring man that turneth aside to tarry for a night" (Jer. 14: 8). When He now makes His modest dwelling place in the midst of the Israelitic community, His action is invested with the intention and promise that He chooses to be present now with His own upon earth and at length to reveal His presence to all flesh.

The holy tent is to be erected in a court demarcated by curtains. Its length is three times its breadth (30 by 10 ells = approximately 18 yards by 6 yards). Its interior is divided by a curtain into two sections, of which the smaller is half the size of the larger, ten ells long, ten ells wide and ten ells high, thus a cube, a "Kaaba". This is the Holy of Holies, the place where God is present. The anterior room is furnished with a table and a candlestick with seven lamps; in the dark posterior chamber is only an ark of acacia wood covered internally and externally with pure gold, and containing the stone documents which testify that Israel belongs to the LORD. It forms the foundation of all God's further revelation to Israel. On the ark lies a cover of pure gold, the ends of which to left and right are fashioned into two cherubs of beaten gold which spread their wings protectively over the ark and hold them extended ready to sustain the glory of the LORD whenever it may descend upon them. This is the place where God has chosen to be present and to speak His living word. This is the place of encounter.

> *And there I will meet with thee, and I will commune with thee from above the mercy seat, from between the two cherubims which are upon the ark of the testimony, of all things which I will give thee in commandment unto the children of Israel*
> (Exod. 25: 22).

No picture of deity is here displayed as in the temples of the heathen, nor are stone tables a kind of fetish, for they lie not upon the wings of the cherubs but as the basic testimony under the cover. The divine throne of grace must be left free. For the LORD is the living God whose name is "I am who I am", and who, as surely as He has promised His presence to His people, is only present as and when He chooses to be present. Therefore even the Holy Scriptures of the two Testaments of God, though they and they alone bear witness to the place in which and through which God reveals Himself, can never be a substitute for the presence of His living Word.

Since the central fact in the erection of the holy tabernacle is that this is the place where God meets with His people, half of the chapters (Exod. 28–30) deal with *the dedication of the man who is to approach the Holy One as the representative of the sinful people*. First (Exod. 28) are defined all the details of the "Investiture" with which Aaron and his sons are to be clothed as they enter the priesthood. In this description eloquent expression is given to the truth that the priest is the representative of the people by the fact that Aaron bears on both shoulders and on his heart the names of the twelve tribes of Israel, engraved in precious stone "for remembrance before the LORD" whenever he enters the sanctuary. And on the golden plate which forms the insignia of office attached to his headband is engraved the inscription: "Holiness to the LORD." This is to rest on his forehead as a sign that he is responsible for all ceremonial observances of the children of Israel and that he mediates to them the favour of the LORD.

The rites of ordination are then described (Exod. 29) which authorize the priest to stand before God and to foster the relationships between God and the people. (That *"kohen"* = priest is cognate with *"kun"* = stand, stand fast, hiph. = confirm is not without significance.) This consecration consists firstly in ceremonial washing; secondly in the *"Chrisma"* (i.e. anointing with specially prepared oil, by which the priest becomes a *"Christos"*); and thirdly in the slaughtering of a bullock and two unblemished rams. The bullock is burnt as a sin offering. One of the rams is burnt as a high offering, and its blood poured out upon the altar. With a portion of the blood of the other ram are smeared the lobe of the priest's right ear, the thumb of his right hand, and the large toe of his right foot. These members of the priest's body must be especially sanctified so that he may hear the voice of the LORD and serve Him faithfully. After his garments have been sprinkled with blood from the altar and with oil, he is permitted to offer "with waving" to the LORD a meal consisting of the best edible portions of the second ram, a loaf of bread, a cake and an unleavened wafer, and then to partake himself of the roasted flesh of the ram and a piece of the holy bread in the sanctuary.

Such are the essential directions for the establishment of the perpetual meeting of the people with its LORD. To Moses it is revealed on the one hand how the place of God's descent should be fashioned, and on the other hand how the man is to be consecrated who is to approach God as the official representative of the people. To this is now added a description of the sacrifice which as *"reach nichoach"*, i.e. as a pleasant savour, is to ascend twice daily to entreat and maintain union with the Deity. Every individual Israelite of twenty years old and over makes his contribution to this, each paying the same amount, a half shekel of silver, the rich not more and the poor not less. For in this case not wealth but bare existence is at stake, and where it is a question of the "covering" of one's life before God it is immaterial what one possesses and deserves; there each one counts as much and as little as the others. It is significant that this contribution becomes due when the individual is given his number on entering the army of the LORD and thus leaves the protection of the common mass, for then the eye of the LORD is directed upon the individual who thus stands in need of a personal "covering" (30: 11–16).

Each day shall have its sacrifice—each morning a lamb shall be consumed with fire and each evening a lamb together with an oil cake and an offering of wine. This is to be the perpetual high sacrifice from generation to generation offered at the entrance to the tabernacle where the people encounter their LORD.

> *And there I will meet with the children of Israel, and by my glory the tabernacle, the altar, Aaron and his sons shall be sanctified. And I will dwell among the children of Israel, and will be their God. And they shall know that I am the LORD their God, that brought them forth out of the land of Egypt that I might dwell among them: I am the LORD their God* (Exod. 29: 43–46).

THE INTERLUDE (EXOD. 32–34)

Whilst upon the mount God shows Moses how He desires to dwell with His holy presence in the midst of Israel, and how He desires to sanctify Aaron to the service of the priesthood, down below at the foot of Sinai Aaron is busy fashioning the golden calf as a substitute for the LORD who acts by the word of His servant. "These be thy gods, O Israel, which brought thee up out of the land of Egypt" is the cry of the people as in a frenzy of joy, with sacrifice, eating and drinking, singing and dancing, they participate in an idolatrous festival which Aaron, with subtle mediation, re-names *"the festival of the LORD"*. How did it come to this? When the "man", who with overwhelming power had led the Israelites through the wilderness, failed after several weeks to descend from the cloud in which he had disappeared, the people were overcome with profound fear, with the sinister feeling of being left a prey to accident. They called upon Aaron to exorcize the demon of their fate, and tore the rings from their ears with enthusiasm. Now before them stands the golden calf, brilliant picture of obstinate, mysterious, fertile power, symbol of mystery and of the historic mission of the people. Now at last Israel also has a "god" which it can see and touch and celebrate, which it understands and in which it understands itself. This experience is like an unutterably blessed gift. Headlong ecstasy knows no bounds. And it is Aaron who removes the last inhibition by declaring that in this religious intoxication the people experience the fellowship of the LORD.

But the LORD is not a mere racial demon. *"Leave Me!"*, He cries to Moses, *"that My anger may blaze forth upon them and destroy them."* An Israel which dances around the golden calf is no longer His concern. "Go down to *thy* people whom *thou* hast brought up out of Egypt" is His command to Moses. The latter however springs into the breach: "No, it is *thy* people, and how can Thine honour endure if Thou extirpate it?" Not by a single word does he attempt to justify his people; on the contrary, he places himself completely on the side of God. When he descends from the mountain anger overwhelms him and he breaks the two tables which were the "work of God". He pulverizes the calf, scatters the dust in water, and makes the people drink of it as an adulteress was forced to swallow accursed water. Then he enters the gate of the camp with the call: "Let every one who is on the Lord's side come unto me". And by the sword of the puritans thus summoned there fall three thousand men.

Despite his burning zeal for the honour of God, or rather because of it, he contends with God in order that He may not cast off His people. For by an eternal decree the LORD has bound up the revelation of His divinity with this "stiffnecked people" ("Remember that Thou hast sworn by thine own self . . ." 32: 13). "Israel I will destroy, and instead make of thee a great people", replies the LORD. But Moses prefers to be erased from God's book rather than that the promise which God gave to the fathers and the people of Israel should be nullified. He uses the promise of personal favour which God grants him in order to constrain Him to lead the people to their goal by His own personal presence, and not by some angel as though they were a heathen people. "Wherein shall it be known that I and Thy people have found grace in Thy sight, except in this, that Thou goest with us, and I and Thy people are separated (treated in a special manner) from all the people that are upon the face of the earth?" (Exod. 33: 16). God having granted him this as a personal favour, Moses now dares the final request: "Let me see Thy glory." The fulfilment of this petition would betoken the death of Moses. So God, placing him in a cleft of the rock, covers him with His Hand until His glory has passed by, and then allows him to behold Him from behind. Though he may not see the face of God, he is allowed to hear the voice of God as He Himself proclaims His "goodness", i.e. the summation of His attributes:

LORD, LORD,
GOD,
merciful and gracious,
longsuffering and abundant in goodness and truth,
keeping mercy for thousands,
forgiving iniquity and transgression and sin,
before whom none is guiltless,
and who visiteth the iniquity of the fathers
upon the children, and upon the children's children
unto the third and fourth generation" (Exod. 34: 6–7).

We perceive a little of what it means that the LORD spoke with Moses "face to face, as a man speaks with his friend" when we listen to the dialogue narrated in these chapters. Veil after veil falls, and the final mystery unveils itself, and in the moment of its unveiling is recognized as the mystery of God which is for ever impenetrable and incomprehensible, the mystery unfathomably hidden in the depths of Godhead:

I will be gracious to whom I will be gracious,
and I will show mercy to whom I will show mercy.

In this fathomless depth is anchored Israel's union with God; otherwise it would have been tugged adrift both there at Sinai and a thousand times since. It is for the sake of this anchoring of his people in God that Moses penetrates to the mystery of God. What would be his own private blessedness if God were to surrender His people and with them His plan of salvation? "If I have found grace in Thy sight, my Lord", he cries in the supreme moment, "then go, Lord, in our midst." He stands in complete solidarity with his people: "Yes, it is a stiffnecked people—forgive us *our* guilt and *our* sin, and let us be thine own." In these words he says to God: I can only be *Thine* if this people is *Thine* and remains *Thine*. Upon this God grants him the renewal of the broken covenant: *"Before all thy people"* (once again God speaks thus, but now in a new sense: for the sake of the mediator, Moses, He accepts His people, *"I will do marvels, such as have not been done in all the earth, nor in any nation: and all the people among which thou art"* (since the mediator has not separated himself from his people, God is ready to abide with His people) *"shall see the work of the LORD; for it is a terrible thing that I do with thee."*

So now Moses can descend the mountain with two new tables of the covenant, which, in contrast to the first, he had to hew himself, but upon which God has written with His own hand the ten words. The skin of his face radiates such a blindingly radiant reflection of the divine appearance that he must hide his face in converse with his people.

These chapters raise the veil from the mystery of Israel. The Sinaitic covenant is one *broken from its inception, yet nevertheless one which endures;* enduring simply and solely by the impenetrable declaration which the mediator wrested from God by stepping into the breach: "I will be gracious to whom I will be gracious". Secured by this anchor, the future history of Israel, despite perpetual apostasy, remains closely united with God. To this the historians of the Old Testament, the prayers and songs, the sermons of the prophets, who from Elijah to Malachi reach out the hand to Moses in an unbroken chain of mediators, all bear witness. And the evangelists and apostles no less. And between the choirs of the prophets and apostles stands the One to whom they point from both sides, the one eternal Mediator between God and man, who from the very beginning was the Mediator between the LORD and His chosen people, Jesus the Messiah. Rejected by Israel, He hangs on the cross as the guarantor of God's faithfulness. His death reveals the final rupture of the Sinaitic covenant and at the same time its eternal inviolability. Paul writes to the Corinthians (2 Cor. 3): When Moses faced the people he veiled his face because the children of Israel were not to see the end of this transient radiance. So there always was, and still is, a veil over the Old Testament until it is recognized that by the death and resurrection of Christ Jesus the veil is removed and the rupture and end of the old covenant unveiled. And do not all New Testament witnesses in pointing to the crucified Messiah reveal the final disruption of the old covenant? Most certainly, and they do so by testifying at the same time that by the crucified and risen Messiah the eternal validity of the old covenant is confirmed. He is God's faithful witness, the revelation and justification of God's faithfulness; in Him the solid foundation of the covenant comes to light, and it becomes manifest that God has maintained His covenant with faithless Israel and will do so eternally, and why this is so. The termination of the Sinaitic covenant in Christ is its completion: "I am come not to destroy but to fulfil the law and the prophets" (Matt. 5: 17). By its completion its limitations are removed. "Thou shalt be my nation of priests for the whole earth." That is the abiding truth; the unfaithfulness of the priest to whom God entrusts salvation does not mean the loss of that salvation. This only serves to show that this salvation is entirely and

utterly the work of God, and in no way an achievement of
Israel. It is the boundless and unconditional grace of God
which He has vouchsafed to His people not for their private
enjoyment, but which He offers to all races of the earth through
the priestly service of Israel. So even the apostasy of the
Israelites mediates the riches of God to the world, and their
failure enriches the heathen (Rom. 11: 12). This miracle
whereby the sins of Israel become charged with salvation for
the world is the import of "those marvellous works, such as
have not been done in all the earth, nor in any nation", by
which God answered Moses' intercession. The "apostle to the
Gentiles", to whom was entrusted the task of freeing the
message of salvation from its confinement to Israel and making
it available to the nations of the world, expounds most fully
this miracle of God's faithfulness. *Romans 9–11 forms the
counterpart of Exodus 32–34.* Like the prophet who there at
the outset wrestles in the narrow valley of the Sinaitic covenant,
the apostle here wrestles at its demission in great heaviness and
continual sorrow of heart for the final unspeakably glorious
revelation of God's faithfulness to His chosen people. As Moses
there bids the LORD blot him out of His book if He is resolved
to give up His plan of salvation for Israel, so here Paul is ready
to be accursed for the sake of his brothers, his kinsmen after
the flesh, the Israelites to whom pertain the sonship and the
glory and the covenants and the law and the service of God
and the promises, of whom are the fathers and of whom Christ
is descended according to the flesh. Is all this to be in vain?
No. God did not cast away the people whom He had chosen
for Himself. That is proved by many a word that God spoke to
the messengers of the Old Covenant and by the whole history
of Israel. And these proofs all find their ground and seal in
the advent of Christ Jesus and the power of His crucifixion.
For the gifts and calling of God are without repentance. He
has concluded all under unbelief that He may have mercy on
all. That is the unfolding of God's answer to Moses, a deed
wrought in Christ Jesus and surpassing all that we can ask or
think: "I will be gracious to whom I will be gracious, and I
will have mercy on whom I will have mercy". It is an answer
which will lead to the final unveiling of the faithfulness of God
towards the Israel who so lightly breaks covenant. "For if
their rejection has become the reconciliation of the world, what
will their being accepted portend but the resurrection of the
dead?"

THE CONSTRUCTION AND DEDICATION OF THE TABERNACLE
(EXOD. 35–40)

The casting of the idolatrous image had called in question the construction of the sacred tent. But the question is answered by the LORD's "nevertheless". "Where sin abounded, grace did much more abound" (Rom. 5: 20). The command to construct the tent is prefaced by the commandment of the Sabbath. We have already seen why. Next the whole people is summoned to free-will offerings in kind and in money towards the work, and to personal co-operation. Each shall find his place in the work, men and women. Each contributes as much as "his heart permits". An artist, whom "the Spirit of God had filled with wisdom, insight and knowledge", Bezalel (significantly of the tribe of Judah!) is commissioned, together with his assistant Ohliab of the tribe of Dan, to produce the sacred furnishings. All is done according to the instructions which Moses received of the LORD, and Chapters 35–39 are simply the echo upon earth of the divine voice in Chapters 25–31. The divine pattern is reflected in the earthly reality like the stars in a mountain lake. And conversely, when the community now, in willing obedience to God's command, furnish the sacred place (*Kultraum*) with the empty mercy-seat, this forms a perfect contrast to that wild scene in which the people in fear and defiance and religious madness fashioned the golden calf as the creature of its own heart. On the first day of the second year after the exodus from Egypt the tent is erected. Moses had already consecrated all its parts by Chrisma. Now the real presence of the Deity supervenes: a cloud covers the tent and the glory of the LORD fills the house.

HE DWELT AMONG US (JOHN 1: 14)

The whole tabernacle and its furnishings are mobile; the staves by which it is carried must never be removed from the rings of the ark of the covenant, in order that whenever the glory of the LORD appears, the mercy seat may be carried towards it. For Israel is on the march, and God's presence is in migration with His people. In contrast to the propensities of all religions, God's revelation through Israel can in no way become petrified. All the utensils for divine worship must remain movable.

In the four hundred and eightieth year (that is, twelve generations of forty years) after the exodus of the children of Israel from Egypt, Solomon built for the LORD a firm, abiding house in place of the tabernacle. This house of God, the resting place of the glory of God which roams over the earth, was both internally and externally closely connected with the messianic royal house. More will be said of that later. But as soon as it became evident that this structure was being misused to fixate and idolize the revelation, and that those who dwelt under its protection were trusting in lies, saying, "Here is the temple of the LORD" (Jer. 7), God permitted the temple to be burnt to the ground by the King of Babylon. Following the Babylonian captivity it was rebuilt in the modest proportions of a village church. And finally Herod the Great rebuilt it more glorious than ever. After forty-six years' work it stood complete—exactly as the One entered the stage who was to disrupt it for ever. Jesus said, "Destroy this temple, and in three days I will raise it up" (John 2: 19).

In Him, Jesus the Christ, "dwelleth all the fullness of the Godhead bodily" (Col. 2: 9). He is the presence of God among men. What Moses saw in the mount and portrayed in the tabernacle was the silhouette of His body. "As the shepherds in the field beheld the multitude of the heavenly hosts, so Moses saw them singing praise and glory and honour in the mount. But in the picture of that age it was shown to the people until Christ should come and put the shadows to flight. The import of the exalted words, "Thou shalt make the house" is therefore: "thus and thus shalt thou foreshadow Christ".[1] In Jesus "the Word was made flesh and dwelt among us, and we beheld His glory" (John 1: 14). Jesus Christ is the place over which God Himself dwells in the midst of sinners, the place from which He speaks, and above all, the place where by the shedding of blood the reconciliation of the people with God is wrought. He is given by God as the *"Kapporeth"*, the covering for sin, the throne of grace where, through His blood, God grants forgiveness to those who trust in Him (Rom. 3: 25).

He is the Mediator, the representative of God and the representative of the people of God. As He is the tabernacle and the throne of grace, so also He is the true High Priest and the sacrifice. Since He came not to reconcile angels but the seed of Abraham, He took upon Himself flesh and blood and became in all things like His brothers, suffering and enduring temptation exactly as we, yet without sin. And in the days of His flesh He offered prayers and supplications with mighty groanings and tears to Him who could bring Him from the dead; and His prayers were heard because He held God in honour. No animal,

[1] Kohlbrügge, *Die Stiftshütte und ihre Geräte.*

but His own faultless self He offered to God by the eternal Spirit. Not through the blood of kids or calves, but through His own blood He entered once and for all into the Holy of Holies and became the author of eternal redemption.

The tabernacle with all its furnishings and services bears witness therefore to the sacrifice made once for all by Jesus Christ, and it is He who confers validity upon all that was done in the tabernacle by His act in founding and ending it. For His high priesthood surpasses the Aaronic; He is called a High Priest after the order of Melchisedek, and does not derive His right to the priesthood by lineal descent from Aaron, but rather is directly appointed by God with the words: "Thou art my son; this day have I begotten thee". So He does not enter into the Holy Place which is made with hands (which is a shadow of the real one), but He enters into heaven itself, there to appear before the face of God for us. In so doing He makes a new living way through the veil, that is His flesh, so that now all who follow Him in faith are filled with the joy of being able to enter the Holy Place (Heb. 2–10).

From all this it is clear that the tabernacle in the camp of Israel and later the temple in Jerusalem are a pledge that in this profane world which refuses to be His holy temple God nevertheless remains present, in a particular circumscribed holy precinct it is true, but from the beginning with the promise that He will yet again fill heaven and earth with His presence. In Jesus Christ God redeems His pledge. At His death the veil of the temple is rent in twain, from the top to the bottom (Matt. 27: 51). The boundaries of the holy precincts fall, and through the message of His resurrection men of all nations, near and far, are called together that they might be made members of His body and compacted together into a habitation of God through the Spirit (Eph. 2). "The Body of Christ, that is the fullness of Him that filleth all in all" (Eph. 2: 22 f.) at once fulfils and abolishes not only the tabernacle and the temple at Jerusalem, but also the Church as a holy precinct separated from the world. For the Church is not an end in itself, but is ordained to foster the sanctification of the world as a priestly mediator. "I saw", says John, "the holy city, the new Jerusalem coming down from God out of heaven, prepared as a bride adorned for her husband. And I heard a great voice out of heaven saying, Behold the tabernacle of God is with men. He dwells with them. And I saw *no* temple therein: for the Lord God Almighty and the Lamb are the temple of it" (Rev. 21).

4

THE SERVICE OF THE SANCTUARY

LEVITICUS

THE Holy One has established His habitation among sinners. But His holiness would annihilate the Israelites if He did not grant them the possibility of appearing before Him "covered" and sanctified. The precepts of the Book of Leviticus define the intercourse of the covenant people with the holy majesty of their God. They begin with a description of the various means whereby man may enter into relationship with God: "If any man of you bring an offering unto the LORD . . ." (Lev. 1: 2). *Korban*, the most comprehensive Hebrew term for "offering", is, as Buber[1] pertinently remarks, "a *concept of relationship (Bezeihungsbegriff)*", i.e. it comprehends the existence of two persons, one of whom seeks to reduce the distance between them by drawing near to the other by means of the *korban* which he "offers".

The first means of drawing near which is mentioned is the *'Ola*, the "one which rises high", the "burnt offering", which consists of an animal whose blood is first sprinkled round about the altar at the entrance to the tabernacle, and which is afterwards burnt and "rises aloft" (=*'ala*). It is the universal offering of veneration. In its place a poor person may take a bird, which however should not be plucked. Raschi, whose commentary is regarded by the Jews as canonical, says, "The smell of burning feathers is sufficient to nauseate the lowest type of person. Why then does scripture command that these should be offered? In order that the altar may be surrounded by the odour of the offerings of the poor."

The second means of approach is the *Mincha* (the "meat-offering"), the gift of homage. The expression is used also of the gift which signifies one's subjection to a person of authority. The *Mincha* consists of fine meal with the addition of oil and incense. A fragment of it is burnt as a memorial in order that God may be reminded of the presence of the worshipper.

Significantly, "the salt of the covenant with thy God" may not be omitted; for the *Mincha* has reference to the "covenant of salt" which established between God and Israel a fellowship

---

[1] Buber, *Ueber die Wortwahl in einer Verdeutschung der Schrift.*

resembling that which is established between two orientals when the one eats salt in the tent of the other.

The third kind are the *Shelamin*, the "peace offerings" or fellowship offerings, which sustain and deepen the "peace", i.e. the living fellowship (*Lebensgemeinschaft*) between those who covenant together by a common meal. Whereas the other gifts are received by the LORD alone (or by the LORD and the priest), in the case of the *Shelamin* the Deity receives only the blood and the fat as His portion, whilst the offerers eat the other parts of the sacrifice.

It is the covenant which makes life possible and sustains it. "Peace" is the healthy, intact life within the fellowship of the covenant. "Sin" is the breach of the covenant, the violation of peace; whoever commits sin has destroyed and forfeited his life. "His blood comes upon his head", i.e. his blood must be shed in expiation; he must lose his life. "Without shedding of blood is no remission" (Heb. 9: 22). If the covenant is violated and the living fellowship between the LORD and His people thus destroyed by a conscious or unconscious sin of the priests or of the community or of a layman against God or of one compatriot against another it must be restored either by the *sin offering or by the guilt offering* (Lev. 4: 5). These two differ from each other in that the sin offering is a pure *expiatio* and expiates a trespass against a divine commandment, whereas the guilt offering is rather a *satisfactio* in the bringing of which the one sinned against is as far as possible to be recompensed for his loss. Corresponding to this difference is a difference in the ritual, and the difference in purpose shows itself particularly clearly in the various ways in which the blood is treated (Strack)[1]

Every sacrifice is brought to the sanctuary by the person who desires to offer it. He identifies himself with his gift by placing his hands upon the head of the animal. The slaughtering and offering of it to the Godhead is however the duty of the priest. How this is to be done in each particular case, and which parts of it he may retain for himself, and where and how he must eat them is defined in Leviticus 6 and 7. The priests who perform this service must be consecrated precisely according to the instructions (Lev. 8 and 9) and each must keep strictly to that for which he is authorized; to act otherwise means death. How rigorously this applied is shown by the case of Nadab and Abihu, the sons of Aaron, who are fatally struck down (Lev. 10) the moment they bring a "strange fire", i.e. a fire they had not

---

[1] *"Kurzgefasster Kommentar zu den heil."* *Schriften des Alten und des neuen Bundes*, Bd. I, S. 305.

been consecrated to bring, before the LORD. The priests must be quite sober for their service, and are permitted to drink neither wine nor any intoxicating drink before they enter the holy tabernacle. For they must be able to distinguish exactly between pure and impure and to give the people correct instructions. The living fellowship into which the LORD admits His people is the antithesis of the blissful intoxication in which the religious man imagines he experiences a *unio mystica* with the Deity (Lev. 10).

The communion with God which Israel enjoys is one which is strictly "holy" and "pure". Therefore precise regulations are laid down concerning *the animals which may be eaten* and which may not (Lev. 11), and concerning *the bodily conditions which render the Israelites unclean* and exclude them from entering the tabernacle (Lev. 12: 15). They are the conditions of child-bearing, leprosy (on account of which the sufferer is set outside the camp), and sexual emissions. Contact with a corpse renders an Israelite for a certain time unfit to appear before the holy Lord of Life. This is connected with the fact "that in the Torah all impurity among men and even among animals finds its consummation in death. Death is the wages of sin" (Strack)[1] The purport of all these regulations concerning purity is "*to admonish the children of Israel, that they may not perish through their impurity by defiling my house which is among them*" (Lev. 15: 31).

All the rites of purification and sanctification culminate in the acts of expiation by which, once a year, on the day of atonement, the whole tabernacle of the Holy One who dwells in the midst of Israel's impurity, is purified, and the accumulated sins both of the priests and congregation are "covered" (Lev. 16.)

The so-called "Law of Holiness (Lev. 17–26, with a supplement in Lev. 27), which is a collection of laws complete in itself and which forms the second part of the book of Leviticus, shows how the whole life of the chosen people *on the soil of the Holy Land* is subject to special sacred regulations because it is a life in fellowship with the holy God "*Ye shall be holy unto Me for I the LORD am holy, and have severed you from other people that ye should be mine. Keep all my statutes and all my judgments that the land, whither I bring you to dwell therein, spue you not out. And ye shall not walk in the manners of the nation which I cast out before you because it had done that which I abhor*" (Lev. 20). This part deals with manners and customs of sexual life,

[1] A.a.O., S. 323.

of killing domestic animals, of hunting, of sowing and reaping, of cattle breeding, of the production of cloth for garments, of hairdressing, of commerce, of the court of law, of cases of death, of taking oaths, of magic and prophecy, of intercourse with old people, with the deaf and blind, and of the treatment of aliens. All that is to be done and left undone is brought into relationship with the LORD, and is regulated from this stand-point. This, too, is the source of the command, "Thou shalt not hate thy brother in thine heart: thou shalt in any wise rebuke thy neighbour, and not suffer sin upon him." Thou shalt not avenge thyself nor bear malice against thy compatriot, but *"thou shalt love thy neighbour as thyself. I am the LORD"* (Lev. 19: 17 f.).

The land belongs to the LORD. Therefore every seventh year a time of high festival must be observed as a Sabbath for the LORD. Every member of the chosen people must possess his particular portion of the holy land, none must be allowed to sink so low that he becomes utterly impoverished and per-manently enslaved. Always after seven times seven years the ancient battle horn shall proclaim the advent of the year of jubilee.

> *In this year of jubilee every man shall return unto his possession and unto his family* (Lev. 25: 10).
> *The land shall never be finally sold, for the land is mine, and ye are guests and sojourners with me* (Lev. 25: 23).
> *The children of Israel are my servants; they shall not be sold as slaves* (Lev. 25: 42).

These two complementary sentences form the pivot of the socialism of the Israelites which is based on the truth that the children of Israel are God's confederates.

As in the book of the covenant and in every Israelite book of laws, the commandments of the Law of Holiness are related to specific promises. If the people keep these precepts they are promised overflowing blessings in the holy land. But if they are disobedient they are threatened with fearful curses. Not, assuredly, a blessedness in a world beyond is promised them as reward, nor the pains of hell threatened. No, rather rain and fruitful seasons and peace on earth, and conversely an iron heaven and barren soil, fear and hunger and dreadful plagues. The perverse will be ravaged by wars and scattered among the Gentiles, yet always in such a manner that they are not utterly annihilated, but are granted the possibility of reform in the hope that *"their uncircumcised hearts be humbled. And I will remember my covenant with Jacob, and also my covenant with Isaac, and also my covenant with Abraham, and I will remember the land. And even when they are in the land of their enemies, I will not cast them away, neither will I abhor them to destroy them utterly, and to break my covenant with them; for I am the LORD their God. But I will for their sakes remember my first covenant, when I brought them forth out of the land of Egypt in the sight of the heathen, that I might be their God, I, the LORD"* (Lev. 26: 41-45).

No word concerning a hereafter or the immortality of the soul. That is the more significant since the Israelites came forth out of Egypt, where the continuance of the soul, the judgment of the dead, reward and punishment in a future world formed the principal themes of religion and art. Man's profoundest religions are the religions of the dead. In complete contrast to all religions of death and the beyond the LORD reveals Himself to His people as the God of Life, as the Creator and Sustainer, Architect, Reconciler and Redeemer of the life of flesh and blood on this earth. Here and now is decided whether He is to be acknowledged as the one Lord and the one Reality. Those who in the obedience of faith give Him the glory live and die to Him, and thus in life and death are His once for all. As soon as it becomes clear that here and now He is their God and they His people, the question of the eternity of their life is answered. For the God of Israel "is not the God of the dead, but the God of the living; for all live unto him" (Luke 20: 38).

CHRIST JESUS WHO OF GOD IS MADE UNTO US SANTIFICATION (I COR. I: 30)

In the presence of the holy God, Israel can live only if God grants the gift of life from day to day and from hour to hour. As a token that the community of sinners in whose midst the Holy One dwells can live only by His grace, there takes place daily before the tabernacle and in the temple a horrible shedding of blood. Vicarious life is perpetually slain so that the Israelites may be granted new life. The vital elements in the laws governing sacrifice are those of mediation and substitution (*Stellvetretung*). The word in the Greek Bible for "reconcile", *katalassein*, means "substitute". The priest mediates between God and man, and the animal which is sacrificed gives its life for the sinner. But it is clear that every sacrifice points beyond itself to the Day of Atonement, and beyond that to the sacrifice which once for all shall cover all sin. No priestly act possesses power and value in itself. All are as it were bills of exchange issued in virtue of the wealth of a rich lord; worthless pieces of paper, a fraud in fact, unless they have legal reference to a capital which really exists. They all point to that one sacrifice which God Himself makes. So by the laws of sacrifice the people of the Old Covenant "were clearly and publicly taught to seek salvation nowhere but in the propitiation which is wrought in Christ alone" (Calvin)[1]. Without this one sacrifice offered once for all, Israel's whole sacrificial cult would be a huge deception. "God was in Christ and reconciled the world unto Himself, not imputing their trespasses unto them, and has established in the Church the word of reconciliation" (2 Cor. 5: 19). Under the Old Covenant this word of reconciliation was proclaimed in the law of sacrifice. Through His life and death Jesus Christ has "covered" the sacrifices of the Old Testament. The Israelites who offered the prescribed sacrifices in obedience and faith drew upon the wealth of grace which God offers believers in Christ and lived upon it as truly as a man who defrays his living costs with Bank of England notes. For the death of Jesus atones not only for our sins but also for the transgressions of the faithful who lived under the first Testament (Heb. 9: 15). In the shedding of His blood lies not only God's justification for pronouncing sinners righteous to-day, but also His justification in allowing the sins of previous ages to pass unpunished (Rom. 3: 25). As it provided an adequate satisfaction for the sins of those born subsequent to it, the sacrifice of Christ possessed also retrospective power. God accomplished His atoning work *once* in Jesus Christ, but *once for all*. "The achievement (of forgiveness) happened once, on the cross; but its distribution to men happened frequently, both before and after the event, from the beginning of the world to its end. For since He had resolved to earn it once, it was immaterial whether He conferred it on men before or afterwards through His word" (Luther).[2] As He now confers it upon us in the sacraments of the New Covenant through His word, so He conferred it upon the faithful under the Old Covenant through His word. A "Christianity" that disdains to hear afresh the witness to Christ in the book of Leviticus is one which in reality refuses to acknowledge Jesus as the Christ of God, as the anointed High Priest by whose mediation alone a man can ever be sanctified by God and for God. The Old Testament law

---

[1] *Inst.* II, 6, 2.
[2] *Wider die himmlischen Propheten* . . . Weimar Ed. XVII, 203.

of sacrifice bears witness that the life and death of Jesus is not the supreme achievement of a "saint" who redeems Himself, but God's all-inclusive act of reconciliation. And this testimony is confirmed by the evangelists when they show how He, the Son of God, comes in sinful flesh, lives in complete solidarity with the sinful sons of Abraham, sits down with publicans and harlots, seeks the outcast and lost, takes upon Himself the impurity and shame of His brothers, burdens Himself with their infirmities, heals the blind and the maimed and the deaf and those afflicted with leprosy and haemorrhage, and raises the dead—all tokens that He has the right to proclaim the acceptable year of the Lord for the liberation of His people (Luke 4: 18 ff.). He takes upon Himself all the guilt, and gives His life as a ransom, a "sin offering", for many (Isa. 53: 10; Mark 10: 45), and when He is afflicted and tormented, like a lamb that is led to the slaughter, He opens not His mouth. "For He made Him to be sin for us, who knew no sin; that we might be made the righteousness of God in Him" (2 Cor. 5: 21). He was the one man whom it became to be sacrificed for the others, of whom Caiphas said, "It is expedient for us that one man should die for the people, and that the whole nation perish not". This he said not of himself, but, being High Priest that year, he prophesied (John 11: 49 ff.). He was unconscious that in condemning Jesus he ended the Aaronic high priesthood and the whole service of sacrifice of the Old Covenant. The sanhedrin of Jerusalem expelling Jesus from the holy precincts unintentionally testified that the previous boundaries of the election and sanctification of the people of God were overthrown, and the previous distinction between within and without, pure and impure, holy and common, replaced by the new distinction between those who believed, and those who refused to believe, in sanctification through Jesus Christ. This became clear to Peter when in a vision he saw a sheet containing a mixture of clean and unclean animals descending from heaven, and received the command, "Kill and eat", and afterwards when he perceived the Holy Spirit falling upon the Gentiles whilst he preached Christ Jesus to them. He apprehended that God no longer distinguished between Jews and Gentiles, but purified their hearts by faith in the LORD Jesus Christ, in consequence of which the yoke of the law "which neither we nor our fathers were able to bear" may no longer be laid upon the necks of the disciples (Acts 10; 11; 15). His grasp of this truth was strengthened, as was that of the pillars of the early church at Jerusalem, by Paul's teaching that whoever believes in Christ

Jesus is dead to the law and alive to God. "I have been crucified with Christ, and the life which I now live in the flesh I live in faith in the Son of God who loved me and gave himself for me." Here communion with the works of the law comes to an end, and anyone who still seeks to be holy through the commands of the law of holiness does not take seriously the sacrifice of Christ. "Cursed is every one that continueth not in all things which are written in the book of the law to do them. But Christ hath redeemed us from the curse of the law, being made a curse for us (as it is written, 'Cursed is every one that hangeth on a tree') that the blessing of Abraham might come on the Gentiles through Christ Jesus" (Gal. 2; 3). The fact that the law is fulfilled by the death of Christ means that the promise to Abraham has broken through the limitations of the law of Moses. The writer of the Epistle to the Hebrews means the same when he says that Jesus is a priest after the order of Melchisedek who through His passion has validated, completed and superseded the Levitical priesthood. Similarly the risen Christ commands His disciples to transcend the limits of the Church of the temple—they are to go to all nations, and claim and sanctify them by baptism in the name of the Father and of the Son and of the Holy Spirit, teaching them to observe all things that He had commanded them, but not to bind them to the Aaronic laws.

Christ Jesus is made of God unto us sanctification. His sacrifice sanctifies us completely without any contributory sacrifice on our side. One would have thought that the Aaronic sacrificial regulations sufficiently indicate that the sanctification of the people of God is exclusively an act of God and no godly work of men. But many a word in both the Old and New Testament has to combat the misunderstanding that the ceremony of sacrifice provides man with an opportunity to perform a pious act as a substitute or supererogation for his normal duties to God and man. Jesus and the prophets attack in scathing words the hypocrisy of disregarding the dictates of justice and mercy and seeking to appease God with sacrifices (1 Sam. 15: 22; Amos 5: 21 ff.; Isa. 1: 11 ff.), of offering as a *Korban* in the temple that which is owing to one's mother and father, of making broad phylacteries and wearing large fringes on the borders of their garments to rob God of His honour (Num. 15: 38), of making long prayers whilst devouring widow's houses, of tithing mint and anice and cummin whilst breaking faith and loyalty, of keeping clean the outside of the cup and platter whilst the inside is full of extortion and excess, of being scrupulously careful to avoid defilement by that which enters the mouth whilst shamelessly defiling oneself with that which comes out of the mouth (Matt. 23; Mark 7).

The sacrificial legislation of the Old Covenant is in no sense a substitute for love to God and one's neighbour; rather it is overwhelming evidence of the source from which alone true love flows: "Herein is love, not that we loved God, but that He loved us, and sent His Son to be the propitiation for our sins" (1 John 4: 10). We live by virtue of this divine act of love in the offering of His only begotten Son, "who His own self bare our sins in His own body on the tree" (1 Pet. 2: 24). *"That* is a work which we cannot emulate. Anyone who attempts it betrays Christ, like the Pope. In the Old Testament, Aaron was a priest who offered sacrifice for the sins of his people, and no one else was allowed to do likewise under threat of the loss of body, life and soul. Though his life set his people an example of high morality, none but he could discharge the priestly office. I take Aaron as my example and ought to follow him, but not in his priestly duties. Similarly we ought to follow Christ, but only in so far as He is our example. But when the Pope persuades the people that he can forgive their sins through the Mass he reverses this distinction and follows Christ in the priestly office instead of in other respects. Therefore, I say, let Christ alone bear this, for He alone is worthy, as Peter says, 'Who his own self bare our sins in his own body'. *Himself*—He tookneit her Aaron nor Moses nor the Pope nor a parson, but made the sacrifice for them Himself" (Luther).[1]

In sanctifying us for God, Jesus the Christ denudes us of all our own "holliness". There remains no longer any distinction between the religious man and the atheist, the Jew and the Gentile, the pharisee and the publican. He embraces them all in His death and thereby purifies them for a new life with God. For them that means a far more radical separation, purification and sanctification than ever the Levitical was. The claim of God: "Ye shall be holy, for I am holy" receives its full validity in Christ, and means now: "Be ye therefore perfect even as your Father which is in heaven is perfect", i.e. except your righteousness exceed the righteousness of the priests and Levites, ye cannot belong to the Kingdom of God. As Christ is not of the "world", so those who are His are not of the world (John 17: 16). As the "chosen nation" and "holy people" they must separate themselves from the "adulterous and sinful genera-

---

[1] Sermon on the Sunday Jubilate 1531, *Predigten D. Martin Luthers,* herausgegeben von Georg Buchwald, 2. Bd., S. 251 ff.

tion" (1 Pet. 2: 9; Mark 8: 38), by their confession of Christ. This separation goes deeper than that between Israel and the Gentiles, it divides Jew from Jew, son from father, daughter from mother. Whoever has heard the call of Christ must be prepared to leave all and take up his cross, to endure being outlawed by his country and excommunicated by his Church. The sufferings of Christ outside the gate of the "holy" city summon all to go out unto Him without the camp, bearing His reproach. In a more radical sense than the Levite they must be ready to forgo the sight of their parents, the knowledge of their brother and the acquaintance of their son (Deut. 33: 9). They must even be prepared to refuse the last offices of piety, like the High Priest who, because of his holy service, might not defile himself with the corpse of his father or mother (Lev. 21: 11). "Let the dead bury their dead; but go thou and preach the Kingdom of God" (Luke 9: 60). If Christ has died for them, they can no longer live unto themselves, but unto Him who died for their sakes. And the "reasonable service" to which they, are now exhorted "by the mercies of God" consists in this, that they "present their bodies, a living sacrifice, holy and acceptable unto God" (Rom. 12: 1). That is their sanctification to be offered unto God with and through Christ.

5

THE MARCH OF THE SACRED HOST

NUMBERS

In the beginning all creatures in heaven and on earth were equipped and enrolled as an "army" for the service of God (Gen. 2:1). After the universal revolt, the Lord of the world "conscripts" one nation as "God's warrior." He Himself, "the LORD of hosts, who sits above the cherubim" (2 Sam. 6:2) commands it from the ark of the covenant as the invisible general. The Book of Numbers gives the numbers of the regiments of the sacred host, reckoning the military age as twenty years upwards, adding the names of the captains, the levy and orders of the Levites (that peculiar kind of regiment which is placed at the service of the priests and consecrated to the external menial service of the holy tabernacle), the rules of the camp and the rules of the march, the signals and commands, the regulations governing exclusion from the camp and the rules of the order of Nazarenes who are consecrated by a special vow, and whose later typical representatives are Samson and John the Baptist. The whole forms the army of the LORD which receives its distinctive character and merit in virtue of the fact that through Aaron the name of the LORD is laid upon it:

The LORD bless thee, and keep thee;
The LORD make his face shine upon thee,
and be gracious unto thee;
The LORD lift up his countenance upon thee,
and give thee peace (Num. 6:22 ff.).

The word of command is given by the LORD Himself through the pillar of cloud. "At the commandment of the LORD the children of Israel journeyed, and at the commandment of the LORD they pitched" (Num. 9:18). When the ark set forward, Moses said:

Rise up, LORD,
and let thine enemies be scattered;
and let them that hate thee
flee before thee.

And when it rested, he said:

Return, O LORD,
unto the many thousands of Israel (Num. 10:35 f.).

THE MUTINY OF THE HOST AND THE COMMANDER'S
TRIUMPHANT PLAN OF VICTORY

How difficult the recruits find it to follow this lead in trust and obedience is revealed in the accounts of repeated murmurings, revolts and despondency. More than once the wrath of the LORD flames forth and decimates the host. And when, at the report of the spies concerning the situation in the promised land, the people begin to weep and to call for a captain who shall lead them back to Egypt, God declares to Moses that He will utterly exterminate the people who still refuse to trust Him, and instead will make of Moses a great nation. But once again Moses casts himself into the breach and achieves the miracle of God's righteousness, that, where sin abounded, grace did much more abound, and the failure of Israel is answered by God's fuller promise of salvation for the whole world.

> *I have pardoned according to thy word,*
> *and as truly as I live,*
> *all the earth shall be filled with the glory of the LORD.*
> *Because all those men which have seen my glory*
> *and my miracles, which I did in Egypt and in the wilderness*
> *and have tempted me now these ten times,*
> *and have not hearkened to my voice;*
> *surely they shall not see the land*
> *which I sware unto them* (Num. 14: 20–23).

This "because" is characteristic of the peculiar logic of God's marvellous righteousness, whereby the crisis of Israel, the sin and the resulting judgment through which God glorifies Himself and blesses all generations, is made to serve the salvation of the world. This is the marvel of the crucified Messiah, for when Israel, revolting against God, cast Him out and caused Him to be crucified on the accursed tree by the heathen, God used *these events* to make Him the Saviour of the world.

THE CONQUERING HERO

In harmony with the preaching of the apostles, several passages in Numbers bear witness that the Messiah Jesus, anointed of God and rejected by Israel, is the true leader who at all times, including the days of wandering in the wilderness, marches with His people, misunderstood, blasphemed and slain, yet judging the disobedience of the Church and carrying forward God's faithfulness to victory.

The apostle Paul's reference, "neither let us tempt the LORD, as some of them tempted" (I Cor. 10:9) in his letter to the Church at Corinth to the murmurings, inordinate desires and blasphemies of the children of Israel recorded in Numbers 11, 14, 21 and 25, receives this comment from Luther:[1] "Note this saying and relate it to the history recorded by Moses, and thou shalt see a marvellous thing, how decorously and delightfully Paul and Moses kiss and offer the mouth to each other. Moses writes, Numbers 14, that the LORD said, this people has tempted me ten times". Here is the word *tetragrammaton*, which can be ascribed only to God, and which the one, sole and true God must thus have spoken. Now comes Paul, and says quite plainly who this God was, namely Christ, for (he says), let us not tempt Him, as some of them tempted. Let anyone find a hole in this who can; I cannot. For Paul says that Christ was the God whom they tempted. And Moses says it was the true and only God. Yet at that time Christ was not yet born, nor Mary, nor even David. Nevertheless Paul says that the Jews who were still in the wilderness, not having reached the land of Canaan, tempted Christ. And he warns us, lest we should do the same and suffer an equally dreadful fate. These words show that Christ is the man alluded to by Moses when he writes that He is the one, eternal, almighty God."

THE SIGN OF VICTORY (NUM. 21)

"And he shall bruise thy head." The *Protevangelium* (Gen. 3: 15) proclaims the victory of the race born of woman over the serpent who is the old wicked enemy (*der alt böse Feind*). And Jesus indicates to a master in Israel in expounding Numbers 21 that the *brazen serpent* is the sign of this victory. "And as Moses lifted up the serpent in the wilderness, even so must the Son of man be lifted up, that whosoever believeth in him should not perish, but have eternal life" (John 3:14 f.). In this figure two things are beautifully portrayed and foreshadowed: the whole misery and need of human nature and Christ's redemptive work and the manner in which it is wrought. For as the Jews were in manifold ways bitten by the fiery serpent, so we are assailed and tormented in diverse ways by the devil and have more poison in us than we received in body and soul by the sting of the serpent in original sin. When sin is upon our conscience we are a prey to death and our life is nothing but hell. Neither guidance nor help is ours. No amount of good

[1] Sermon in the Hauspostille, 1st Sunday in Trinity, 1535.

P

works can avert our damnation until we experience the wonder and grace of that other serpent which is neither poisonous nor harmful and possesses merely the form of a serpent. So God spoke to Moses, saying, "Make thee a fiery serpent, and set it upon a pole; and it shall come to pass, that every one that is bitten, when he looketh upon it, shall live". Why does He not choose a symbol other than the serpent? Paul answers in Romans 8: 3 that He condemned sin with sin, dispelled death with death, overcame law with law. Jesus Christ, the Son of God, became like one of us who are condemned men, and hung on the cross like a poisonous, evil and pernicious worm (Ps. 22: 7). He appears in the very similitude of the serpent, the devil, who in paradise caused man to perspire. Despised and condemned by the world, He is crucified with the murderers as a transgressor" (Isa. 53: 12).[1] And, most significant for the method of Old Testament exposition, Luther adds: "The Lord thus shows us (by this exegesis) the correct viewpoint for the interpretation of Moses and all the prophets, namely that Moses with all his pictures points to Christ, so that *He forms the centre of the circle*, around which all revolves and towards which all points. And whoever looks to Him belongs to the circle".

THE RED HEIFER

In the name of Rabbi Channina, Rabbi Acha says that when he ascended to heaven to receive the law, Moses heard the voice of God and "sat down to study the passage relating to the 'red heifer' and offered this interpretation in the name of Him who spoke the words".[2] This chapter in fact presents a remarkable allusion to Christ Jesus. We read that an unblemished heifer which had never been placed under the yoke should be slain outside the camp. And when its blood has been sprinkled by the finger of the priest Eleazer seven times towards the tabernacle, not only is its skin and flesh to be burnt to ashes, but also the *blood* and dung, together with cedar wood, hyssop and scarlet, is to be burnt—a thing which otherwise was never done. The ashes are then to be removed by a man who is clean, and preserved outside the camp. And now whenever a member of the holy community defiles himself by contact with the dead, he is to purify himself with these ashes mixed with water, on the third and seventh days, after which he is free from

[1] *Luther's Evangelien-Auslegung*, zusammengestellt von Chr. G. Eberle, S. 433.
[2] Bammidbar rabba, sol. 224, col. 1, zitiert nach Eisenmenger, *Entdecktes Judentum* 1 Teil, S. 6.

the stain and eligible again to enter the house of the LORD and resume intercourse within the community.

The allusion to Christ is manifest. He who is without spot and is the only one who never came under the yoke of sin, offers Himself to God without the gate on the accursed tree; not under compulsion like an animal, but in voluntary obedience, "through the eternal spirit" as the Epistle to the Hebrews expresses it, i.e. in contrast to the evanescent spirit of the animal, He commends His eternal spirit as He dies into the hand of His Father (Luke 23: 46). And so His spirit becomes "the quickening spirit" (1 Cor. 15: 45) for His brother men in the bondage of death, and the Church receives a water for sprinkling which "purges our conscience from dead works to serve the living God" (Heb. 9: 14). By what works could we purify our conscience from the stains of sin and death? Nothing but being sprinkled with the blood of Christ can absolve us, and nothing but the transfer of the merit of His obedience to us can open the door of God's service and to an active participation in the Church of the living. That is the gospel which is proclaimed in the passage concerning the red heifer and confirmed in the sacraments of baptism and communion.

CONCERNING VOCATION: THE STEWARD AND THE SON

The accounts in the Book of Numbers of the official position of the ministering mediators bear witness to the work and person (*Amt*) of Christ. Consider the revolt of Korah's faction, a group of Levites, who in the name of the universality of the priesthood, claimed the right to participate in the burning of incense during divine service, a function for which they were not authorized. The earth opens its mouth and swallows them with their families and all their possessions. The next day the whole community band themselves menacingly together against Moses and Aaron with the cry: "Ye have slain the Lord's people". The wrath of the LORD blazes forth upon the whole nation and would have annihilated it had not Aaron with his censer stood between the living and the dead. By the "Tannhäuser miracle" of Aaron's rod, when it buds and brings forth blossoms and almonds overnight in the tabernacle, God confirms his special election to a particular office (Num. 16: 17).

But it is the special position accorded to Moses which is most vehemently assailed. Nor only are there perpetual murmurings against him among the people, but Miriam and Aaron reproach him for his marriage and claim that through them God can speak equally well as through him. Thereupon God punishes Miriam with leprosy and tells her that, in contrast to the prophets to whom He speaks in visions and dreams, *Moses is the servant to whom is entrusted the whole house, and to whom He speaks mouth to mouth* (Num. 12: 6–8). This supreme position of trust with its incomparable responsibility made *the man Moses the meekest among all men on the face of the earth* (Num. 12: 3). How heavily the burden of his responsibility weighs upon him is revealed in one of the dialogues in which, mouth to mouth with the LORD, he lays bare his heart:

> *Wherefore hast thou afflicted thy servant?*
> *and wherefore have I not found favour in thy sight,*
> *that thou layest the burden of all this people upon me?*
> *Have I conceived all this people?*
> *Have I begotten them,*
> *that thou shouldst say unto me, "Carry them in thy bosom,*
> *as a nurse carries the sucking child,*
> *unto the land which thou swarest unto their fathers?"*
>
> (Num. 11: 11–12)

The LORD relieves Moses somewhat by placing a part of the spirit that is in him upon seventy elders, so giving them a share in the responsibility. Upon two of them the spirit descends although they did not come to the tabernacle. Moved by the spirit, they prophesy in the camp, and Joshua cries out, "Moses, my Lord, forbid them". Moses, however, replies, "Art thou jealous for my sake? *I would to God that all the people of the LORD were prophets, and that the LORD would confer his spirit upon all of them*". The answer reveals the injustice of the reproach that Moses desired to have God solely for himself and planned to dominate the people. On the contrary, he is distressed to the point of despair that the people, despite all that God does, fail to enter into the fellowship of the spirit with Him, and direct their thoughts and desires to the flesh-pots of Egypt rather than to the LORD. The law indeed he has given to the people, but he is unable to confer on them "grace and truth" (John 1: 17) whereby they might live from God and to God in gladness and faithfulness. His heart cries out for the "New Covenant" which God promised Jeremiah: "Not according to the covenant that I made with their fathers in the day that I took them by the hand to bring them out of the land of Egypt; which my covenant they brake, and I had to compel them, saith the LORD: but this shall be the covenant that I will make with the house of Israel in later days, saith the LORD:

I will put my law in their inward parts, and write it in their hearts; and I will be their God, and they shall be my people. And they shall teach no more every man his neighbour, and every man his brother, saying, Know the LORD: for they shall all know me, from the least of them unto the greatest of them, saith the LORD: for I will forgive their iniquity, and I will remember their sin no more" (Jer. 31: 31–34). Moses, who gave to Israel the divine ordinances, yearns for *Pentecost*, knowing that his work can only find its fulfilment when "suddenly there shall come from heaven the sound of a rushing mighty wind, to fill all the house where they sit, and fiery tongues to sit upon each of them" (Acts 2).

Moses, as we have already seen, was more than just one of the prophets. God defines his official standing in the community in the words: *"He is my servant (ne'eman) in my whole house"*, i.e. (for the Hebrew expression cf. 1 Sam. 3: 20) he is authorized by the LORD for his ministry to the whole house, and, in conformity with the dignity of his duties, enjoys direct communion with the LORD, who speaks with him not in visions and parables but mouth to mouth. So God answers not only the question of Miriam and Aaron, whether He could not speak equally well through them, but also the question of Moses: "Have I begotten this people, that Thou shouldst say unto me, 'Carry them in thy bosom, as a nurse carries the sucking child'?" For though he has not begotten the nation, Moses holds in fact the office of "nurse" of *"Omen"* for the people of the LORD, or as God expresses it, he is *"Ne'eman"* (which is the niphal participle of the same root of which *'Omen* is the *qal* participle) "authorized for the ministry of the whole household of the LORD". One only possesses higher dignity and greater honour in the house of God, as the Epistle to the Hebrews explains, namely Jesus the Christ, who in contrast to the "servant" Moses, is "the Son" and as such stands over the whole house. As Moses was a "faithful servant appointed to witness to that which should later be declared", so Jesus as the faithful Son is the Word itself which God finally speaks, the heir whom He has set over all, by whom also He made the worlds, and who, being the express image of His person, upholdeth all things by the word of His power (Heb. 1: 1–3). He is exalted both over the ministering spirits, the angels, and over the "servant" Moses, and shares equal glory with Him who built the house (Heb. 3: 3). To Moses therefore was entrusted the responsibility, as "nurse" and guardian of the people of God to guard and guide it in the days of its childhood (as Calvin calls the era of the Old Covenant) until the day when it should come of age with the appearing of the Son and its confession of Him.

It is this function of guardianship until Christ should come which Paul characterizes in the Epistle to the Galatians (3:23 ff.), as the function of the law, when he says that it is *"our paidagogos to bring us to Christ"*. *Paidagogos*, which Luther not very felicitously translates as Taskmaster, is simply the Greek rendering of *'Omen*, the guardian of the child which has not yet come of age. And if we translate the passage in Galatians into Hebrew, a felicitous play on words is revealed, which however is no mere play but the pregnant expression of the reality. "Before *'Aemuna* (which is the noun from the root *'amen* and signifies confirmation or faith) came, we were preserved and embraced under the Torah (ordinances, law) until the coming of the *'Aemuna* which should be revealed. Wherefore the Torah was our *'Omen* to bring us to Christ, that we might be justified by *'Aemuna*. But after that *'Aemuna* is come, we are no longer under an *'Omen*. For ye are all children of God by *'Aemuna* in Christ Jesus." From this vantage point the passage already referred to in the prologue to John's gospel is seen to have a more pregnant significance: "The law was given by Moses, but grace and *'Aemet* (another noun from the root *'amen*, which signifies existence, truth, faithfulness) came by Jesus Christ".

So it becomes clear that the guardianship of Moses and the law leads to the revelation of our sonship in the Son, and that the functions of the servant and the Son and the faithfulness of both have their source in the demonstration of the faithfulness of our LORD and Father, so that obedience to Moses and the law finds its fulfilment in the confession of faith in the Messiah Jesus.

That the offices which belong to the constitution of the Old Covenant do not find their *raison d'être* and fulfilment in themselves is further shown in the Book of Numbers by the account of Miriam's death and burial in Kadesh and Aaron's removal from office and death on Mount Hor (Num. 20). He is not allowed to enter the promised land because when the people, in fear of dying of thirst, murmured against God, he lost his trust in the LORD and did not honour Him. He was not alone in this, for Moses at the same time struck the rock twice in angry despair crying, "Ye rebels! Must we fetch you water out of this rock?" For this, he also is not allowed to lead the people to their goal: from the summit of the mountains of Abarim he is to have one glance of the promised land before he is gathered to his fathers. There is no word concerning the recompense of the "faithful servant" for all the labours and sufferings of his hard ministry. The only success resulting from his work which he is allowed personally to enjoy is to see the goal from afar. Yet not a word of complaint does he utter against this judgment, or seek to gain for himself anything more. In silence he acknowledges that God is right. From first to last he is concerned only for one thing—the glory of God, which stands or falls with His ability to accomplish the salvation promised to the fathers of Israel. What does it matter whether He chooses to use Moses to this end or not? Therefore Moses asks nothing for himself, but all the more earnestly begs one thing:

Let the LORD, the God of the spirits of all flesh, set a man over the congregation, who may lead them out and lead them in; that the congregation of the LORD be not as sheep which have no shepherd (Num. 27: 16–17).

God again answers his petition, and gives him the command: "Take Joshua (Hosea receives this name because of the promise) . . . and let thy glory rest upon him, that all the congregation of the children of Israel may be obedient" (Num. 27: 18–21).

From the gospel we know that the LORD by this answer gave exceeding abundantly above all that Moses could ask or think. For with these words He promised to send the conquering hero of His Kingdom, whose name shall be Jehoshua, Jesus, because He was so named of the angel before He was conceived in the womb (Luke 2: 21). He will have compassion on His people when He finds them desolate and scattered, like sheep without a shepherd (Matt. 9: 36). He seeks each one that is lost until He finds it. And when He has found it, He lays it on His shoulders and bears it home rejoicing (Luke 15: 3–7). He is the Good Shepherd who gives His life for the sheep. "The whole congregation" obeys Him, for His pastoral care extends far beyond the confines of Israel: "And other sheep I have", He says, "which are not of this fold: them also I must bring, and they shall hear My voice; and there shall be one fold, and one shepherd" (John. 10: 16). He is the "one Shepherd" by whom God Himself gathers His flock (Ezra 34: 11). In Him is fulfilled the word: "I will slay the shepherd, and the sheep shall be scattered" (Zech. 13: 7; Matt 26: 31), but because He lays down His life the Father loves Him (John 10: 17), "and brings again from the dead that great shepherd of the sheep through the blood of the everlasting covenant" (Heb. 13: 20).

So by His death He saves the flock, and every pastoral office in the congregation, from Joshua, the son of Nun to the final scattering and gathering together finds its ground and completion in His ministry.

THE STAR OF JACOB

The most glorious testimony in the Book of Numbers to the coming conquering hero of God's kingdom glistens in *Balaam's* blessing.

We have already seen how when the spies returned with their report, the people broke out in weepings and murmuring and wanted to return to Egypt. Joshua and Caleb, who tried to awaken confidence in the help of the Lord, were almost stoned. In reponse to Moses' petition, the LORD modified His resolve to exterminate Israel and decreed instead that the corpses of all those above twenty years old should decay in the wilderness. But He added an oath that despite this the glory of the LORD should fill the earth. This, however, arouses the people's obstinacy, and they decide to force their way into the promised land in their own strength, without the ark and without Moses if necessary. In vain Moses utters his warnings. They are defeated and cut in pieces by the Amalekites and Canaanites. Those who survive are led by Moses to the oasis Kadesh, the modern 'Ain Kdes, which lies west of the Jordan valley at about the altitude of Petra. There they live "upon a little island beautiful as paradise, severed from all intercourse with the outer world by a sea of desert" (Gressmann).

Moses' ministry is, however, not yet ended. He is to lead Israel still nearer to the frontier. In vain he seeks permission from the King of Edom for his "brother Israel" to pass peacefully through his domain along the "King's road" (the great highway in a region previously Turkish is known to-day as the Sultan's road) with the promise that they will turn neither to the left nor right of the defined road nor pass through the fields or vineyards, and will pay for the water needed by man and beast. Edom, however, refuses to allow his brother Israel to pass through the land. Moses avoids a bloody conflict with the Edomites by marching round their country, and endeavours to approach the borders of the promised land from the east instead of from the south. The enemies who still block his way are overthrown by the edge of the sword. So the children of Israel reach the plains of Moab and encamp east of Jordan opposite Jericho.

The Moabites are filled with "dread" at the sight of Israel, for they feel that a strange higher power is at work. This "company" (Num. 22: 4) is manifestly proof against every assault of outward force, and can be overthrown only with spiritual weapons. In order to cut the nerve of Israel's life (the "blessing") Balak ben Zippor sends for the most famous magician of the eastern mountains, a man of Edom (as should be read in Num. 23: 7 for Aram). Israel's situation resembles that of its tribal father Jacob many years before when, returning from Mesopotamia, he reached the frontier of the Holy Land, and at Jabbok wrestled the whole night with a man for the blessing: "I will not let thee go except thou bless me". Since the blessing of Abraham the "blessing" forms the real substance (*eigentliche Substanz*) of Israel. Without the blessing it is the most wretched of all nations; with the blessing it is, despite all its own weakness and sin, the invincible bearer of blessing for all nations of the earth. "So now", says Balak to Balaam, "go and curse this people for me. For I know that whom thou blessest is blessed and whom thou cursest is accursed." The Balaam who possesses this power is a descendant of *Esau*. Has the time arrived when the cry of Esau shall again be raised, this time to wrest the blessing from Jacob? Has not Israel forfeited the blessing a hundred times through all that has been done in the wilderness? Assuredly—yet nevertheless (and this is the miracle of God's faithfulness, which is incomparably more wonderful than the fact that Balaam's ass opens its mouth to speak), the LORD transforms the curse in the mouth of Balaam into blessing. Despite all Israel's infidelity the blessing of Abraham and the blessing of Jacob remain. Balaam is constrained to repeat word for word the promise made by God to Abraham and handed on by Isaac to disguised Jacob (Gen. 12: 3; 27: 29).

Blessed is he that blesseth thee,
And cursed is he that curseth thee (Num. 24: 9).

For

God is not a man, that he should lie,
nor a son of man, that he should repent.
Shall he not do what he has promised?
Or fail to fulfil what he has spoken?
Behold, I am commissioned to bless;
He has blessed—can I do other? (Num. 23: 19 ff.).

No power in the world can abolish Israel's blessing, for it is anchored in God's Word and faithfulness. Nothing therefore can change Israel's character as given in the blessing. "In the peculiar characteristics of each individual and each class resides the peculiar 'Blessing' of that person or class. And here Balaam describes the features which constitute Israel's characteristics and 'blessing' "[1]:—

> *a people dwelling alone,*
> *and not counted among the heathen* (Num. 23: 9).

To this is added that moment which takes Israel's history out of the realm of mere fate:

> *Enchantment is not found in Ja'acob,*
> *Nor magic charms in Israel;*
> *What he ordains he intimates*
> *to Israel and Ja'acob* (Num. 23: 23).

Fulness of life and innumerable progeny further characterize Israel's "blessing":

> *Who can count Ja'acob's dust?* (cf. Gen. 13: 16).

His sons are "upright" and hold steadfastly to the line of their destiny and thus avoid disintegration:

> *Let me die the death of the upright,*
> *and let my last end be like his* (Num. 23: 10).

Israel's vocation as "the warrior of God" upon earth confers on him triumphant power:

> *A nation arising like a lioness*
> *and exalting itself as a lion* (Num. 23: 24).

For, and here is the blessing of blessings:

> *The LORD his God is with him,*
> *and the exultation of the king is in him* (Num. 23: 21).

Here we touch the whetted point of Balaam's words, which speed like arrows towards the future preparing the victory of God, like the arrows from the bow of King Joash when the dying Elisha guided his hand (2 Kings 13: 14 ff.). Their climax and culmination is reached in the last two speeches (Num. 24):

> *The speech of Balaam, son of Beor,*
> *a man whose eyes are open wide,*
> *the speech of him who heard God's words*

[1] S. Mowinckel, *Der Ursprung der Bileamsage*, Zeitschr. f. AT. Wissensch. 1930, S. 233 ff.

and knew the knowledge of the Most High,
who saw the vision of Almighty God
with eyes half closed but clear of sight:
I look at him—but not yet now,
I glimpse his face—but not yet near;
A star of Jacob enters on its course,
a comet mounts from Israel's bounds,[1]
and shatters Moab's temple
and strikes the head of every son of Seth;
and Edom is possessed completely,
and Seir lies helpless in the hand of foes,
and Israel displays her might,
and looks for mastery to Jacob's house (Num. 24: 15–19).

The saying of Isaac (Gen. 27: 37) which made Jacob (Israel) "lord over Esau (Edom) and reduced all the brothers of Esau to slaves" here finds its confirmation, as does also the separation of Lot (whose descendants are the Moabites) from Abraham. In conclusion (Num. 24: 12 ff.) Balaam repeats the curse against Cain, who was the first to be driven out accursed from the Holy Land. Before the "open eyes" of the Edomite seer the conquering hero of the tribe of Jacob blazes forth like a comet in the night sky. To whom does this allude?

Referring to the regal passage in the second speech (Num. 23: 21), "The LORD his God is with him; and the exultation of the King is in Him", Sigmund Mowinckel remarks: "The context makes it abundantly clear that the king here referred to is not the earthly king, but Yahweh". He considers it equally easy and safe to conclude that the king referred to in the third and fourth speeches is not Yahweh or the "Messiah", but "quite evidently the king of Israel, especially the one who was contemporaneous with the poet", and this, in Mowinckel's opinion, is "David, who overthrew Moab and Edom, and made them subject to Israel". Mowinckel sees in this difference a proof that the first two songs have a different author from the last two. We agree with his contention that the "King" in the second speech is the LORD, and in the third and fourth a figure who is to appear upon earth as King of Israel. We further concur in his statement that the words used to describe this figure point immediately to *David*. This is the case even in

---

[1] "Shebet" in Hebrew means rod, staff, sceptre as well as comet—cf. A. B. Ehrlich's marginal comment on Num. 24: 17 and B. Gemser in ZAW. 1925, S. 301 where as also by Fr. Boll, reference is made to the parallels in German phraseology—
"Den Kometen streckt er wie eine Rute
Drohend am Himmelsfenster aus" (Schiller).

Jacob's blessing concerning Judah, which heralds the shiloh, the "the Shining One", to whom the line of the bearers of Judah's sceptre leads (Gen. 49: 10). This saying already points immediately to David, though not quite so clearly as the last two speeches of Balaam with their reference to the victory over Moab and Edom and the King of the Amalekites, Agag. But it is equally clear that these speeches point through David to a more distant future. Balaam sees David "in a vision".

Though he does not see beyond, his words point beyond David to another Figure who, as seen by Jacob and Balaam, stands so exactly in a line with and behind David, that he is both defined and hidden by David. This is the Messiah, "David's son", through whose advent the Kingdom of God in Israel and the subjection of the world to the Kingdom of God is accomplished.

But if we now see the four speeches of Balaam as they have been handed down to us as a unified prophetic whole uttered shortly before the chosen people entered the promised land from the wilderness, then we realize that, at a time when in Israel itself no one had the remotest conception of it, they bore witness to the time when the theocratically organized people of God would have a king at their head who would demonstrate in a new way, and in contrast to all the kingdoms of the other nations, that the LORD Himself is the King of Israel, and that it is His will through the leadership of Israel to bring all nations into subjection to His rule. The kings upon the throne of David have, it is true, in equal measure with the people, shrouded this messianic purpose of the kingdom rather than illumined it. None the less, there runs from the blessing of Jacob, through the speeches of Balaam, through Hannah's hymn of praise (1 Sam. 2: 10), through the words of Samuel to Saul when the latter failed to kill Agag (1 Sam. 15, especially verses 28–29), through Nathan's answer to David's plan to build a house for the LORD (2 Sam. 7), through the last words of David (2 Sam. 23), through Isaiah's prophecy of the branch of the root of Jesse and Micha's words about the eternal LORD who shall come from Bethlehem, a coherent straight line of messianic testimony to the gospel story of Christ. It is no line drawn in the air (*Luftlinie*), for it touches temporal history (*Zeitgeschichte*) at specific points, and each testimony is conditioned by temporal history and points to an event of the present or near future. At the same time each testimony points beyond this temporal event to the "End". This belongs in a measure to their style and is consonant with the fact that the triumphal king of the last days (*Endzeit*) is already present with the people of God in every decisive moment and leads them to the "final" decision.

That the congregation which handed on the tradition understood the speeches of Balaam messianically is also admitted by Mowinckel[1] when he states that a later age interpreted the words concerning Edom and Moab eschatologically as referring to the annihilation of the world powers arrayed against God. This finds expression in the masoretic text in the words "at the end of the days" (Num. 24: 14), which in his opinion, however, is "unquestionably a gloss". That the Greek translators understood Balaam's speeches eschatologically is obvious from the fact that in the passage which affirms that the coming king is superior to Agag, they have substituted "Gog" for Agag. Gog, according to Ezek. 38 f., is the king who assembles a gigantic army with the intention of destroying the restored city of God. He is overthrown by God who then finally establishes His kingdom of peace. It is not our purpose, however, to "make capital for the apocalyptic interpretation" (Mowinckel) from this Greek version. The speeches of Balaam themselves, even without any mention of Gog, offer clearly enough their testimony to the Messiah Jesus.

Jesus the Christ is "the dayspring from on high", the radiant star from whom the tender mercy of God shines out to those who sit in darkness and in the shadow of death, to guide their feet into the way of peace, that they, being delivered out of the hand of their enemies, might serve Him without fear (Luke 1: 67 ff.). And in the final words of Jesus, attested by the last book of the New Testament, He says:

I am the root and the offspring of David,
  the bright and morning star (Rev. 22: 16).

This confirmation makes us the more certain of the prophetic word of the Old Testament; "and ye do well", says the apostle, "that ye take heed, as unto a light that shineth in a dark place, until the day dawn, and the day star arise in your hearts" (2 Pet. 1: 19).

We also do well to reflect that directly after Balaam had pronounced the blessing of the LORD, Israel ran after Baal Peor and began to play the harlot with the daughters of the Moabites who invited the people to sacrifice to their gods (Num. 25). By his zeal for the LORD, Phineas averted the catastrophe and as a reward received the right to the priesthood

[1] A.a.O., S. 248, Anmerkg. 5.

237

for all time. But that did not prevent his descendents in the days of Samuel from being excluded from the altar because they had dishonoured the priesthood, nor did it prevent Phineas, the son of Eli, together with his brother from being slain in a single day as they carried the ark of the covenant. "Him that honours me will I honour; he that despises me shall be put to shame" (I Sam. 2).

It was a heathen magician from the eastern mountains who proclaimed the star of Jacob, and there remains for the people of God a grave warning in the fact that it was once again magicians from the east who came to Jerusalem seeking the new-born king of the Jews because they had seen His star and were come to worship Him. Their arrival startled all the holy city, for its inhabitants had no notion that the great event had occurred. Herod's answer was to murder the infants of Bethlehem, and the chosen people's answer was to hand over their divinely annointed King to be crucified by the heathen. "And I say unto you, that many shall come from the east and west, and shall sit down with Abraham, and Isaac, and Jacob, in the kingdom of heaven. But the children of the kingdom shall be cast out into outer darkness. And behold, there are last which shall be first, and there are first which shall be last" (Matt. 8: 11; Luke 13: 30).

PREPARATIONS FOR THE DIVISION OF THE PROMISED LAND (NUM. 26–36)

Before his departure Moses is charged with the duty of preparing for the division of the promised land. For this purpose he commands the High Priest to ascertain once again the total of the whole congregation of the children of Israel. To each tribe is then assigned a portion of ground whose size depends on the number of men it can place in the field. The frontiers of the entire holy domain are sketched in chapter 34. The division is to be undertaken by named leaders of each tribe on the principle of the lot under the guidance of Eleazar and Joshua. We have already seen how deeply concerned the lawgiver was that no family should forfeit its claim to a portion of the holy land—this was the purpose of the decrees concerning the year of jubilee. Now to this is added the provision that in a case where a man dies leaving no sons, *the daughter becomes heir*. It then becomes her duty to marry only within her father's tribe: "so shall not the inheritance of the children of Israel remove from tribe to tribe" (Num. 36: 7). We may here mention that there is another chapter of the Book of Numbers which devotes itself to the rights of the women, namely the thirtieth, which decrees that the vow of a married woman and of an unmarried daughter and of a housemaid is valid only if the husband has silently given his consent, whereas the vow of a widow and of a divorced woman is unconditionally binding.

In the division of the land the tribes *Reuben* and *Gad* and the half tribe *Manasseh* have a special position. They express the desire to settle east of Jordan because of the suitability of the land there for cattle breeding. Moses permits this on condition that they join with their brothers in the struggle for the conquest of the land west of Jordan (Num. 32). From the Song of Deborah (Judges 5: 15–17) we learn that at the crucial moment they preferred to sit by their sheep pens, and followed the shepherd's pipes rather than the battle trumpet.

The *Levites* form another special case. They are numbered differently—not from their twentieth year, but every male child from the first month. To them pertains no inheritance of land, for *"the LORD is their inheritance"* (Deut. 10: 9). They are to a certain extent Israelites (*potenzierte Israeliten*) of higher standing through their separation for the priesthood; and as all the Israelites are "the guests of the LORD", they are the guests of the Israelites. "They are the most perfect example of a guest race (*Gaststamm*) within the Israelite community" (Max Weber).[1] They are to be dispersed over 48 cities (with their exactly fenced meadows) among all the tribes, and, supported by the tithe, are to be free for their spiritual service (18: 21; 35: 1–8). Six of these 48 cities are places of sanctuary to which anyone may flee who has unintentionally killed a man. In this connection very precise directions are given to distinguish manslaughter from premeditated murder, in order that the right of sanctuary, the purpose of which is to reduce shedding of blood, may not be *misused to circumvent the Noahtic command* (Gen. 9: 6). *This is to be permitted in no circumstances:* "for whoever *sheds blood pollutes the land, and the land cannot be cleansed of the blood that is shed therein, but by the blood of him that shed it* (cf. Cain: Gen. 4: 10–14). *Defile not therefore the land which ye shall inhabit, wherein I dwell: for I the LORD dwell among the children of Israel"* (Num. 35: 33–34).

Divine service is the keynote of Israel's life in the holy land, and every year lived there is no ordinary "civil" year, but an "ecclesiastical year". Moses therefore provides his people with

[1] A.a.O., S. 184.

a *calendar* which expresses this truth in an impressive and practical manner and enables the layman to know which festival is due and which sacrifices are to be offered (Num. 28: 29).

Before he can hand over the nation to his successor who is to lead them over the Jordan, Moses must fulfil the commission entrusted to him. To this belongs the duty of taking *vengeance on the Midianites*. This is a debt which emerged from the wanderings in the wilderness, and which must therefore be settled by Moses before his departure. The campaign against the Midianites is at the same time an example of the way in which Israel is to conduct the impending holy war (Num. 33: 50–56), and in particular how the people are to treat the women and children and the captured cattle and the booty in order not to sin in their appropriation. For the "enemy" upon whom Israel is to execute the vengeance of the LORD is, together with all his possessions, "sinful", and Israel would be mortally infected with this sin if the foreign men and boys were to be enrolled in the congregation of the LORD, or if the men of Israel were to enter into fellowship with the foreign women who were already married, or if they were to appropriate the enemy's cattle and implements without purifying it by dedicating it to the LORD either by water or by fire. In any case, anyone who has killed a person or touched one of the slain is unclean for seven days and must purify himself, whether he be an Israelite or one of the prisoners. This chapter (Num. 31) is intended to set the standard for the battles for the conquest of the holy land, though a few decrees are changed.

And finally Moses gives a complete list of the places through which he led the people of God in their journeyings from Egypt through the wilderness to the plains of Moab (Num. 33).

So the faithful steward of the house puts his books in order and makes his final preparations for the future before he has to leave the scene of his labours.

6

MOSES' SERMON

DEUTERONOMY[1]

THE last book of the Torah contains, according to its own title, speeches which Moses delivered on the other side of Jordan before the whole congregation of Israel in order to "engrave this Torah upon their hearts with perfect clarity" (Deut. 1: 5), just as one "sharpens" the letters which are inscribed on a table in order to make them clearly legible (this is the meaning of the Hebrew word employed, which is otherwise found only in Deut. 27: 8 and Hab. 2: 2). The Greek description of the whole book as *deuteronomion* is the translation of the Hebrew word "Mishne", which means a repetition, a double, a copy. When we examine more closely this "sharpening" of the law we recognize immediately that it is simply preaching, declaration, teaching and exhortation: *"Hear, O Israel"* (Deut. 4: 1; 5: 1; 6: 4; 9: 1). These three words say substantially everything. On the 1st day of the 11th month of the 40th year of the wanderings in the wilderness (1: 3), when the last members of the generation which personally experienced the miracle of the exodus are dead (Deut. 2: 14), and Moses knows that in a few days he will share their fate (Deut. 3: 23–29), he addresses himself to the generation of Israel still living and present and to the generations which shall follow in order by a review of the events since the departure from Horeb (Deut. 1: 6–3: 22), to impress unmistakably upon them that what happened on the mountain was a *promise* which will be fulfilled when the present generation and each succeeding one sees it afresh as a living *reality in the obedience of simultaneity. "Ye stand* to-day *before the LORD"* (Deut. 29: 1–14) *and shall perpetually remember that "the LORD our God made a covenant with us in Horeb. The LORD made not His covenant with our fathers, but with us, even us, who are all of us here alive this day"* (Deut. 5: 1–3).

That means that true Israelites in every generation are contemporaneous with the events on Mount Sinai, and stand before the voice which there speaks not in the remoteness of historical distance but with the vital responsibility of one who is addressed *to-day: "Thou* stoodest before the LORD thy God

[1] Herbert Breit, *Die Predigt des Deuteronomisten*, München, 1933.

241   Q

on Mount Horeb; *thou* has heard his words; *thine* eyes have seen his lightnings" (Deut. 4: 9–11). It has become clear from our survey of the Pentateuch that this doctrine of simultaneity (*Gleichzeitigkeit*), far from being a theologoumenon of the "Deuteronomist" is the essential meaning of all the narratives, without which one can understand neither the meaning of the "pre-history" (*Urgeschichte*) nor the meaning of the patriarchal narratives nor the meaning of the narratives of Moses. For they are all recounted in such a way that the attentive reader is driven to this realization: they speak of my fathers, and therefore of me. The New Testament Church read them in this way and thus regarded the Pentateuch as a divine message directed to themselves. Neither Rabbi Gamaliel nor his pupil Paul had to attribute this significance to them as a kind of afterthought, for this is their own evident and fundamental meaning, and the last book of the Pentateuch maintains it as a "doctrine".

In the light of this it becomes evident that the question, so often discussed by critics and apologists, of the "authorship" (*Echtheit*) of Deuteronomy, i.e. the question whether the "historical" Moses delivered the addresses recorded in this book or whether they are the work of a later century, misses the real point of the fundamental contention of the book, which is that the attempt at an historical understanding of God's covenant with Israel through Moses and the law rests upon a misconception and obscures the real meaning. Moses preaches, and whoever will hear him must listen to his sermon and not attempt to "know him after the flesh" (2 Cor. 5: 16). It may be that Deuteronomic speeches were first published at the reformation under King Josiah in 622 (2 Kings 22 and 23), for which there are several indications, or it may be that they were published at another time. In any case they show that there was a time in Israel when the sermon of Moses was once again listened to. And thereby they testify that "Israel" is always present whenever Moses speaks in the living present as the preacher of God's promises and commands and men listen to him.

> *"The LORD thy God will raise up unto thee a Prophet from the midst of thee, of thy brethren, like unto me; unto him ye shall hearken"* (Deut. 18: 15).

Without this promise the testament of Moses would be dead, and the tables of the Torah a granite memorial and not a testimony. By the fulfilment of this promise the Word of God based on the law is proclaimed and heard in every generation when and where God wills.

For this, says the sermon, is the marvel of Israel, its incomparable "being", that here are men upon the earth who are called of God and destined to a new life by the fact that *God speaks with them* and they are not consumed. "For who is there of all flesh, that hath heard *the voice of the living God* speaking out of the midst of the fire, as we have, and lived?" (Deut. 5: 26). "For ask now of the days that are past, which were before thee, since the day that God created man upon the earth, and ask from one side of the heaven unto the other, whether there hath been any such thing as this great thing is, or hath been heard like it? Did ever people hear the voice of God speaking out of the midst of the fire, as thou hast heard, and live?" (Deut. 4: 32 f.). Assuredly all the passages attest that this miracle happened at one time only (*einmalig*); this direct speaking of God from the fire when "the mountain burned with fire unto the midst of heaven" (Deut. 4: 11) will not be repeated precisely in this manner. But all the days of their life the children of Israel to their remotest generations share in the convulsions of that dreadful day which gave them birth when God's own voice spoke to them once and for all time in the living present. Called into life by the voice of God, to hear which is more terrible than the terror of death, they can live only in so far as they hear this voice. "Only take heed to thyself, and keep thy soul diligently, lest thou forget the things which thine eyes have seen, and lest they depart from thine heart all the days of thy life: but teach them thy sons, and thy sons' sons; specially the day that thou stoodest before the LORD thy God in Horeb, when the LORD said unto me, Gather me the people together, and I will make them hear my words, that they may learn to fear me all the days that they shall live upon the earth, and that they may teach their children" (Deut. 4: 9 f.). The thunder of Sinai must roll through all the words of the prophets, and wherever the commands and promises of the law are proclaimed the living voice of the LORD must be heard. It is the incomparable privilege of Israel above all nations that through the "law" it may participate in this dialogue with God. "Where is a mighty nation to be found whose gods approach so near as the LORD our God whenever we call upon Him?" (Deut. 4: 7). Israel's relationship to God is totally different from that of any other nation in that it consists solely in the fact that God speaks: "Ye heard the voice of the words, but saw no similitude; only the voice"

243

(Deut. 4: 12). Therefore for Israel God can never become an "object" in any kind of image or in the worship of the stars "which the LORD thy God hath divided unto all nations under the whole heaven" (Deut. 4: 19). In contrast to the nations which fashion their idols, the LORD has melted Israel in the "iron furnace" of Egypt and made it ready to be moulded by His Word (Deut. 4: 20). He does not allow Israel to "fashion" Him; for "He is a consuming fire". Israel's part is to hear His voice and to answer Him with the utter obedience of perfect trust.

That means to trust God and to love Him. The LORD is "a jealous God" (Deut. 4: 24). In *pure love* He made the covenant with Israel, and His people must recognize His love in all its purity, namely as free and groundless *election*. "Behold, the heaven and the heaven of heavens is the LORD's thy God, the earth also and all that is therein. And yet the LORD had a delight in thy fathers only, to love them, and he chose their seed after them, even you, out of all nations" (Deut. 10: 14 f.). "The LORD did not set his love upon you nor choose you because ye were more in number than any people; for ye were the fewest of all people: but because the LORD loved you, and because he would keep the oath which he had sworn unto your fathers" (Deut. 7: 7). Neither do you enter the promised land "because of your righteousness and sincerity of heart". Remember rather how on the way through the wilderness you proved a "stiffnecked" people. It is in virtue only of God's forgiveness that you are and remain His people (Deut. 9). Thus "ye have not chosen me, but I have chosen you" (John 15: 16); and herein is love, not that Israel loved God, but that God loved Israel. From this only a double conclusion is possible, a conclusion which *must* be drawn: "Let us love him and let us love one another" (1 John 4).

"Know therefore that the LORD thy God, He is God, the faithful God, which keepeth covenant and mercy with them that love him and keep his commandments" (Deut. 7: 9). Since His unswerving faithfulness is the power which holds Israel, the latter's relationship to Him can consist only in *faith*, in absolute trust and obedience to Him. In the wilderness God has trained His people to this faith "as a father chasteneth his son" (Deut. 8: 5). He deprived them of every possibility of trusting in their own strength or in any power but the divine. "He humbled thee (weakened thee), and suffered thee to hunger, and fed thee with manna . . . that He might make thee know that man doth not live by bread only, but by every word that proceedeth out of the mouth of the LORD, doth man live" (Deut. 8: 3). Israel should remember this, and not become proud when he enters the land of culture. And because the LORD is with him, he is to fear nothing and no one. But he is not to trust in his own strength. The "culture" which he is commissioned to develop is a plant of grace whose fruits are trust and obedience, faith and love. *The land* itself into which the people are led reflects this, for in contrast to Egypt, where the farmer waters his seeds by means of irrigation wheels which he constructs and operates himself, Canaan is "a land of hills and valleys, and drinketh water of the rain of heaven; a land which the LORD thy God careth for: the eyes of the LORD thy God are always upon it, from the beginning of the year even unto the end of the year" (Deut. 11: 10–12).

Thus Israel can live only if in all its life and activity it loves God alone.

Hear, O Israel, the LORD our God is the only LORD: and thou shalt love the LORD thy God with all thine heart, and with all thy soul, and with all thy might (Deut. 6: 4–5).

The LORD claims His people completely. He alone can do so, for He is One, and He alone "is God; there is none else beside him" (Deut. 4: 35). All that Israel is springs from His love, for His love created His people out of nothing. Therefore he belongs completely to His love. And with the claim of love He embraces the people and every single *individual* in his whole personality far more effectively than He could by a mere moral challenge. For to love God "with all thine heart" means "with both impulses, the good and the evil" (Bab. Talmud, Berak IX, v).

That Israel, in distinction from all other religious possibilities, is to worship the LORD alone, and obey His word, is the truth which the "speeches of Moses" emphasize. And it was by no accident that Jesus took from them the three words with which He withstood the temptation of the "prince of this world". The words of Moses after forty years in the wilderness form the solid foundation from which Jesus proceeds after forty days in the wilderness to win the victory for the sole sovereignty of God (Matt. 4: 1–11).

In *chapters 12 to 26*, where the sermon of Moses returns again to the *promulgation of the law*, repeating some ancient laws and adding certain new ones since Israel is about to occupy the land, one truth which is to be driven home finds imperious expression—Israel is allowed neither to take over from the heathen religious conceptions and customs nor to devise for itself any pious rites. His one task is simply to keep to the commandment of the LORD, and, directing all his faith, love and hope to Him. who is the sole LORD, to ascribe to Him the glory and to seek unity as a people. "Ye shall utterly destroy all the places wherein the nations . . . served their gods, upon the high mountains, and upon the hills, and under every green tree. . . . Ye shall visit only the *one place* which the LORD shall choose as a habitation for his name, and there alone shall ye offer sacrifice" (Deut. 12: 2–5). There alone in future shall the passover be observed, not as a family festival but as a festival of the congregation which was born on the night of the passover. Similarly the other high festivals shall unite the whole people in one place before the face of the one LORD and that in exalted joy, as is repeatedly emphasized: "Thou shalt be joyful, most joyful" (Deut. 16: 1–17).

The fellowship of the compatriots among themselves stands or falls with the common veneration of the one true God. "If there arise among you a *prophet or a dreamer of dreams*, and giveth thee signs and wonders, . . . saying, Let us go after other gods . . . or if thine nearest relation, thy brother, thy son, thy daughter, or thy wife in thine arms, or thy friend who is as thine own soul, entice thee secretly saying, Let us go and serve other gods, . . . thou shalt slay him without mercy; thine hand shall be the first upon him to put him to death, and afterwards the hand of all the people; and thou shalt stone him to death" (13). The *Monarchy* which will arise from the wish of the people will bring a peculiar danger—the desire to be militarily and politically strong after the manner of neighbouring peoples. To minimize this danger, it is decreed that the king is to be under the law and how he is to be subject to the law of the LORD (17: 14–20).

As on the one hand the slightest seduction to a false faith in God threatens to destroy the chosen people and disrupt the relationship of its members among themselves, so on the other hand love to God is the inexhaustible spring of *love to one's neighbour*. Many commandments with which we are already acquainted show what it means in practice to take seriously the truth that the legal basis upon which one should treat other people and animals and the land is the gracious will of our Maker and Redeemer. In the Deuteronomic setting, more general expressions give place to the word *"brother"* (compare Deut. 15: 12 with Exod. 21: 2; Deut. 24: 7 with Exod. 21: 16; Deut, 23: 20 f. with Exod. 22: 24), in order that the sense of the binding nature of the command and the consciousness of the *setting apart of Israel* might be deepened. Unfortunately in times when men no longer understood the meaning of the divine election of Israel, this was misunderstood as a mark of national exclusiveness (*völkische Beschränkung*).[1] These multifarious commandments, from the greatest to the least, from the laws of the year of jubilee to the prohibition to remove a mother bird with her brood from the nest (Deut. 22: 6), from the choosing of the one place where the name of the LORD is to dwell to the founding and cleanly maintenance of "the place whither thou goest" (Deut. 23: 12 f.)—all are given to Israel in order that he may *live* in the promised land (Deut. 5: 30) as a people separated and *holy* unto the LORD (Deut. 26: 19), and praising him by obedience among the nations (Deut. 4: 6–8).

"See, I have set before thee this day life . . . and death, in that I command thee this day to love the LORD thy God and to walk in his ways" (30: 15). In contrast to the heathen, by the Word of God in the Law Israel is faced at every moment of its existence (to-day!) with an eternal decision. The Word of God denudes Israel of every possibility of deciding or mastering his own destiny, whether by mantic inspiration or magic, whether by science or art or technology, whether by speculation, mysticism or mythology. *"For this commandment which I command thee this day is not too high and not too far removed. It is not in heaven, that thou shouldest say, Who shall go up for us to heaven, and bring it unto us, that we may hear it and do it? Neither is it beyond the sea, that thou shouldest say, Who shall go over the sea for us, and bring it unto us, that we may hear it and do it? But the word is very nigh unto thee, in thy mouth, and in thy heart, that thou mayest do it"* (Deut. 30: 11–14).

> *The secret things (mysteries) belong unto the LORD our God: but those things which are revealed belong unto us and to our children for ever, that we may do all the words of this law* (Deut. 29: 28).

God's voice calls Israel away from all ways of his own choosing. The LORD who called him places him before the narrow gate leading to the narrow way which means life. As an unforgettable sign of this, the chosen people enter the promised land through the *narrow pass between the mount of blessing and the mount of the curse* (Deut. 11: 26–32). Inexhaustible is the blessing which Israel is promised from the peak of Gerizim if

[1] Gerh. v. Rad, *Das Gottesvolk im Deuteronomium.*

the people are willing to obey the voice of the LORD. And in the curses which from the summit of Ebal are threatened if the people fail to serve the LORD in joyful obedience, hell itself opens its mouth—scattered among the nations from one end of the world to the other, branded by God, inwardly and outwardly restless they shall live without hope of demise (chapters 27–29).

Abandoned to the wrath and scorn of men and the devil, driven by terror to the gates of death, they will die and yet survive. That is the mystery hidden in God, that He always leaves open the *possibility of conversion*. "If thou shalt mortify thyself, and return unto the LORD thy God, and obey his voice . . . with all thine heart and with all thy soul, then the LORD thy God will turn thy captivity, and have compassion upon thee, and will . . . gather thee from all the nations, whither the LORD thy God hath scattered thee. And though thou wert driven out to the far corners of heaven, the LORD thy God will gather thee from thence" (Deut. 30). It is just this truth, that the faithfulness of the LORD is a rock, a rock from which Israel was born and on which he is wrecked and raised, that is proclaimed with sublime literary power as a final testimony which is to ring through all ages as long as Israel breathes.

THE SONG OF MOSES (DEUT. 32)

In this document the prophetic seer, who surveys the progress of the chosen people from its beginning to its goal, as from the mount he viewed the promised land from end to end, declares in summary fashion the decisive deed by which the Creator and Redeemer of the world reveals Himself in the election of Israel. He enjoins heaven and earth to listen, for His words proclaim the secret of all history.

> *I will publish the name of the LORD:*
> *ascribe ye greatness unto our God* (Deut. 32: 2).
> *He is the Rock . . .*
> *a God of truth and without iniquity.*

In distant "primeval ages" He appointed Israel to His heritage.

> *When the Most High divided to the nations their inheritance*
> *when he separated the sons of Adam,*
> *he set the bounds of the people*
> *according to the number of the children of Israel* (Deut. 32: 8)

The Greek version reads: "according to the number of God's

angels", which we may compare with Ps. 82. And whilst the
Most High appoints angels as governors of the other nations
and lands, He rules Israel directly in His own Person.

> For the LORD's portion is his people,
> Jacob is the lot of his inheritance (Deut. 32: 9).

That this is intended in the sense of *pars pro toto*, i.e. that the
LORD has not abandoned the other lands and nations to themselves and their "gods", but purposes rather in His own time
to embrace them in the same personal jurisdiction which He
now exercises over Israel, is clear from the Hebrew construction, which asserts that God has set the bounds of the nations
according to the number of the children of Israel. In such
mythical profundities is rooted that election of Israel, whose
purpose it is to reveal the nature and dominion of God.

The following verses recount the deeds by which God dis-
closed in the realm of history that He leads Israel personally
as His people:

> He found him in a desert land,
> and in the dreadful howling wilderness;
> he embraced him, he nursed him,
> he kept him as the pupil of his eye.
> As an eagle stirs her brood to flight,
> and hovers o'er her young,
> so he spreads his wings,
> takes the young thereon
> and bears them high in graceful motion.
> So the LORD alone doth lead him forth;
> no other god is with him (Deut. 32: 10–12).

Then comes the time in the mountains of the promised land
when He fosters him with honey from the rock and oil from the
flinty rock, with milk and cream, with the fat of lambs and
rams, with finest wheat and foaming ruddy wine. And now
occurs the incredible event—this nation, satiated and corpulent,
grows insolent and deserts the God who made him. He reviles
the rock of his salvation and provokes His jealousy and wrath
by sacrificing to strange gods and devils of the field. He ignores
the rock that begat him and forgets the God who bore him with
travail (Deut. 15–18).

Seeing this, the LORD resolves to reject him:

> I will hide my face from them,
> from the sons that know no loyalty.

> *They have moved me to jealousy with that which is no God;*
> *I will provoke them with that which is no people.*
> *For fire is kindled in mine anger,*
> *and hurtles down to hell itself.*
> *It shall consume the earth with all her increase,*
> *and set on fire the groundwork of the mountains.*
> *Mischief will I heap upon them,*
> *and all my arrows spend upon them.*
> *When enervated by fierce hunger*
> *devoured with burning heat*
> *and plagued with pestilence*
> *I will send the teeth of beasts upon them*
> *and poisonous serpents of the dust.*
> *The sword without and horrid fears within*
> *shall overthrow the young man and the maid,*
> *the sucking child and grey-haired veteran* (Deut. 32: 19–25).

Yet in spite of this—and here is the surpassing miracle—the
LORD does not utterly annihilate His people. Why not?
Because of His glory and faithfulness.

> *I would have said I will blow them far away,*
> *and obliterate their memory among men,*
> *were it not I knew the mockery of the enemy.*
> *For their enemies would misconceive the deed,*
> *and say, Our hand is high, and the LORD hath not accom-*
> *plished this* (Deut. 32: 26, 27).

If Israel should be delivered into the hand of the great
powers, this fact might easily be misinterpreted as a proof that
these powers are stronger than the God of Israel. Therefore
Israel's fortune is reversed, that it may be manifest that God
is the unshakable rock on which Israel is shattered, a rock
whose incomparable power is revealed in the fact that God
raises up again His shattered people on the immovable rock of
His faithfulness.

> *Is this not hidden in my treasured store,*
> *and sealed among my treasures?*
> *Mine is the vengeance. I repay . . .*
> *The LORD will rule his people's way,*
> *and clemency unto his servants show* (Deut. 32: 34–36).

This turning of Israel's fortune, which is hidden in the depths
of God, brings to light the perfect revelation of His sole divinity:

See now that I, e'en I am he;
no god is there beside me.
I kill, and make alive,
I wound, and heal again,
and none can pluck ought from my hand.
To heaven I raise my hand, and speak:
"As truly as I live for ever!" (Deut. 32: 39 f.).
Rejoice, O nations, with his race;
His servants' blood is now avenged.
Revenge he turns against his foes,
but reconciles his people and their land (Deut. 32: 43).

After this song, Moses like Jacob before his death, proceeds to bless each of the tribes.

THE BLESSING OF EACH SINGLE TRIBE (DEUT. 33)

Like Jacob, he confers the most abundant blessing and "the good will of him that dwelt in the bush . . . upon the head of Joseph, upon the crown of the head of him that was anointed above his brothers" (Deut. 33: 13–17). Significantly he emphasizes the spiritual distinction and appointment of Levi. But most important is the frame in which all is cast—the tribes, each with its distinctive life imprinted by the blessing, are bound and confederated into a living unity by their invisible heavenly *King*, the LORD who is present in all their earthly history. This is the meaning of the *introduction* to the blessing, which describes how the LORD approaches from Sinai by Seir and Paran with dazzling radiance and a blaze of fire, accompanied by His holy angels, and is welcomed as King in Jeshurun by the heads of the people and the united tribes of Israel in solemn festival (Deut. 33: 2–5). The same spirit animates the close, which is a hymn to the God of Jeshurun,

who rides through the heaven to thy help . . .
The eternal God is thy refuge,
and underneath are the everlasting arms . . . (Deut. 33: 26–27).

Under His governance,

Israel dwells in safety, alone the fountain of Jacob.
Hail to thee, O Israel! Who is like unto thee?
A people saved by the LORD (Deut. 33: 26–29).

This setting in the Kingdom of God (*verfasstsein unter dem Königtum Gottes*) was given to the tribes of Israel by Moses as their "Law", as their incomparable *"nomos"*, as is expressed in verse 4. He united them as the people of the great King. The import of the Torah, the *nomos*, is the consummated Theonomy, for which Josephus coined the word "theocracy" when, as a Jewish eye-witness belonging to the Graeco-Roman world, he described the fall of the Jewish state in the year A.D. 70.

THE DEATH OF MOSES (DEUT. 34)

Moses climbs Nebo, to the summit of Mount Pisgah, and from there surveys the deep, broad valley of the Jordan. And the LORD said unto him, "This is the land which I sware unto Abraham, unto Isaac, and unto Jacob, saying, I will give it unto thy seed: I have caused thee to see it with thine eyes, but thou shalt not go over thither."

So Moses, the servant of the LORD, died in the land of Moab; according to the word of the LORD (literally, "according to the mouth of the LORD", which the rabbis interpret thus: "At this hour the LORD pressed a kiss upon the lips of Moses, and took his soul with the kiss of His mouth").[1]

And He buried him in the dale, and to this day no one knows his grave. The graves of the patriarchs are known to their heirs, but none knows the grave of Moses.

And there arose not a prophet since in Israel like unto Moses, whom the LORD knew face to face.

---

[1] Bin Gorion, *Die Sagen der Juden*, Mose, S. 371.

7

THE FULFILLER OF THE LAW

"THE goal of the Law is Christ" (Rom. 10: 4). "The first adoption of the chosen people (in the calling of Abraham) depended upon the grace of the Mediator. And the law was added about four hundred years after the death of Abraham not in order to distract the chosen people from Christ, but to keep the spirits of men in eager expectancy of His advent" (Calvin).[1] Against the attempt of the priests to materialize the revelation in ritual and to denude it of moral content; and against the attempt of the scribes "to turn the law into a lie by their lying pencil" and to protect themselves from the word of the LORD by hiding behind the "Law" (Jer. 8: 8 f.); and no less against the attempt of the false prophets to replace the voice of their Covenant LORD by the voice of their own heart or the voice of the people or the voice of their age, from time to time the Word of God itself broke forth "like a fire, like a hammer which breaks the rocks in pieces" (Jer. 23: 29). It shattered time and again the religious and secular foundations and illusions of the Israelites by its witness to the one fathomless foundation in the election of Israel by God's free choice: "I am the LORD thy God, and have made the covenant of promise with thee".

In Jesus Christ that Word of God in which all is grounded became flesh. He is the ground and the fulfilment of the Law. Subject to the law (Gal. 4: 4), He is yet master of the law. His royal freedom as the Son consists in this, that as a faithful servant obedient unto death, even the death upon the cross, He has no other desire than to do the will of the Father, and thus the obedient Son redeems the rebels and slaves to the liberty of the children of God. Since His advent is the fulfilling of the law, it is the complete contrary to any dissolution of the law. His life and teaching confront the sinner with the infinite claims of God's love. The "to-day" of the sermon of Moses receives in the preaching of Jesus and His apostles its final intensification: "But *Now!* But I!" To-day becomes the "final" day. "This day is this scripture fulfilled in your ears." The hour of Jesus is the presence of God for all time, and is therefore the "last hour". His Word, and the proclamation of His

[1] *Inst.* II, 6. 2; 7, 1.
Compare also the excellent thesis by Wilhelm Brandt, *Das Gesetz Israels und die Gesetze der Heiden bei Paulus im Hebräerbrief*, München, 1934.

death and resurrection place the hearer before the final decision. It would thus be folly to imagine that He came to destroy the law or the prophets. He is come not to destroy, but to fulfil. And when the righteousness of His disciples does not exceed that of the Jews who are most fastidious in their observance of the law, they cannot be members of Christ's Kingdom. As surely as He represents the challenge of God's love in all its majesty, so will He not set one jot or tittle of the law aside until all be fulfilled. For every letter of the law attests the complete appropriation of man by the love of God, which is in Christ Jesus. The Beatitudes would be tinkling cymbals if they did not proclaim: "Be ye therefore perfect, even as your Father which is in heaven is perfect".

By His words "But I say unto you", Jesus makes it impossible for those who listen to Him to understand that which those of old said as mere history or morals, but speaks it afresh to them in such a way that they are confronted with the decision of eternity. His concern is not to adorn the ancient precepts with a slight addition here or there, but to take that which was said long ago and to proclaim it anew with the authority of the Author. Listening to Him, we can no longer apprehend the law as a collection of religious ideals or ethical norms, for His "I say" impels us to hear the ancient words as the living voice of "I am".

With His "But I say unto you", the Author removes the previous limitation of His law. Was not every word from the beginning spoken in the sense of *pars pro toto*? And now He discloses the new possibility of covering the whole by that which previously regulated but a part. The oath (Greek *"horkos"*), for example, and the prohibition of perjury had established a barrier (Greek, *"herkos"*), and thus fenced off a certain area in which the word of man (who is a liar) should be true. Now Jesus says, "Swear not at all . . . but let your communication be, Yea, yea; Nay, nay; for whatsoever is more than these cometh of evil", and thus abolishes the limitation and the special area it enclosed. In doing so, however, He places the whole realm of human speech and thought under the command of veracity. By removing the limitation He reveals in all its potency the original purpose of the Lawgiver. *"He takes every command as a promise"* (Blumhardt, jr.) and fulfils the law by unfolding in all its fullness the promise therein contained. Similarly, in the decree which made divorce more difficult by requiring a letter of divorce to be written there lay the promise that, despite the hardness of men's hearts, the principle would be acknowledged that what God has joined together no man should put asunder. And, once again, in the command to punish every bodily injury by retribution, there was contained the promise of the complete conquest of evil by the new possibility of forgiveness. And similarly in the prohibition of hatred among brothers lay the promise of the possibility of loving every brother man, friend or foe, with the love of the heavenly Father who causes His sun to rise on the evil and on the good.

That the divine possibility (that which is possible only to God), will yet once again become regulative of human affairs is the ground and promise of the law of Israel, and all testimonies to the dealings of the LORD with His chosen people are but the "testament" in which this possibility finds its charter. Jesus the Christ came to open this testament and to execute it to the letter.

So the fact becomes transparently clear that this possibility is and remains entirely *God's* possibility. No ground is left for the attempt to suit the claims of God to the strength of man "Be ye therefore perfect, as your Father which is in heaven is perfect". Jesus insists upon the utter seriousness of God's love, and leaves no loophole for misunderstanding: God does not set before man an ideal, either high or low; but claims him utterly by His love. He asks of him not this or that, but his whole self. When God loves us, He demands that we love Him with all our heart in return, and our neighbour as ourselves. Nothing less than this absolute love can fulfil the law. Whoever detracts in the slightest from this fails to take the love of God seriously. Truly, the Son *frees* His brothers from the bondage of the law; but anyone who fails to look into the perfect law of liberty and to continue therein, deceives himself (James 1: 22–27). For he alone is *free*[1] who loves as he is loved by God, and is unconcerned about himself. "And they were astonished out of measure, saying among themselves, Who then can be saved? And Jesus, looking upon them saith, With men it is impossible, but not with God: for with God all things are possible" (Mark 10: 26 f.). Only the act of God, only the miracle of *His* love can fulfil the law. This act of God is the crucified Lord Jesus. "We have a law, and by our law He must die", declared the Jews to the Roman governor. Their words condemn their conception of the law, and yet unwittingly proclaim, as do the evangelists, the truth of God that nothing but the sacrifice of the Son can satisfy the law of the Father and fulfill His will. "The zeal of the LORD will accomplish this" (Isa. 9: 6). And this zeal of

[1] See above, pp. 68–73.

the love of God judges him who is most zealous for the law, and makes the morally wealthy poor (Phil. 3). The greatest love turns to serve the needy, and none but the poor in spirit are rich in God. The first Beatitude fulfils the first commandment as its *ground* and *source*.

A. SELECT INDEX OF PROPER NAMES

Names of authors quoted or alluded to, and of non-Biblical books known only by their titles.

B. NAMES OF PERSONS AND PLACES

Familiar Biblical names are not entered in the list if the references to them are merely casual. But they are inserted when they are necessary for the full presentation of a fact or an idea.

262